MR ADAMS'
FREE GRAMMAR SCHOOL

The design by the London artist, George Murray, was used on the front cover of The Novaportan *from July 1930 to December 1957.*

MR ADAMS'
FREE GRAMMAR SCHOOL

David and Ruth Taylor

Phillimore

2002

Published by
PHILLIMORE & CO. LTD.,
Shopwyke Manor Barn, Chichester, West Sussex

© David & Ruth Taylor, 2002

ISBN 1 86077 221 8

Printed and bound in Great Britain by
MPG Books
Bodmin, Cornwall

CONTENTS

LIST OF ILLUSTRATIONS

ILLUSTRATION ACKNOWLEDGEMENTS

We are indebted to the following for permission to use illustrations in their possession: Bodleian Library, University of Oxford, Gough Maps 28, p.241, plate 1; Shropshire Records and Research Centre, plates 2, 3, 4, 68; Royal Institute of British Architects Library Drawings Collection, plate 15; The *Shropshire Magazine*, plate 16.

For drawings within the text we are indebted to: Shropshire Records and Research Centre, pp.9, 32; Shrewsbury School, pp.27, 28, 29; *The Shrewsbury Chronicle* pp.50, 80; Literary executors of D.H. Robinson, *The Sleepy Meese* (Waine Research Publications, 1988), p.55; Mrs Ann Quickenden for wood engravings by Agnes Miller Parker, pp.107, 130, 152, 206; *The Newport Advertiser*, p.179; Peter Maddocks for cartoon, p.196. Drawings on pp.33, 39, 58, 64 are taken from J.A. Comenius *Orbis Sensualium Pictus (Visible World)* facsimile of the 12th edition. London, 1777 (The Bodley Head, London).

We thank Lin Cawthorne for the drawings made especially for this book on pp.16, 74, 78.

ACKNOWLEDGEMENTS

In 1996 we were invited by the School Governors to write a history of Adams' Grammar School. To do this we had to assemble an archive and we are grateful to them and the Headmaster for providing a suitably furnished room and to Elizabeth Kosinski for being a most supportive and skilled archivist. We found most of the early information about the school in the hand-written minutes of the various committees of the Haberdashers' Company. These are mainly in the Guildhall Library, London, but other documents are held by the Company itself. We are greatly indebted to Stephen Freeth and his staff in the Guildhall manuscript room, and to John Cope, the Company's archivist. They made our visits to London enjoyable as well as productive. We are also grateful for the assistance of Tony Carr and his staff at Shropshire Records and Research Centre. Our stays in London were made possible by the hospitality of our daughter and son-in-law, Catherine and Steven Randall and our nephew, Christopher Jones.

We have come to know and appreciate the many people who, over the centuries, have contributed to the life of the school. Apart from William Adams himself we have met successive Headmasters and Ushers, local landowners, clergy, townspeople and pupils as well as tenants on the Knighton estates. Condensing the history of nearly 350 years into a 256-page book has meant, unfortunately, that we have had to leave out much that was of interest, for which we apologise.

We have collected many drawings and photographs, including some not published before – in particular an eighteenth-century drawing of the school found in the Bodleian Library, Oxford. Many of the colour photographs were taken over a number of years by David, some of the recent ones with a digital camera kindly loaned by the school's Information Technology Department. We are greatly indebted to the School Bursar, Allan Snell, for using his computer skills to render our illustrations suitable for modern publishing techniques.

Our grateful thanks for help and encouragement go to the steering committee of Alan Snead, Peter Watson Jones, Harry Wood (all past Chairmen of Governors) and Roger Johnson (currently a Governor). We are indebted for specialist help to: Chris Jobson, archivist while at Adams' until 1988, and valued adviser since; James Lawson, archivist and librarian at Shrewsbury School for putting his vast fund of knowledge at our disposal; Martin Thorpe for translation from Latin and Greek and research on classical authors; Jo Wisdom, librarian at St Paul's Cathedral; Sir George White, Past Master of the Clockmakers' Company; David Smith for sharing his knowledge of the Adams family, and Dr Chris Stray of Swansea University for information on early textbooks. We are very grateful to the retired Clerk to the Company, Mike Barrow, to past Headmasters Robert Glover and Jeff Roberts, and Corinna Peterson, widow of Alec Peterson for their memories of the school, to the present Headmaster, Jim Richardson and also to members of staff past and present, including Keith Reynolds, Lynton and Stella Seymour Whiteley, Bryan Banks, Tom Bate, Neil Gibbs, Rodney Jones and Barbara Anderson, widow of Ron Anderson. We have drawn on information assembled by Graham Mottershaw while at the school and are sad that he has not lived to see the outcome of this project. We have also benefited from the A. W. C. Johnson archive, kindly donated by his family. We were all but overwhelmed by the response from Old Novaportans to our call for memories of school days. A list of names is at the back of the book, we are grateful to them all. The newly appointed archive room at the school is ready to store still more information.

We are happy to acknowledge the help we received from members of Newport History Society, in particular Sue Cleaves, Martin Elkes, Bryan Lloyd, Tavia McClean and Heather Williams; also from Ann Warner, Malcolm Miles; and Jenny Colls at the Bodleian Library. Peter Bowyer, John Evans and Steven Randall gave us vital instruction at crisis points in the use of the computer.

Lastly we wish to thank all our friends and family who have endured our enthusiasms with fortitude and our daughter, Catherine, whose patient and professional editing has combined constructive criticism and encouragement and without whom this project would not have been completed.

DAVID AND RUTH TAYLOR
LILLESHALL, MARCH 2002

FOREWORD

In 1656 William Adams, born in Newport, Shropshire, and a considerable benefactor to the town, established the Free Grammar School which bears his name. That the school is now flourishing is a tribute to William Adams' vision, and also to the Haberdashers' Company which is still responsible for the governance of the school and the management of the Foundation assets.

This book is the story of that school over the last four centuries; it is a fascinating story of both good times and bad. To a large extent it reflects the fortunes of all grammar schools during this period, and whatever one's view of these institutions, it is certainly true that for many people over the last century the grammar school has been the bench-mark against which all other secondary schools have been measured.

The fascination of the story is not confined to the fluctuations of the school's fortunes. When the school opened William Adams presented it with a Lantern Clock which still shows the time in Big School, originally the school room. This timepiece was at the forefront of the technology of its day. It is interesting that the school has for many years had a bent towards science and technology which is evident today in its status as a Technology College.

The Governors of the school have long felt the need for an authoritative account of its history. In 1996 they recognised that in David and Ruth Taylor there were two people pre-eminently qualified to undertake such a work and were delighted when they accepted the commission. The Haberdashers' Company enthusiastically supported this initiative and has made funds available to make possible the necessary research.

It was indeed a most propitious time for the undertaking. The authors, Ruth, a retired teacher and historian and David, for twenty years the Headmaster of the school, have been closely involved with the school since 1974. This background and the fact that they have also been able to gather first-hand information from many other people involved in running the school over a long period has given them an unrivalled opportunity to write this work.

The research that the authors have undertaken has been immense. It has involved much travelling to collect material from a variety of sources, much of which will be new even to those who know the school well. They have given their time and expertise freely and have asked that any proceeds from the sale of the book should be used for the benefit of the school.

The book is a valuable contribution to the history of secondary education in this country and is not only a most interesting story in its own right, but is also a mirror to life in the community of Newport.

Anyone with an interest in education or familiar with Newport will find the narrative compelling reading.

Alan Snead
Chairman of the Steering Committee
Anglesey, March 2002

One

WILLIAM ADAMS AND HIS FAMILY

On 29 October 1656, at a special meeting of the Court of Assistants, the Master and Wardens of the Worshipful Company of Haberdashers in London agreed to take on the overall direction of William Adams' newly founded Free Grammar School in Newport, Shropshire.[1] They still do so, although in the 350 years since then their role has altered from time to time. Without their backing the school would not be the flourishing centre of learning it is today.

Who was William Adams and why should a London merchant
found a school in Shropshire?
Little is known about William Adams' background or about him personally. He was registered as an apprentice in July 1606 to Thomas Allen, haberdasher of the parish of St Mary, Colechurch, in the City of London, and his father was noted as John Adams of Newport, Shropshire, Yeoman. We know that his brother John was later referred to as a retail dealer of Newport, so it is possible that their father was a trader as well as a small landowner and that the eldest son, John, took over his business while William, the second son, was sent to London to make his own way in the world. If William was no older than 21 years of age at the time of his apprenticeship, which was normal, and in his 77th year when he died in August 1661, as noted in Newport parish register, his date of birth must be July/August 1585. No record of his baptism has yet been found.

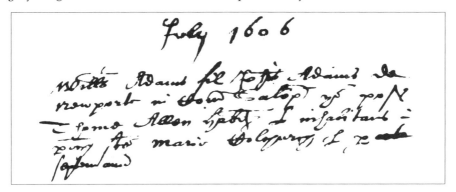

Apprenticeship of William Adams, from Haberdashers' Company's register of apprenticeship bindings.

1

It is not surprising that a young man from the provinces should come to London to make his living. The population of the capital grew during the 17th century from approximately 300,000 to about 550,000 inhabitants. When infant mortality and recurring outbreaks of plague are taken into account, it is obvious that the numbers of Londoners must have been topped up from outside the capital. In the month that William was apprenticed we find that 46 young men were apprenticed to members of the Haberdashers' Company, and of these only six were from London (and Southwark). The rest came from 21 other counties including places as far afield as Yorkshire, Devon and Herefordshire.

What we do not know is why William Adams should have become a Haberdasher rather than joining any other Company. One clue might be a certain William Justice who became a Freeman of the Company 11 years before William Adams did. We know no more about this William Justice, but he could well have been the son of William Justice of Newport (died 1615)[2] and a hitherto unknown older brother of the Roger Justice who married William Adams' sister Alice. Roger and Alice's son, another William, later rose to prominence in the Haberdashers' Company, and we shall hear more of him later. So it seems that there may already have been a link between Newport and the Haberdashers' Company.

Our William became a Freeman of the Company in 1613, later becoming a Liveryman and a member of the Court of Assistants. He was Fourth Warden in 1644 and in 1649 was elected as Alderman of the City of London, though he paid a fine rather than taking up the duties of the office. This was fairly common practice for someone who thus had the honour of the title without the commitment of time and energy it involved. He never became Master of the Company.

What was the Haberdashers' Company?

In the Middle Ages in most towns as well as in London, craftsmen and traders formed associations known as guilds to protect their trade or industry. In London they came to be known as Livery Companies from the distinctive costume or livery they wore on special occasions. When they emerged as separate from the Mercers in the late 14th century, the Haberdashers dealt with all types of clothing accessory, such as laces, pins, points, caps, purses, buttons, beads, bells and combs. As fashions became more complicated the greater was the demand for all these things. By becoming a separate company the Haberdashers acquired the right to control the quality of goods and admission to their trade. Anyone carrying out that trade had first to be apprenticed to a member of the company and then, when accepted as a Freeman, to abide by its rules. To be a Liveryman was another step up, with the right to wear the company's livery and, along with the Liverymen of the other London Companies, to elect the Mayor, Sheriffs and other city officers. They had the right to a greater number of apprentices and attended more social functions than Freemen. At the head of the Company was (and is) the Master and four Wardens, chosen each year by the Court of Assistants, an inner group of Liverymen. The normal advancement to Master was through the offices of Wardens. By the end of the reign of Henry VIII the Worshipful Company of Haberdashers was established as eighth in the hierarchy of the Twelve Great Livery Companies of the City of London.

At first the Haberdashers had their own shops and supplied the packmen who attended fairs and peddled their wares throughout the country. As time went on many began to trade in a much wider field, becoming wholesale importers of goods, including wool. By the 17th century all types of merchant could be members of the Company.

We have no idea what William Adams' speciality was. All we can gather from his funeral oration was that he was a self-made man, blessed with 'a very fair Estate – the fruit of Industry, not purchased by fraud or injury or oppression – but by a diligent and laborious hand'.[3] We know he had a shop, which would imply that he was in the retail trade, but he could have dealt wholesale as well. Certainly towards the end of his life he was immensely wealthy.

Why did William Adams found a school?

Thomas Horton, in William Adams' funeral sermon, describes how, after William Adams had made provision for his many relatives, 'his next care was of the public and doing good abroad: for which purpose after good and serious and very private advice taken with such friends as were fit to be consulted in such a business, he pitched upon a design of founding a free grammar school at Newport in the County of Salop, the place of his nativity.'

If we wish to know why William Adams founded a school in preference to any other charity we need look no further than the prevailing interest in education and the tradition of founding grammar schools which reached its peak in the 17th century. In the Middle Ages people had left land to monasteries in the hope of receiving benefits from the prayers of the monks, but by the 15th century bequests to monasteries had gone out of fashion. People turned to founding chantries, whereby a priest would say mass for the soul of the founder and any others named in the bequest. Newport's chantry and College of St Mary is an example of this. By the time that the chantries were abolished in 1548 it was considered popish idolatry to believe that masses for the dead could affect their destiny in the afterlife. At the same time the New Learning, led by Erasmus at the beginning of the 16th century, spread enthusiasm for pure classical Latin instead of the church Latin of medieval times. It became the language of diplomacy and international learning.

By Elizabeth's reign the two main areas of charitable giving were in education and help for the poor. The founding of schools combined three aims, educating the young in good humanistic learning, replacing outdated popish prejudice with Protestant beliefs and giving a chance for a poor boy to better his position in society. Many a labourer's son went from grammar school to university as a sizar (servant) to a more wealthy student and was able to get a degree, which usually led to a career in the church. As many endowed schools were founded in the first half of the seventeenth century as in the whole of the previous century.

Members of the Haberdashers' Company took part in this increase in giving. A number of their charities were founded to spread the word of Puritanism. Some established lectureships which functioned outside the parochial system, and others left money to buy advowsons (the right to appoint parish clergy) so that godly ministers could be chosen and have adequate salaries for their work. The living at Albrighton, Shropshire, has since then been in the hands of the Haberdashers' Company, and the Governors of Newport Grammar School would frequently visit Albrighton at the same time as they came to inspect William Adams' foundation. This still happens. Two grammar schools were founded by Haberdashers during this period. The first was at Bunbury, Cheshire, by Thomas Aldersey in 1594, and the second, and much more substantial establishment, was at Monmouth, by William Jones in 1614. William Adams must have been aware of the Company's care in administering these two schools, so he was following in Haberdasher footsteps in founding a school of his own. It is interesting to note here that the Haberdashers' Aske's Schools now at Elstree and Hatcham were not founded as grammar schools by Robert Aske in 1690. He founded an almshouse for 20 poor single Freemen of the Haberdashers' Company and a school for 20 sons of poor Freemen. This had a chequered history and was reorganised as four schools, two for boys and two for girls, in 1873.

The Family of William Adams

William Adams never married so in addition to founding the Free Grammar School at Newport he was able to use his considerable wealth in helping other members of his family and founding a number of charities. In fact the picture that emerges is that of everybody's favourite uncle! He made ample provision for his nephews and nieces, in educating them in a suitable manner, helping them to set themselves up in life and seeing that they made suitable marriages.

There are numerous Adams families in Shropshire and North Staffordshire and so far it has been impossible to locate earlier members of William Adams' own family with absolute certainty. There were no Adams in Newport at the time of the Lay Subsidy of 1524, but there were yeomen of that name at Edgmond and Little Aston. A century later there were many Adams families in Newport itself, mostly tradesmen. They had links with the Adams who had been potters at Burslem in Staffordshire since the 15th century.[4] The family tree set out here has been pieced together from a variety of sources and is confirmed by the bequests in William Adams' will.[5]

William spent considerable money and energy in supporting the children of his elder brother John. He sent Walter to Grammar School in London,

William Adams' Family

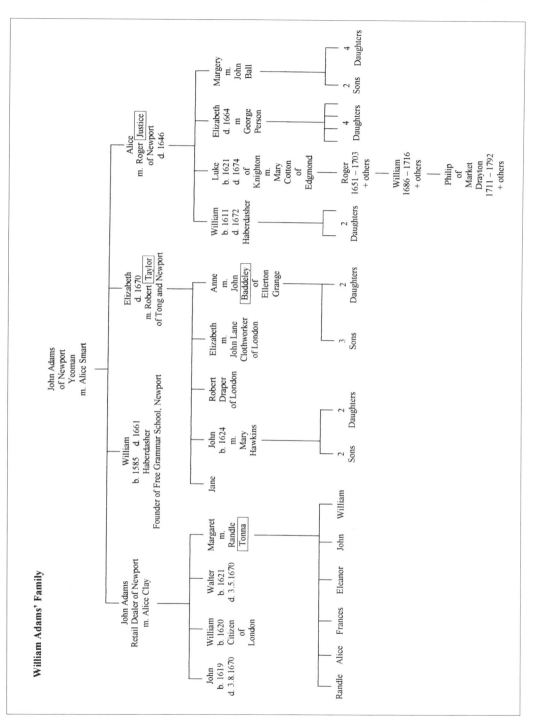

> # Walter Adams of Ifcoyd Gent: being born in this town, gave to the poor 5l.

From a dole board in Newport Parish Church.

and afterwards to Emmanuel College, Cambridge. He became a Fellow of Emmanuel College and in 1658 Minister of Hampstead near London. Emmanuel College was known for its Puritan leanings so it is no surprise to find that a year after William's death Walter refused to accept the 1662 Prayer Book, which restored the Church of England services and doctrines to what they had been before the Commonwealth, and resigned his post. He was one of nearly 2,000 ministers nationwide who were ejected from their livings for this reason. John Malden, minister of Newport since 1658 and an eminent and respected Puritan in the area, was one, as was Thomas Gilbert, minister of Edgmond. Walter Adams was not destitute after this and he was able to live the life of a country gentleman thanks to the generosity of his uncle. He retired to live at Iscoyd Hall in Flintshire, a few miles from Whitchurch, which William had bought in 1657. This was a sizeable estate, which is shown on Richard Blome's 1673 map of Shropshire. Unfortunately the Hall no longer exists; it was pulled down in the 18th century to make way for the new Iscoyd Park.

In his diary, Philip Henry,[6] another dispossessed minister who now lived at Broad Oak Farm, very near the Iscoyd estate, noted on 15 August 1663, 'I visited Mr Adams lately come from London, hee hath brought with him great store of books'. 3 May 1670 brought this sad entry, 'This day dy'd Mr Walter Adams of Iscoyd an ingenuous and worthy neighbour & my good Friend'. Walter had inherited Iscoyd on the death of his uncle William and at his own death bequeathed it to his niece Alice Tonna. Among other small bequests to people living at Iscoyd Walter left £5 to the poor of Newport,[7] which is still commemorated on the Benefaction Board in St Nicholas' Church. Walter also, in 1669, gave the clock for the new Market House in Newport built according to the will of his Uncle William. John, Walter's elder brother who died three months after him, also left money to the poor of Newport in his will.[8] He also left gifts to the members of the Tonna family and local Iscoyd inhabitants so it seems that he, like Walter, lived at Iscoyd. John in 1663 had added to his uncle's benefaction by giving the clock and dial at the Free Grammar School in Newport. William, the third brother, in 1665 gave the Bell for the new Market House in Newport, with the effigy of a man to ring it. Unfortunately it was burnt in the great fire of Newport later that same month. But in 1885 the bell was stated to be still in use at the Town Hall 'and has the following inscription round its rim: "William Adams gent. of London gave this Bell 1665".[9] What has happened to it since? The inscription could indicate that William lived in London and not with his brothers at Iscoyd.

William Adams may well have helped the children of his sister Elizabeth to make their way in London. Robert became a member of the Drapers' Company and Elizabeth married John Lane, a Clothworker of London. It seems he had little need to help his nephew John Taylor, mercer of Newport and Elizabeth's eldest son. In the 1672 Hearth Tax returns John Taylor is listed as having 13 hearths; only one inhabitant of the town, William Stanton, having more at 16 (and he was noted in the Lay Subsidy list of 1661 as an Innholder). This implies a far bigger house than most, the average for Newport being two to three hearths per dwelling. It puts him almost on a par with the big landowners such as Thomas Talbott Esq of Longford with 18 and Mr Piggot of Edgmond and John Cotes of Woodcote with 19 each.[10] William Adams stated specifically in his will that the new Market House that he ordered to be built was to be 'so placed that no prejudice in the least may come to the lights of the house and shop wherein my kinsman the said John Taylor now dwelleth',[11] so even in this he was careful not to damage his nephew's livelihood. John Baddeley of Ellerton Grange, married to Elizabeth's daughter Anne, was, like the Tonna family, obviously a farmer. His sons were used from time to time by the Haberdashers in London to report on the state of their woods on the Knighton estate.

William Adams' greatest gift turned out to be to the Justice family. We have already referred to the fact that William Justice followed in his uncle's footsteps and became a Haberdasher in London. He was Master of the Company in 1663/64, and an Alderman of London 1662-1664. Luke Justice was granted the lease of the lands at Knighton, Staffordshire, and later Woodseaves, Shropshire, which William Adams bought to pay for his benefactions in Newport. William donated them to the Haberdashers' Company, and for a fixed rent of £175 per annum Luke Justice could rent them out to other tenants and reap the benefits. The original lease of 16 March 1657 was for 21 years. A second lease for 70 years was granted to him in 1667, and a third lease for 70 years was granted to his grandson William in 1714. When this lease ran out the Haberdashers decided to re-let the lands for a higher sum. As the value of money changed the Justices had been able to charge much more for the land but the Charity had been limited to the original sum. On the basis of this the Justice family was able to build a considerable fortune and position for themselves in local society. By the end of the 18th century, after they lost the tenancy of the Knighton estates, they owned lands in Hinstock, Market Drayton and Woodseaves. Henry Justice lived at The Grove, Market Drayton before building Hinstock Hall in the early 19th century, but his son Philip had to sell the estate in 1862 as he was living beyond his means.

Three families of William Adams' brothers and sisters benefited directly from his arrangements in founding the School. The children of John

Coat of arms of the Justice family.

Baddeley, Luke Justice and Randle Tonna the younger were to have priority of admission, along with children born in Newport or Chetwynd End, to the Free Grammar School.

William Adams' extended family did not merely receive money and help from him, they were actively involved in helping him set up his charities in the town. For instance among the many transactions involved in buying land on which the school was to be built was one of 1655 in which Luke Justice, yeoman, and John Taylor, mercer, bought a house, which was later transferred to William Adams. Three of his other nephews were also in the consortium of 10 London businessmen who had previously bought property in Newport, Church Aston and the Iscoyd estate and then sold them to William Adams in 1657 to allow him to spread the cost of his enterprise. By that time the schoolhouse had already been built on the site of the *Angel Inn.*

William Adams left £550 in his will for the building of a new Market House in Newport. He again used his family. Three of the trustees were his nephews: Luke Justice of Knighton; John Baddeley of Ellerton and John Taylor of Newport, the others being well known names in the town, Robert Hawkins, William Staunton and William Brown.[12] The Market House, with the Town Hall on top and room for the sale of corn between the pillars underneath, was to be sited in St Mary Street and, as we have already noted, was not to interfere with the light for John Taylor's house and shop. There were strict instructions that the building was to be started within a year of William's death, and according to a model provided by him. The pillars of hard stone 'shall or may be got in my land at Knighton and the Building over them to be of brick stone and timber'. If these instructions were not carried out his executors (in fact this was William Justice) were to spend the money in other ways, half on a Market Hall in Market Drayton, and £150 on books for the library of Newport Free Grammar School. It was built as instructed, and opened on 28 November 1663[13] and, although it was badly damaged in the Great Fire of Newport in 1665, it served the town until the 19th century.

William Adams' Town Hall (replaced in 1860).

Did William Adams have a coat of arms?

No evidence has been found by the College of Arms that either William Adams or the school have ever been granted a coat of arms, but the coat of arms used by the school was similar to that of other branches of the Adams family such as Adams of Greenfield, Adams of Sambrook and Adams of Wem. They all have three cats (or catamountains) passant gardant. The earliest seal of the Governors of the School now in existence dates from the 19th century, so we have no evidence of what was used at first. We do not know whether William Adams personally used a coat of arms.

By the 16th century Heralds from the College of Arms would tour the country periodically to check that those bearing arms had the right to do so. The draught copy of the 1663/4 Heralds' Visitation of Staffordshire gives a pedigree of three generations of our William's family, from John Adams senior through to John and Walter, living at Iscoyd, and William and Margaret. This pedigree is noted as 'certified by John Adams'. With it appears a sketch of a shield and crest incorporating three cats, similar to that on the Governors' seal but with minor additions. The pedigree was printed in the final copy of the Heralds' Visitation of Shropshire that year but with no shield or crest. A John Adams of Newport disclaimed any arms at the 1664 visitation held at the Lent Assizes in Shrewsbury. This must surely be our William Adams' nephew who either had been using arms without sufficient evidence to justify it or, when offered a grant of arms (as sketched), had declined because of the expense or because he was not interested. It seems highly likely that the question would not have arisen at all if he had not been living the life of a gentleman at Iscoyd Hall thanks to his uncle William![14]

William Adams' other benefactions

William Adams' will, dated 6 July 1660, reveals his extraordinary wealth. The total identifiable in cash was £15,719 6s. 8d., in modern terms well over £1 million. This sum does not take account of the value of the property he bequeathed, still less of the buildings and grounds at the Grammar School and the Knighton estates which he had bought earlier. Even so he envisaged some residue after his legacies; that was to go to William Justice his nephew and partner. William Justice was made sole executor. As partner he kept his half share of the business, but also an extra £6,000 from William Adams' part of it. John Lane and Walter Adams were made overseers of the will to assist William Justice. A summary of his bequests is given in Appendix A.

None of William Adams' extended family was omitted from the will. No wonder Thomas Horton at his funeral was able to say 'he hath ... with so much wisdom love and impartiality bequeathed a very fair estate among his relatives and friends, as that it is believed there's not one of them, but rests abundantly and thankfully satisfied'. It can be seen that he kept a very tight account of his financial affairs, as in several cases he adds in sums he has already given to calculate the total that person receives. In addition to family, dependants, and friends in Shropshire and London he left £150 to Christ's Hospital, of which he was a governor. The pieces of plate were duly presented to the Haberdashers by William Justice on 17 October 1661: a silver basin and two ewers. These were included in the list of plate belonging to the Company in October 1715 (by now valued at £117), so they had avoided the major refashioning of 1714 into 'something convenient and useful', but we can find no later reference to them, so maybe they were melted down soon after.[15]

The Adams families of Wem and Newport

Before leaving the Adams family it might be useful to answer a question that is often put. Had William Adams, founder of Adams' Grammar School, Newport, in 1656, any connection with Thomas Adams, founder of Adams' School, Wem, in 1650? The answer must be that there is no direct link. There are many Adams spread over Shropshire at this time. There must however have been some connection between the Wem and Newport families because they used a similar coat of arms. Born within a year of each other they obviously knew each other in London: William in his will refers to Thomas as 'my worthy friend and kinsman' and to his younger brother William as 'my loving kinsman'. This was in July 1660, soon after Charles II was restored to the throne. Earlier, however, they appear to have been on opposite sides in the great divide between King and Parliament in the Civil War.

Thomas Adams was a member of the Drapers' Company, and Lord Mayor of London in 1646. He was a supporter of King Charles I and regularly risked his position in the City by sending sums of money to him and later to the future Charles II. Thomas was one of the 20 substantial citizens of London who were sent over to Holland to greet Charles II in 1660 when it became obvious that the Commonwealth experiment in government could no longer survive. He was made a knight and then a baronet that same year so he was well thought of by the King. He was considered an important representative of Shropshire in London. After the Great Fire of Newport in 1665 the King published a Brief which was circulated nation-wide, asking for money to help the people of the town. He appointed Sir Thomas Adams, along with Alderman William Justice and another Alderman, to receive contributions from Londoners. Sir Thomas died in 1668, and his son William inherited the title and lands, principally in Norfolk. Thomas Adams was also a great supporter of the established Church and its clergy, whose fortunes were at a low ebb in the Commonwealth period.

William Adams, on the other hand, seems to have been Puritan in sympathy, although we know nothing about his political position. His friend Dr Thomas Horton was a noted Puritan, being appointed Vice Chancellor of Cambridge University during the Interregnum,[16] and most members of the Haberdashers' Company at the time seem to have been of a similar persuasion.[17] Bishops had been abolished by Parliament before the Civil War was ended and the reform of the church handed over to the Westminster Assembly. This was a body of mainly Presbyterian ministers with some laymen that drew up a Directory of Worship which superceded the Prayer Book, a Catechism and a Confession of faith. Those clergy who would not accept this were deprived of their livings (just as the Puritans were ejected after the return of the Prayer Book in 1662). William Adams in the statutes of his Free Grammar School in Newport ordered that the pupils be instructed first in the lesser, and then in the greater Catechism of this Assembly. This of course was not surprising as these arrangements were made while Oliver Cromwell was Lord Protector. What is surprising is that this Westminster Catechism appears to have been used even after the Restoration of King Charles and into the 19th century, when the Governors queried why it was still being taught!

Thomas Adams and William Adams appear to have supported different sides in the Civil War, but by 1660 attitudes had changed. Many who had been strong supporters of Parliament and the Commonwealth had become disillusioned by the end of Cromwell's reign and on his death there seemed no alternative to the return of Charles II if there was to be an orderly state. Many Puritans, as we have seen, refused to accept the return of the Prayer Book in 1662, but many, including William's friend Thomas Horton, agreed to it in the hope of moderate reform. William himself was very quick to approach the King for royal approval for his Grammar School, and there is an often repeated story that he gave Charles £1,000. Maybe Sir Thomas helped to introduce him to the King.

So perhaps the Shropshire families in London, then as now, did get together despite some differences of opinion. It certainly seems that Thomas' brother William, one of three William Adams in the records of the London Drapers' Company at this time, was part of the business consortium that helped our William Adams, as well as being his 'loving kinsman'.

To conclude this chapter on what little we know about William Adams as a person we refer to a book published in 1662, but obviously written before the death of William Adams. This was *The History of the Worthies of England* by Thomas Fuller.[18] Under Shropshire, after Sir Thomas Adams, Knight, is the entry for William Adams, Esq, born at Newport in this county. After a brief description of the School and the arrangements made for it by William Adams, he exclaims, 'But who can hold from praising so pious a performance' and bursts into verse ...

> Some cottage schools are built so low,
> The Muses there must grovelling go.
> Here, whilst Apollo's harp doth sound
> The sisters nine may dance around:
> And architects may take from hence
> The pattern of magnificence.
> Then grieve not, Adams, in thy mind,
> Cause you have left no child behind:
> Unbred! unborn is better rather,
> If so, you are a second father
> To all bred in this school so fair,
> And each of them thy son and heir.
> Long may this worthy person live to see his intentions finished and
> completed, to his own contentment!

Two

THE FOUNDING OF THE SCHOOL

We now turn to the arrangements made by William Adams in founding his Free Grammar School and the rules he laid down for its maintenance. Chapter Four will deal with how he financed it from the profits of the Knighton estate.

The school officially opened on 25 March 1657, the first day of the New Year according to the Old Style Calendar in use in England until 1752. This was the date that the statutes, instructions as to how the school was to be managed, came into force and from which the Schoolmaster's salary was paid, but it seems from a note in his diary that the first Headmaster, Thomas Chaloner, may have already opened the school in January. The newly erected building provided teaching space in the Schoolroom (later called Big School and now Big School Library) for 80 'foundation' scholars. First priority was given to boys (no girls) born in Newport and Chetwynd End, widening to boys born within three miles of the school if there was still room, then within five miles, and then to the whole of Shropshire. The Master could also take in other pupils so long as this did not interfere with his teaching of the foundation scholars. There was no mention of boarding but it was normal for boys from a distance to board with a master or lodge in the town. Boys usually started at the age of eight or nine.

It took some time to fit all the arrangements into place. We know William Adams was buying property in Newport as early as 1652. This was the *Angel Inn*, which formed the main part of the land on which he built his new school. He added other strips of land in the years that followed and, as we have seen, used relations, friends and business acquaintances to purchase some of the property to spread the financial load. He bought it all back in 1657, and on 20 May of that year formally handed it over to the Master and Wardens of the Haberdashers' Company as Governors of his Free Grammar School. This transaction was enrolled in Chancery on 1 June 1657, as the Court of Chancery had general oversight of all charities in the country.

Legal Arrangements

To establish his school on a proper legal footing William Adams had had to obtain official sanction from the government. Thus on 7 November 1656 Letters Patent were issued by Oliver Cromwell, Lord Protector of the Commonwealth. These Letters stated that William Adams 'out of his sincere intention to the public good, and the education and instruction of youth is willing

Seal of the Governors of William Adams' Charity.

and desirous, at his own costs and charges to erect and build a large and convenient schoolhouse for a Free Grammar School to be forever hereafter kept in the town of Newport'. He wished to settle the lands and tenements, which were of a yearly value of about £200, on the 'Master and Four Wardens of the Fraternity of the Art or Mystery of Haberdashers in our City of London'. The Lord Protector 'being most willing and desirous to encourage and promote the pious and charitable deeds of the said William Adams … willed, granted and ordained that for ever hereafter there be and shall be in our Town of Newport in the county of Salop one Free Grammar School'. William Adams, during his life, was to appoint the Schoolmaster and Usher of the school, and make what rules he saw fit for the running of the school. After his death this was to be the responsibility of the Governors, that is, the Master and Four Wardens of the Haberdashers' Company. The Governors were to be 'One Body Corporate and Politique' with their own Common Seal for 'sealing of their affairs and businesses', capable in law to hold all possessions in perpetuity for maintaining the charity and carrying out its business, 'the statutes for not putting lands in mortmain … notwithstanding'.

The statute of mortmain had originally been passed early in the 15th century. It enacted that anyone leaving possessions to a corporate body, such as a monastery, had to obtain a licence from the king. This was, in effect, to compensate the Crown for the lack of future income, as a corporate body never died and therefore never paid death duty. It held a 'dead hand' (mortmain) over the property. William Adams obtained a licence of mortmain from John Cooke of Holkam, who was overlord of the Manor of Knighton.

Barely a year and a half later, in September 1658, Oliver Cromwell died, and England was once again plunged into political uncertainty. Richard Cromwell took his father's place as Lord Protector but soon proved to be ineffectual. He had no charisma and very little administrative or political ability. He resigned, and after eighteen months of chaos, when the Army and the remains of Charles I's last Parliament, nicknamed the Rump, quarrelled over power, a completely new Parliament was called, elected by Royalists as well as Commonwealth supporters. This Convention Parliament immediately asked Charles II back from Holland to be King, and the Restoration of the Monarchy on 29 May 1660 was accepted with relief by everyone. William Adams had a problem: all government acts since the fall of Charles I were now illegal. He moved very quickly to get his Free Grammar School, which by now had been going for three years, legally confirmed. This was done by the Convention Parliament between May, when Charles II returned, and December when it was dissolved, in 'An Act for the Incorporating of the Master and Wardens of the Company of

Haberdashers, London, to be Governors of the Free-School and Alms-houses in Newport, in the County of Salop, of the Foundation of William Adams, and for settling of Lands and possessions on them for maintenance thereof, and other charitable Uses'. This was very similar to the Letters Patent of Oliver Cromwell, but there was an important new final clause:

> And lastly, be it enacted by the Authority aforesaid, That the said Mannor and Grange of Knighton, with the Appurtenances and all other Lands and Hereditaments, setled, and conveyed by the said William Adams to the said Governors and their Successors for the purposes aforesaid, be, and at all times hereafter shall be freed, discharged, and aquitted of, and from the payment of all, every, or any manner of Taxes, Assesments, or charges, Civil or Military whatsoever, hereafter to be laid and imposed by Authority of Parliament, or otherwise. And that the said Mannors, Messuages, Lands, Tenements, and Premisses, and the Owners and Occupiers thereof, or any of them, shall not at any time hereafter be rated, taxed, or assessed to pay any sum or sums of Money, or be otherwise charged in any way whatsoever, for or in respect of the said Mannors, Lands, and Hereditaments, or any of them, for or towards any manner of Public Tax, Assesment, or charge whatsoever, any Statute, Law, or Ordinance to the contrary hereof in any wise notwithstanding.

To get this so quickly through Parliament, and obtain this extra concession of exemption from taxation, which still applied until the late 20th century, even to the Knighton lands after they had been sold off by the Charity, William Adams must have had considerable influence. How did he manage it? A later story claims that he gave Charles II a gift of £1,000. This could well be true, as Charles was chronically short of money and generous when he could afford to be. The earliest written account of the story we have found so far was in the *Shrewsbury Chronicle* of 12 December 1772.[1] It should be noted that the *Chronicle* got the name of the founder of the school wrong, not the last time that Thomas Adams of Wem and William Adams have been muddled. The context confirms that it is the founder of Newport Grammar School who is the subject of the story.

> When Charles II was informed of the great benevolence of Sir Thomas Adams, he sent for him and asked, whether he had not greatly injured his fortune? To which he answered, That it had rather increased it; and if his majesty would procure him an act of parliament to exempt his estate from taxes, he would give him £1000. Whether the king took it we are not told but the act passed, and all the estates left by Sir Thomas, for the support of his charitable foundation, are still exempted from taxes.

Edward Jones, local historian of Newport in the 1880s, repeats the story, involving William, not Thomas, Adams and £1,000, but there is no indication of where he got his story from.[2] Incidentally, the article in the *Shrewsbury Chronicle* goes on to tell of a 'dreadful fire' that broke out in

Inscription on Beaumaris Road gate pillar (original position unknown).

Newport on 18 May 1765. The few details it gives show that it was referring to the fire of 1665! It is amazing that it could be 100 years out in a date supposedly so recent. The whole report illustrates the pitfalls of accepting without question what is printed in the local press!

This exemption from taxation of the lands funding the school must be seen against the difficulties the Haberdashers' Company was experiencing at the time. During the Civil War and Interregnum taxation had increased enormously, and many of the charities administered by the Company could not pay these taxes out of their own resources. For instance, at one point the Company had to cut the salaries of the Lecturers and Schoolmasters of the William Jones foundation at Monmouth, because the charity could not afford to pay them in full after paying the taxes demanded. In 1657 the Company tried without success to obtain remission of taxes on land in Huntingdonshire which supported the Newland charity.[3] As a member of the Court of Assistants William Adams must have been well aware of all this and he succeeded where no other Haberdasher charity had done so. A reminder of this is the stone of uncertain date which is now incorporated into a brick pillar at the Beaumaris Road gates of the school. On it is inscribed 'Here endeth the School Liberty'. Incidentally, there is no record of Thomas Adams having an Act of Parliament passed for his school at Wem, and his charity is not exempt from taxation.

The Convention Parliament had not been summoned by the King, so a new Parliament in 1661 confirmed all the laws of 1660, the founding of Newport Grammar School along with a Navigation Act, an Act prohibiting the growing of tobacco and an Act to restrain excessive usury (i.e. charging excessive interest on a loan). William's foundation was well and truly enshrined in the laws of the land.

The provisions of William Adams' charitable foundation

William Adams set down the arrangements for his charity in Newport in the First Deed of Uses[4] on 27 November 1656, less than three weeks after the issue of Letters Patent.

£175 each year, from the rents of the lands at Knighton, was to finance everything.

The details were as follows:

£20 to the preacher of Newport as long as he shall, every week, catechise the scholars, children and servants of the town, so that 'they might be instructed in the grounds of religion and the Christian faith'. If he refused this duty the Governors were to use the money instead for the benefit of the poor of Newport, or in some other way for the good of the town.

£60 for four years from 25 March 1657, then £40 per year for the Schoolmaster.

£20 per year to the Usher.

At any failure of either to perform his duties properly the Governors could use the money for other purposes, as in the case of the minister.

£24 for the binding of three poor boys, born in Newport or Chetwynd End, as apprentices in London or Shrewsbury or some other town of manufacture. They were to be between 12 and 18 years of age, chosen by the minister, Schoolmaster and churchwardens and at least five other of the 'ablest and most discrete persons' of the town. Once in seven years there were to be no apprentices paid for, as this money was to be used to pay the expenses of a visit by the Governors or other Haberdashers from London, so that they could inspect the school, the masters and all the other commitments of the charity in Newport.

24 shillings a year to be paid to 'four godly and learned ministers' and 'three other the best knowing, judicious and qualified people' (later changed to six clergy and four laymen) to act as Visitors, i.e. local people who could visit and inspect the school. The money was to be used for the expenses of the visitation. They were to visit several times a year, as they saw fit.

20 shillings a year for a poor scholar to ring the bell to call the boys together.

20 shillings a year for a poor scholar to sweep and clean the schoolhouse and the seats, benches and desks.

Both these were to be appointed by the Schoolmaster.

£5 a year set aside for repairing the schoolhouse and almshouses, at the discretion of the Governors. Money left over was to be kept 'in bank' until needed, or the Governors could help the Schoolmaster or Usher, if well deserving, with repairs to their houses.

£20 for the maintenance of four scholars from the school at Oxford or Cambridge. This was to start in 1661, presumably to give time for the first boys to be brought up to this level. One scholar appointed each year was to receive an Exhibition of £5 a year for four years. William Adams was to choose them during his lifetime, after that the Schoolmaster and Visitors should do so during the last ten days of February. The choice was to be sent for approval to the Governors. The College where the student was studying was to send written confirmation in subsequent years that he was still attending, and worthy of the Exhibition. If an Exhibitioner died or left college, his money was to be divided among the others, so that they could then receive more than £5 a year.

£20 16s. a year, i.e. £5 4s. each, to four aged and poor people: two men, widowers or bachelors, and two women, widows or maids, who are to live in the almshouses to be built on each side of the gate entering into the court in front of the schoolhouse. After William Adams' death these were to be chosen by the same people who chose the apprentices, and their names were to be sent for approval to the Governors.

£20 a year to be paid to 20 poor people of the Haberdashers' Company.

£2 a year to the clerk and beadles of the Haberdashers' Company.

If there was any shortfall in the rents received, the £24 for placing out apprentices was to be cut or cancelled for that year.

Were the salaries paid to the Master and Usher of William Adams' Free Grammar School generous? If we compare them with others in Shropshire they certainly seem so. Thomas Adams' foundation at Wem, six years before, carried similar salaries: £40 for the Head, £20 for the Second Master and £10 for the Third Master. Wem was, incidentally, the only school in Shropshire besides Shrewsbury School which provided for more than two masters. Shrewsbury School, by the second half of the 16th century one of the largest grammar schools in the country, paid Thomas Chaloner's successor, Richard Pigott, £60 as Headmaster and £20 as Catechist, the other masters getting £45, £30 and £20 respectively. Previous to this the Head probably still received the Elizabethan salary of £40. Of the ten other Shropshire grammar schools only Ludlow (£25 a year in 1661), Bridgnorth (£24 in 1638) and High Ercall (£20 in 1663) paid their Masters about half that of the new schools, and the others lagged far behind. A survey of Warwickshire schools in the 17th century has found that the majority of headships there were worth only £20 a year, although some, e.g. King Edward VI Grammar School, Birmingham (£50 in 1655), exceeded this.[5]

The endowed salary, i.e. the salary paid by the foundation charity, was not the only source of income available to a schoolmaster. The foundation scholars were to pay on entry 2s. 6d. (18d. to the Master and 12d. to the Usher), poorer children being charged only 12d., but the Master could charge what he liked to boys outside the foundation, and if they boarded he could gain even more income. We do not know what the boarding arrangements were at Newport. The payment of an entrance fee seems to have been customary in most schools. Shrewsbury School in the 1630s had a sliding scale of entry fees from 10s. for the son of a lord to 1s. for those of low degree born in the county. The charging of tuition fees by the term or year was not commonplace among endowed schools until the 18th century.

The other way a schoolmaster could gain additional revenue was by holding a benefice (serving as a parish priest) at the same time. This was frowned upon in most school statutes. William Adams laid down that the Master and Usher were not to take on any other 'charge or employment to the hindrance of his or their performing of the duty of the said place'. This was interpreted by the Governors in different ways at different times. They used it as an excuse to get rid of Thomas Millington as usher in 1667, but many other Masters and Ushers did hold office as ministers in the church. One wonders how much time they gave to their parishioners!

William Adams' donation of £20 a year for the minister of Newport must have been very welcome for until then his income had been only £10 with, since 1633, an additional £5 given by William Robson of the Salters' Company, London (another Novaportan who had made good in London). This lack of funds was due to the fact that, before the Reformation, Newport's church was staffed by a college of priests. When this college was dissolved by the Chantries Act of 1547, the Crown put the rectory, the glebe land and all tithes and dues up for sale. The new owners took all the profits (£50 from tithes alone in 1655) and had to pay only £10 annually to the minister of Newport. This compares most unfavourably with other parishes in the area. In 1655 Edgmond's income was £307, Cheswardine's an amazing £700, Longford's was £60 and Lilleshall's £88.[6] At last in 1700 a public subscription was raised among the people of Newport to buy back these possessions of the church and thereafter the minister received a better income. A list of the contributors can be seen on the benefactions board in St Nicholas' Church.

The English School

In the 1920s and '30s the school claimed that it had been founded in 1442 and merely refounded in 1656. Was this true? The short answer is no, but we must examine where the story came from. To understand it we must return to Newport's college of priests.

1442 was the year in which a certain Thomas Draper was given permission to buy the Church of St Nicholas from Shrewsbury Abbey and found a college of priests with a Warden and four Chaplains. The first Warden was appointed in 1452 and he and his successors were parish priests of Newport.

The Chantries Act of 1547 provided that in every place where a guild or fraternity had recently kept a grammar school some guild lands or income could be assigned to continue it. The four commissioners who investigated Newport certified that a grammar school had 'always been kept' by Richard Robins, one of the Fellows of the College of Newport, (although there had been no mention of a school when the college was founded). No record of a charter for the school has been found but it must have continued because whoever owned the site of the college and its lands had to pay £5 for the schoolmaster each year as well as £10 for the minister. William Robson also gave £5 to the schoolmaster when he gave £10 to the minister. In 1635 the current owner of the college lands told the Court of Exchequer that the four previous owners had never paid the £15 but he was ordered to do so. One hopes that the State had continued to pay the two salaries even if the owners of the land had not kept to their side of the bargain![7]

Was this the school that William Adams himself went to at the end of the 16th century? We do not know, but it seems likely. Certainly by the 1650s he saw the need for a completely new school. In his First Deed of Uses of 27 November 1656 he states that it was 'by experience found that the Booth Hall where the school for the said town was formerly kept was very ill convenient if not hurtful both for the town schoolmaster and schol-ars'. So he had built a new one, but he did not ignore the old one. In his will he left two closes of land in Norbroom to the English School, 'usually kept in the Booth Hall', so that the rents would provide income of nine pounds a year. This was so that the children of the poorest people in New-port 'of civil and honest demeanour may be there freely taught to read English'. The lands he gave are now under the Barnmeadow estate, ap-proached along School Ground Lane. He asked the Haberdasher Governors of his Grammar School to keep an eye on the English School and its affairs on their seven-yearly visits to Newport. Richard Barnfield made further benefactions to the English School in 1665 so it had a steady income.

This school continued as a 'feeder' school to the Grammar School, although many boys never went on to learn Latin. It was finally closed in 1878. If any school could claim to have been founded in the 15th century it would be the English School, not William Adams' Free Grammar School.

The Master and the Usher

The appointment of the Master (headmaster) and the Usher (assistant mas-ter) was carefully regulated by statutes laid down on 2 February 1657. They are summarised here, but sections 2, 3, 5 and 8 deserve detailed study and are printed in full in Appendix B.

The Master had to be an MA of either Oxford or Cambridge (there were no other universities until the 19th century). The Governors were to exam-ine and appoint him, and after a six-month trial period the local Visitors were to send them a certificate of approval so that they could confirm the appointment under the common seal. The Usher was to be a BA, serve a three-month trial period, and the Master was to join with the Visitors in signing the certificate of approval. Either could be removed from his post if he behaved badly or took other employment which hindered him in the performance of his duties. Both had to be constantly resident and in attend-ance, except for very good reason. The Visitors could take action if there were complaints about them. They were not to be absent at the same time.

The Schoolmaster was to have the bigger house and garden and the Usher the smaller one, rent free. Each was to sign a bond for £100 to maintain the property and leave the goods and furniture, including the books in the library, in good condition when he left. This was a normal way at the time of ensuring that an obligation was carried out, but it seems an extremely large sum of money when you consider what their income was. The £100 was not actually paid, as a deposit is nowadays, but could be called upon if needed when the property was examined at the end of the arrangement. The Master and Usher were to be responsible for repairs to their houses but in practice this arrangement was not always carried out, the Governors tending to pay for the larger repairs. It was the cause of quite a lot of argument over the years. The tendency was to leave the buildings unrepaired, and by the end of the 18th century they were in a very bad way.

A long section of the statutes was devoted to the care of the library, which is printed in full in Appendix B and will be dealt with in Chapter Three. Finally, William Adams laid down that if there were any differences of opinion about these statutes the Governors were to have the final say, after consulting the Visitors. All this became very relevant in the notorious case of John Langley early in the 19th century. The statutes were still being referred to late in that century.

Several bonds signed by a Master or Usher still exist, together with inventories of their property. It is interesting to see what were considered essential fitments and furniture in those days.

> September 25th 1657 A catalogue of the goods belonging to the Head School master, his house of the Free School in Newport to be kept and preserved by the present master from time to time.
> Imprimis In the hall a drawing table
> Item Kitchen two dressers and a shelf
> Item Parlour a long table
> Item Cellar a beer stall
> Item In several separate chambers seven new bedsteads corded
> Item In the closet in the parlour a form and shelf
> Item In the closet at the stair head shelves for books
> Item on the doors of the hall, hall chamber and kitchen chamber and the gallery with locks and keys also on the closet door at the stair head
> Item the hall and parlour now wainscotted with benches of wainscott in the hall
> Item A lock and key for the library door
>
> > by me Thos Chaloner

On the same day a catalogue of goods in the Usher's house was made out:

> Imprimis In the hall one long table
> Item In the kitchen two dressers and a shelf
> Item In the cellar a beer stall
> Item In five several chambers five new bedsteads
> Item In the little study three shelves
> Item the hall new wainscott with benches of wainscott therein
> Item Lock and key for the library door, the hall door and also four several locks for four several rooms
>
> > by me David Peirce[8]

A drawing table would be one with leaves that pull out to extend it, whereas a long table would be a basic type of trestle table whose size could not be altered. A closet was a cupboard. A beer stall was a shelf to hold beer barrels. Wooden bedsteads had cords threaded across them to provide a base for a mattress. The number of beds provided presumably catered for a large family and servants, rather than for boarders. Wainscott means oak or oak panelling. This was just basic furniture: stools, chairs,

chests for storage and straw or feather mattresses would be supplied by the Master and Usher themselves.

Despite these precautions, a little later when Samuel Edwards and Ambrose Rea, Master and Usher, signed inventories and bonds to keep their houses in good repair, we find the following:

> 30 April 1669 Upon examination of the goods mentioned in this inventory was found to be wanting in the usher's house
> One Bedstead and one cord from another Bedstead, two keys to two small locks
> In the master's house was found to be wanting
> One Basse Viol, one sack in the kitchen, one bedstead and three bed cords, one stall of bees given and sett in the master's garden, two locks and keys, one from the hall Chamber door and the other from the Gallery door, which are removed to two outdoors.[9]

A 17th-century wainscot chair.

Presumably these losses were not the fault of the incoming masters but of their predecessors, but whether any action was taken against them we have no record. The previous Master had retired through ill health, and the Usher was his son. Maybe no one liked to press them on these losses.

The Pupils and the Curriculum

William Adams' final statutes, signed on the same day as those concerning the Master and the Usher, gave detailed instructions on how the school should be run, the curriculum, the school day and the behaviour of the scholars. These are set out in Appendix C and will repay careful study.

The statutes still hang, in their original case, at the end of Big School Library. They are practically indecipherable today but in 1937 the enterprising editors of the school magazine, the *Novaportan*, got some senior boys to transcribe them and published them in the December edition of that year. Some of the wording had been rubbed out by then, but luckily we have other copies of the original statutes.

They raise some interesting questions. Were they what was to be expected in a school of this period? Whom had William Adams consulted before drawing them up?

He must have been affected by the ferment of educational ideas that surfaced during the Commonwealth and possibly by the many publications designed to improve teaching methods such as *Orbis Sensualium Pictus* (*The World in Pictures*) written by the Czech John Comenius, the leading European educationalist. This little book aimed to make learning an exciting journey by the use of pictures; used properly it would not have been stuffy or dull. In 1659 a version in Latin and English was issued by the schoolmaster

Charles Hoole who the following year himself wrote the influential *New Discovery of the Old Art of Teaching School.* At the time Charles Hoole was running a very successful private school in Tokenhouse Gardens, Lothbury, London, 'where the generality of youth were instructed to a miracle'[10] – this was just round the corner from Lawrence Lane where William Adams lived. In a small community like 17th-century London, William Adams can scarcely have been unaware of Hoole's work. Was he one of the friends 'fit to be consulted' about William's design for founding a grammar school? Hoole was appointed Schoolmaster at Monmouth in July 1663, at the request of the local community, but had to leave the following year when he refused to give up his church living.[11]

Whether William Adams had a view on educational methods is not clear from the statutes – school statutes in general did not specify the methods of teaching to be used, only the content. However, it is interesting to note that clause 14 of the statutes states specifically that 'the master shall read and teach classical authors, in order to [?aid] grammatical learning and knowledge of the tongues …'. Many educationalists at this time, including the poet John Milton, were speaking out against the sterile teaching of grammar rules without applying them in reading useful Latin authors at the same time.

William Adams' statutes were similar to those of earlier schools. He laid down that Latin, Greek and Hebrew should be taught, although Hebrew was not normally included in a grammar school curriculum. Its inclusion may reflect William Adams' religious viewpoint. We have no evidence that it was actually taught at Newport, although the library had several Hebrew texts.

In common with all endowed schools, William Adams' Free School at Newport had a strong religious ethos. Prayers were said at the beginning and end of each day, the Westminster Assembly catechism was learnt every Saturday afternoon and pupils attended church twice on a Sunday. As with many schools, the pupils were expected to give an account on Monday morning of what they had learned at church. Some school statutes state specifically that boys should take notes of the sermon, ready for class discussion the next day. John Brinsley, in his *Ludus Literarius* of 1612, gives detailed instructions as to how this should be done, so that the sermon was not only an occasion to hear God's Word, but also an opportunity to improve a boy's note-taking ability and his analytical skills. Younger boys who could not write well were expected to make mental notes, the others would be expected to translate their sermon notes into Latin! No wonder 17th-century society took a keen interest in theological matters.

The six classes or forms into which the school was divided would have been just that – six forms or benches to sit on – and each boy was seated in order of his ability so 'going to the top of the class' really meant something. It is interesting that William Adams actually set down that there could be an appeal to the Visitors if a pupil felt he had been unjustly treated. We can pick up echoes of the fierce competition that was felt about this in contemporary writings. Adam Martindale, who has left a detailed description of his schooldays in pre-Civil War Lancashire, tells of how he was so upset when two 'arrant dunces' were placed above him in class that he got his father to remove him from the school.[12] In that case it appeared that the poorly paid schoolmaster had been given money by the fathers of the two boys to elevate them to the top positions in the class. This story also illustrates the difficulties that could arise in treating free and fee-paying pupils equally.

William Adams' instructions that boys who were capable of speaking Latin should speak only that amongst themselves, and that once a month there should be speeches and open discussion, were typical of schools at that time. In fact the 'proposing grammar or historical questions one unto another' so that there was competition amongst them very much ties in with what Charles Hoole recommended in his book. Hoole suggested 3 o'clock on Friday afternoon as suitable for weekly disputations between teams of boys, as a sort of game. Hoole (and Brinsley before him) thought these disputations should be on grammar, phrases, poetry and even capping verse.

The school year, set out in clauses 7 and 8, was also normal for grammar schools at that time: holidays of up to ten days at Easter and Whitsuntide and 16 to 24 days at Christmas, but no summer holiday. It is interesting to note that William Adams does not use the term Christmas, but 'the time called the Nativity': Christmas and its attendant jollity was frowned on as popish by the Puritans. On Christmas Day 1656 Parliament met as if it were an ordinary day, but many members did not turn up and many tradesmen were keeping it as a holiday. Soldiers were sent round London on Christmas morning to search all kitchens and ovens and to carry away any meat they found being cooked.[13] But all these attempts at repressing traditional festivities did not last. William Adams was obviously following the usual grammar school dates and wisely ignored the current Puritan fashion. The timetable was typical:

> 10 March - 10 September: 6am - 11am and 1pm - 5pm
> 10 September - 10 March: 7am - 11am and 1pm - 5pm
> (7.30am - 11.30am in the two shortest months)

Every Thursday afternoon was to be a 'time of recreation'.

The stipulation that 'no candles shall be used for teaching in the school at any time' must have been a precaution against fire. One would think it would shorten the school day considerably in the winter, but it did not do so as much as the boys might have hoped! Books were very scarce, most learning was done by chanting aloud in unison, so that there was no need for much light – especially if the Master organised the school day round this problem.

As for behaviour, the statutes speak for themselves. There was obviously some fear that mixing with local boys would have a bad effect (maybe lead to fights?). The expulsion for disobedience on the third occasion, after parents or friends had been kept informed, has a very modern ring to it. Schools were definitely expected to teach pupils good manners and behaviour; this was firmly entrenched before the Reformation. Erasmus' book *de Civilitate Morum puerilium* was translated into English in 1532 as *The Cultivation of Manners* and was in regular use thereafter. Charles Hoole recommends that it be read by schoolboys in class. It emphasises self-respect and consideration for others as the basis for true courtesy. This sounds very familiar to a modern ear.

Clause 3 banning children with 'noisome [smelly] or infectious diseases' shows that they knew that quarantine was an effective way of preventing the spread of disease even though they had not discovered its cause.

The very first sentence of these statutes poses a question. In what way was the school to be 'free for the teaching of Latin Greek and Hebrew' if even those fourscore scholars had to pay an admission fee? There has been much debate on what was meant by a 'free school', as most of them charged for admission. The answer must be that the endowment produced a regular income for the teacher, so there was no charge for tuition for the free scholars. A private school with no resources would have to charge a recurring tuition fee.

Before leaving William Adams' statutes, which were very much in line with those of previous schools, it is good to find that these themselves were held in high regard by others. The Trustees of Bolton School, Lancashire, which had been in decay, and was refounded in 1646, spent some time investigating the regulations of other schools so as to formulate the best possible statutes for their school. There is no record of what they actually drew up, but Robert Lever, one of the Trustees, sent a copy to his brother James in London, asking for his opinion. James writes in December 1681 saying that he had very little experience of this and was sure the Trustees knew far more than he did and had taken good advice in drawing them up. He goes on to say, 'All the service that I can do you and all the satisfaction that I can give you is this, that I have seen the Orders of another School, and can assure you that your Orders are as full and almost in everything run parallel with theirs. One Mr Adams, of London, builds not long since a free school at Newport, and endowed it, he being a haberdasher himself, hath settled the government of that school in the Haberdashers' company, and your Orders are in substance the same with theirs, wherein there was any little variance I took some few notes of ...'.[14] He goes on to enumerate some of William Adams' statutes. As there is no record of the statutes of Bolton School at this time we do not know whether they used this advice, but at least it indicates that William Adams' foundation was known and respected in London.

Three

THE SCHOOL BEGINS

The First Headmaster: Thomas Chaloner

'... a learned and facetious man'

With the above words Richard Gough, in his celebrated history of Myddle near Shrewsbury, describes Thomas Chaloner, the first Headmaster of Adams' Grammar School. By 'facetious' Gough meant, in the language of the time, 'witty and urbane'. We know much more about Chaloner than William Adams because, from 1637 to 1645, he was Headmaster of Shrewsbury School which has preserved the school register that Chaloner also used as a diary for many years. No records have survived at Newport.

Chaloner was born in 1600, the son of a clergyman, and entered Shrewsbury School in 1614. He went on to Jesus College, Cambridge, graduating as BA in 1620 and MA in 1624. There is evidence that he was ordained priest at Peterborough in 1626 and around 1634 made Headmaster at the school in Geddington, Northamptonshire.

From this apparent obscurity, Thomas Chaloner moved in 1637 to become Headmaster of Shrewsbury School which was then the largest school in England, with a national reputation. Chaloner soon made a good impression on the Shrewsbury people and the Corporation thanked St John's College, Cambridge, whose right it was to appoint the Headmaster, for sending 'so able and every way qualified a schoolmaster'. In each of the next three years well over 100 new names were entered in the school register including Richard Roderick who went on to become the first Headmaster of Adams' Grammar School, Wem, founded by Sir Thomas Adams in 1650. It is a nice thought that the first Headmaster of Adams' Grammar School, Newport taught the first Headmaster of Adams' School, Wem!

At the start of the English Civil War in 1642, King Charles I came to Shrewsbury to raise money and men. The people of Shrewsbury received him with enthusiasm and Thomas Chaloner lodged five eminent members of the King's court in the school and his own house. Because the school finances were flourishing, he made a loan of £600 to the King.

During the two years following the King's visit, town after town in Shropshire and North Wales fell into the hands of the Puritans. The people of Shrewsbury held out for a long time until Parliament forces captured the town during the night of 22 February 1645. Chaloner's Royalist sympathies were too well known for him to continue as Headmaster of the school and

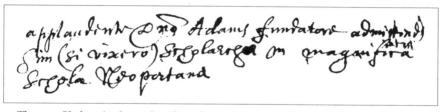

Thomas Chaloner's diary describing his appointment to the 'magnificent school at Newport'.

he was ejected from his position and deprived of his possessions. He immediately left Shrewsbury with his wife and family.

During the next eight and a half years they lived in nine different places in Shropshire, Staffordshire and North Wales. Wherever they stayed Chaloner started a school or became Headmaster of an existing one.[1] It seems to have been his restless disposition rather than his Royalist views that usually precipitated a move. When he left Shrewsbury, Chaloner removed the school register and took it with him; thereafter it became his diary, in which he recorded his personal affairs as well as school matters. He wrote mostly in Latin, occasionally in English, and used Greek when he wanted to be rude! He wrote about his sons' debts, his daughter's unsuitable marriage and his battles with Puritan authorities. In a week of self-analysis he confessed to drinking too much. But there was also wit, a buoyant spirit and a love of Latin puns!

Wherever he was he attracted large numbers of pupils, many of whom followed him from school to school. By 1653 he was headmaster of Ruthin School in North Wales, his ninth post since leaving Shrewsbury. In 1655 he was again in danger of ejection for his Royalist beliefs and went to London to petition Cromwell. Cromwell left the decision on his future to the local Major-General who allowed him to remain at Ruthin.

Immediately after recording this Chaloner noted, 'Mr Gilbert has secured my appointment (if I live long enough) as Headmaster of the magnificent Newport School; this favour being granted by the Lord Protector and Council through the good offices of the Major-General and with the approval of Mr Adams, the Founder'. Thomas Gilbert, Rector of Edgmond, often nicknamed 'the Bishop of Shropshire', was an assistant Commissioner for the 'ejection of scandalous ministers and Schoolmasters' (i.e. Royalist sympathisers) and therefore a man of considerable power and influence. Chaloner had done well to secure his active support in obtaining Cromwell's assent to the appointment.

Thomas Chaloner at Newport

Chaloner recorded that he visited Newport on 24 July 1656 and no Ruthin entries appear in his register after that. He wrote down the names of 45 Ruthin boys who were to go with him, including his fourth son, David. A scribbled note at the side of this list said, 'I have written this on January 6, tomorrow God willing, the school will open'. This suggests that Chaloner

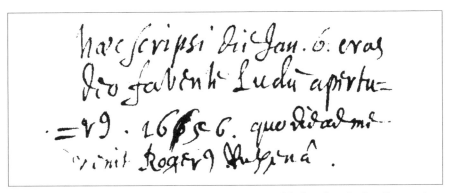

Thomas Chaloner's note on 6 January 1657 (New Style) that the school will open the next day.

started his duties on 7 January (the day after Epiphany, the usual start to a school term). This is almost three months before 25 March, when the school statutes officially came into force. So did the first boys arrive on 7 January or 25 March and was Chaloner paid between those dates?

In many ways Thomas Chaloner was a surprising choice as Headmaster of a new school. He was 56 years old and had little solid achievement to point to in his 12 years of restless wandering. We can only conclude that, despite all this, Chaloner's reputation as an outstanding teacher was undiminished. His first Usher was David Peirce who had been with him at a previous school, and whom he had supported at Cambridge, but by September 1658 he had been replaced by Chaloner's eldest son Thomas who had for three years been Master of Nantwich School. He was 31 and no doubt possessed the energy needed to build up a new school. He must have been an assertive character because he took over his father's register and recorded his own appointment in it. He then wrote a list of 242 boys' names, in no discernible order. The previous three leaves had been torn out of the register so possibly Chaloner junior made a fair copy of what his father had written down untidily as each boy joined the school. This list is often cited as evidence that there were 242 boys in the school by 1659. We think this is most unlikely.

If we look at the Shrewsbury School register for 1636-1664 we see that the lists are of admissions and not the names of boys who were in the school at a given time. Only the date of entry and the admission fee paid is recorded. There is no alphabetical order even for boys arriving on the same day. Since Thomas Chaloner operated this system at Shrewsbury and his other nine schools it is reasonable to suppose he would continue to do so at Newport. We should therefore look at the list of 242 names as an admissions list that was started in 1658 and stopped in March 1663 when Chaloner senior returned to Shrewsbury, taking the register with him. Many boys must have stayed a very short time at the school – we know this was the case at other schools. There is also the point that William Adams had provided for 80 pupils and had stipulated that if numbers rose above 130 the Headmaster had to appoint a third master and pay for him personally. There is no evidence that this happened. The school could not have accommodated 242 pupils for teaching nor provided board and lodging for the considerable number who would have had to board. (Newport was then a town of around a thousand people and could not have produced that number of day boys.)

If there were never 242 boys in the school at any one time, how many were there when the school opened? At the back of Chaloner's register on an unnumbered page, in his handwriting, is another shorter list of 25 boys headed 'Scholars of the foundation in the free grammar school of Newport'. It is dated 26 June and although no year is given it is most probably 1657, soon after he signed his bond to keep the Master's house in good repair. Fifteen are boys he brought from Ruthin; only six can be identified as

List of the twenty-five scholars of the Foundation.

having Newport family connections – Cranmer, Malden (possibly the son of the Rector), Piggott, and the three Stantons. We therefore suggest that the school started with 25 foundation scholars rather than the 80 that William Adams had planned for.

The arrival of his son at the school may have allowed Chaloner more time for teaching and academic pursuits. In December 1658 he sent two complimentary addresses in elegant Latin verse to Mr William Dugard, Headmaster of Merchant Tailors' School, London, who had recently published a Lexicon of the Greek Testament for use in schools.[2] Both were published in the 1660 edition of the book. In one of them Chaloner says that he has been teaching Greek to boys for 35 years, it has turned his hair white and the bell for the end of school has often brought release from the long tedium of hard labour to the exhausted schoolmaster. He thanks Dugard for helping teachers but particularly 'I, whose little boat, hitherto tossed by endless storms and suffering the terrors of sky and sea, now rests safe in New Port'. Whatever else had happened to him, Chaloner had not lost his love for a play on words.

Charles II was restored to the throne in May 1660. In September 1662 the Puritan Headmaster of Shrewsbury School was suspended from his duties and Thomas Chaloner was invited to return. He was clearly ready to leave the safe haven of his 'New Port', but for an unexpected reason, for he recorded in his register that 'I, Thomas Chaloner, after 19 years in exile, return to my old place' and continued 'The undermaster at Newport behaved in such a high-handed and troublesome manner towards me that, unable to stand association with him any longer, I moved here with my second wife and some young sons of gentlemen'. As we know, the undermaster was his eldest son Thomas! Returning to Shrewsbury in March 1663, he admitted 43 boys to the school in a single week, of whom fifteen had been with him at Newport. He had not lost his power to attract pupils. His second period at Shrewsbury was to last barely eighteen months for he died in October 1664 and was buried at St Mary's Church, Shrewsbury.

The School Buildings

Many school foundations started from modest beginnings with pious intentions but inadequate funds. They often had only a room in the local church, as at Wem. They would have had little equipment, few books, and a master who was paid a meagre salary. There were a number of such schools in Shropshire.

Newport's Free Grammar School had a very different beginning. William Adams provided a new purpose-built and visually striking building as the following contemporary account by Thomas Fuller shows:

> 1. The building is of brick, with windows of freestone, wherein the school is threescore and ten in length, and two and twenty feet in breadth and height. 2. Over it a fair library, furnished with plenty and choice books. At the south end, the lodgings of the schoolmaster, whose salary is sixty; on the north the usher's, whose stipend is thirty pounds per annum. 3. Before the front of the school a stately *crypto-porticus*, or fair walk all the length of the school, with pillars erected; and on the top thereof a leaden terrace, with rails and balusters. 4. Two alms-houses for poor people, at convenient distance from the school, with competent maintenance. 5. Two gardens a-piece, for schoolmaster and usher, with well nigh two acres of ground for a place for the scholars to play in.[3]

Adams' Grammar School is rare among ancient grammar schools in that its original building is still in school use. The 'lodgings of the schoolmaster' was the Headmaster's house up to 1979 and is now used for school offices. The Usher's house was smaller than that of the Headmaster and now contains the main staircase (probably a late 19th-century addition) to the schoolroom on the first floor, now the library. This was for over two hundred years the only teaching room, hence it was referred to as Big School. The adjacent room reached by stairs in the centre of the east wall was the library referred to by Fuller and remained so until 1991 when Big School was converted into a library.

We have no plan or drawing of the original building. However, we have discovered in the Bodleian Library, Oxford an undated drawing by an

18th-century artist, Francis Perry, entitled 'The East Prospect of NEWPORT Schools in Shropshire' (plate 1). All we know about the artist is that he died in January 1765, so he must have made the drawing within about one hundred years of the school being built. We know very few repairs were made to the school in these years – up to 1730 far less than the allocated £5 per year was spent.[4] We can therefore safely say that Perry's drawing shows us what the school looked like when it was first built. In it we can easily identify the two almshouses, with their elaborate semi-classical façades, and the school building behind them. The Headmaster's house is at the left of this building and the Usher's house at the right, joined by a covered walkway or portico (the *crypto-porticus* in Fuller's description), with the library above. The portico was glassed in to form an extra room in 1928 and until recently had the rather prosaic name of Room D. (Rooms A, B and C are on the second floor.) In the main building the roof slope is much steeper than today, coming down to the top of the first storey and enclosing the library. The roof was altered in major work done in the 1820s and a flat roof put over the library. Plates 2 and 3 give some idea of the changes made. These are dealt with in Chapter Six. Perry's depiction of the clock tower is different from the one we see today, springing from below the roof line instead of sitting astride it. Fuller makes no mention of it. Perry's drawing is that of a draughtsman, with ruler-drawn lines and exaggerated perspective, looking more like the design of a building to be erected than one already in existence. The *Dictionary of National Biography* describes Perry as painstaking and industrious, so we may assume he was striving to be accurate. The two small buildings between the almshouses and the school appear to have been the brewhouses for the Headmaster and Usher. The tradition of teachers brewing their own beer is a long one, but in those days of polluted water it was a necessity.

Perry's drawing gives no idea of the state of repair of the school, but within fifty years it was described as being in a dangerous state. That such a grand building should decay so rapidly suggests poor building techniques when it was erected. These suspicions were strengthened by what the architects found when major repairs were made to Big School and the Headmaster's house in the 1970s.

The appearance of William Adams' magnificent building in the centre of the town must have made a considerable impression on the inhabitants and it would have formed a startling contrast to the lesser buildings around it. It could have been mistaken for a gentleman's residence, for its symmetrical design of a recessed five-bay centre with two three-bay wings was much in fashion in the mid-17th century. We have found interesting similarities between Adams' and Sir John Moore's School at Appleby Magna in Leicestershire which was founded in 1697 by Sir John Moore, liveryman of the Grocers' Company and eventually Lord Mayor of London. It was designed by Sir Christopher Wren, modified by a local architect Sir William Wilson, and built in the style of the 1650s, very similar to Adams' (plate 71). If Wren was willing to design a school at Appleby it is possible that a London architect

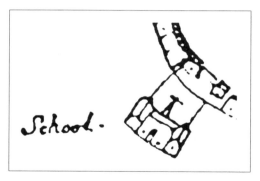

Rear view of the school from William Hill's map of 1681.

would have worked for Adams, but we have no information about this.

Although it cannot be seen from Perry's drawing, a later sketch of 1827 (plate 3) shows that neither the Headmaster's nor the Usher's house had doors facing the High Street. The entrances to these must have been within the portico. The building occupied the whole width of the site and other buildings abutted it on both sides. This was so up to 1919 and 1926 when the adjoining properties were bought (see p.122). The simple representation of the school in William Hill's map of 1681 (plate 68) shows a large central arch which ties up with the bricked-up archway we see today (plate 77). The boys' entrance to Big School on the first floor must have been at the back of the building, with an external flight of steps reached by a passage under the portico. These must have been the stone steps which were reported as worn and dangerous in 1832, to be replaced by wooden ones.[5] The plans on the conveyance maps of 1919 and 1926 appear to show such a passage. The Ordnance Survey map of 1881 (p.112) shows a path at the back of the school between the gardens of the Headmaster and Usher, by means of which boys could reach their playground and field.

At Appleby the roof space was divided into boarders' cubicles about 12 feet square, which can still be seen. It is possible that Adams' was the same. The windows visible in Perry's drawing confirm that the roof space was put to some use. It also gave access to the bell tower.

The Headmaster's and Usher's Houses
Inside the Headmaster's house there are three areas that can confidently be said to be original: the oak-panelled parlour on the ground floor, the drawing room on the first floor and the magnificent oak staircase, whose open well and strap-work design is typical of the mid-17th century (see p.74). The two rooms, or withdrawing chambers, are in the conventional positions for a house of the period. Later the parlour became the dining room and since 1984 has been the Headmaster's study. Behind the panelling there is a bricked-up stone fireplace with a flattened arch, typical of the period. It was uncovered in 1954, and again in 1980 when the Headmaster had the carved overmantel installed. This had been in the Annexe ever since it was bought from a house in the town by A.D.C.Peterson (Headmaster 1946-52). The drawing room above the parlour on the first floor has an elegant plaster frieze which was possibly added in the early 19th century (see p.78). It is at present a Deputy Head's office.

The Usher's house was not as elegant as the Headmaster's and was smaller, particularly on the first floor, to accommodate the schoolroom. There was a

way through to the schoolroom from
this house, but not from the Headmaster's. Looking at it today it is difficult to visualise how the Usher's accommodation was arranged as it was
gradually absorbed into the school
from the 1870s onwards.

Big School
What is now the school library was
for most of the school's history the
only teaching room. It was designed
to hold the 80 pupils envisaged in
the statutes. These statutes have
pride of place at one end of the
room (plate 75). This is the heart of
the school. From Big School a short
flight of stairs leads to the room that
held the original library and which
since 1991 has been an 'electronic
library' – the Resources Centre. On
the east wall of Big School is what
has been known to generations of
boys as Bill's Will (plate 76). In fact,

A wall-mounted lantern clock.

it is not the will of William Adams but a dole board which was brought here
from the parish church in 1915 and lists some of his bequests. From the
1950s to the 1990s copying out Bill's Will was a common sanction used by
prefects.

On a bracket high on the west wall of Big School Library is a fine brass
lantern clock made by a leading London clockmaker Thomas Knifton
(plate 72). On its face is inscribed, 'This was given by William Adams the
founder of this Schoole and is to be used for the benefit thereof 1657'.

There is no record of any other school that has received such a gift from
its founder. Lantern clocks were not cheap and apart from public institutions
only the wealthy could afford them. The Adams' clock is described in various books on the history of clocks as being of particular interest because it
carries the donor's name and because William Adams is the only one of
Knifton's many customers to be identified.[6] Originally the clock would have
been secured by a hook at the back to the wall some eight feet above the
floor. The original clock had only an hour hand and would have been a
poor timekeeper. This type of clock predated the pendulum clock by a few
years, using instead a balance wheel escapement. It was driven by weights
hanging below it. This might have been a temptation to boys but apparently
the clock was in an oak case.[7] Although the clock was supposed never to
leave the school it was found at Grange Farm on the Knighton estate in

1842 (probably taken there by the Justice family). It had been away from the school for so long that when it was discovered it was thought to have been in a school at Knighton! Fortunately the Company deputation decided that the clock should be 'brought into the Library at Newport School to be preserved as a memorial of the Giver'.[8] Thus the clock is still, after almost 350 years, in the place for which it was intended. Like many early clocks it has been 'improved' (a spring-driven movement and a minute hand were added in 1901) and also copied. We discovered a counterfeit in 1975 in Guildford, but the shopkeeper did not want to know!

The School Library

A first-floor library over a colonnade was a very fashionable design in the 17th century and can be seen in several Oxford colleges.

It is a mark of the importance William Adams attached to the library that it occupies a quarter of the entire teaching area. Most new schools had no library and few books, but within a few years William Adams' library contained 1,400 volumes. It was one of the finest in England at a time when a collection of 100 books was rare and 1,000 was exceptional, comparable with that of an Oxford or Cambridge college.

Like many other worthy founders of schools in that era, William Adams was a hard-headed businessman who had made his money in the workaday world so why did he attach so much importance to a library? The first reason was clearly religious. Latin, Greek and Hebrew were necessary to read the New and the Old Testaments. But Latin was also the language of international discourse in secular as well as religious matters and the Adams' library possessed books printed in Belgium, France, Germany, Holland, Italy and Switzerland. There was also a social reason for a library in a school. Wealth was the way to gentility. A basic education might be sufficient to make money, but to be accepted as a gentleman a man had to be well read.

William Adams gave the Headmaster and his successors the responsibility of looking after the library (see Appendix B 8). In a book fixed to one of the desks they were to record, first of all the books given by the Founder and then details of all other books given to the library. The books were not on any account to be removed from the library but scholars were to be allowed from time to time to enter and use the books 'for the better profiting in their respective way of learning'. The boys must not 'write in, scratch or deface, with pen or other ways' any of the books, and once a week 'the dust may be beaten from off the said books'. Both the Headmaster and Usher were provided with a lock and key for the library. If these instructions had been properly carried out we might have had more than the seven books that survive today. We know that the recording of the books began well enough because two catalogues have survived.[9] They are both dated July 1657 but contain details of books acquired up to 1704. Although they are not completely identical, one appears to be a fair copy of the other. We also have catalogues dated 1767, 1839, 1843 and 1873.

Verulamÿ novum organon. 1620 Folio.
Ejusd. opera moralium et civilium Tomus. Folio
Ejusd. sermones fideles. 1641
Ejusd. Hystoria naturalis, sive Phanomina Universi: 8°
Idem de augmentis Scientiarum. Lugd. Bat. 16...

Books by Francis Bacon, Lord Verulam, in the 1657 library catalogue.

The 1657 catalogue starts, as required, with a list of the 58 books given by the Founder. The first nine are Greek and Latin dictionaries together with books on grammar and rhetoric. The rest, listed in no discernible order, are the works of famous Greek and Latin authors such as Virgil, Sophocles, Cicero and Aristotle, edited by eminent 16th- and 17th-century scholars. Only three were in English, including John Speed's *History of England with the mapps in two volumes* (London 1636). Interestingly, Adams did not donate any religious books. After the Founder's gifts there is a curious entry in Latin recording a donation by Richard Powford, the writing master at Shrewsbury School and probably a friend of Thomas Chaloner. It is not a book but '*machinae lignariae et tabulae Pergamenae*' i.e. wooden machines and parchment tablets. The machines were probably frames on which to rest large books, whose angle could be altered by wooden screws.[10] Book titles would be listed on the tablets which would be mounted at the end of each set of shelves. A reference to the library in 1808 suggests that some if not all the books were chained (plate 11).[11]

The catalogue goes on to list 92 other books (several in more than one volume) provided by 53 other donors. Some of them must have been friends or business contacts of William Adams or Thomas Chaloner. They were not only local people but Adams' relatives and London friends, while Chaloner could draw on his Shrewsbury supporters and others he had met during his wandering years. Sir Thomas Mackworth (who had been a boy at Shrewsbury School) presented a bass viol. The donor list shows that the new school had the support of the 'great and the good'!

An interesting inclusion in the catalogue is the famous *Eikon Basilike* (Image of a King) which was published immediately after the execution of Charles I and encouraged general sympathy for him, running to 50 editions in a single year. The great Puritan poet John Milton wrote *Eikonoklastes* in response but it only sold two editions. Given the seditious nature of the gift it is not surprising that only the donor's initials (T. C.) were noted – this could have been Chaloner himself! However the library also contained books with a very different viewpoint, such as *The Saints' Everlasting Rest* by

Works by Oughtred and Kepler bound together with Galileo's Starry Messenger (Nuncio Siderio), *in the 1657 library catalogue.*

Richard Baxter (1615-91) which was a Puritan classic and Fox's *Book of Martyrs* which commemorated the Protestant martyrs under Queen Mary. Presumably the breadth of religious thought in the library reflected that in the school itself. Despite the requirements that Hebrew be taught there is no record of a book in Hebrew until 1660 when John Malden (minister of Newport 1658-62) presented one.

The majority of gifts are listed under the date July 1657 but there are further short lists for 1658 and 1659, with a longer one in 1660. After 1660 there are no further entries until 1664 by which time Thomas Chaloner had returned to Shrewsbury and Francis Potts had succeeded him. It is in this list that inconsistencies arise for it contains books published in 1681 and 1682. With no change in the handwriting there follows, without a gap, a list headed 1672. This list of well over 1,000 books is arranged in order of authors' names, but thereafter there is no discernible order. The donors' books, having been recorded separately, were probably on a separate set of shelves. Searching for a book whether by author or subject would have been a lengthy business. Sadly, we conclude that the books were treated as objects to be stored rather than used. The catalogue was an inventory not a guide. We do not know who chose the books, when they were bought or where the money came from. They represented a considerable capital investment. It is sometimes said that William Adams left money for the purchase of library books, but we have found no evidence of this.

What makes this library so remarkable and unusual in a small country grammar school is the number of books on science, philosophy and mathematics. It was a library in tune with the intellectual climate of the times – not only had there been a political revolution in England, there had been a scientific one too which radically changed people's attitude to the natural world. Adams' school library had a first edition of Francis Bacon's *Novum Organum* (1620) in which he outlined a 'new method' not deductive from fixed premises as in the classical logic of Aristotle, but inductive, moving from individual observations to general laws, in a way we recognise today. One of the finest examples of Bacon's 'new method' was William Gilbert's

Book by William Harvey, author of The Circulation of the Blood, *in the 1657 library catalogue.*

de Magnete, the first experimental study of magnetism. It was published in London in 1600 – and the Adams' library had a first edition! There was also the *Optics* and three works on astronomy by Johann Kepler (1571-1630) who laid the foundation of modern astronomy in his three laws of planetary motion. With Kepler's *Disceptatio* was Galileo's *Starry Messenger (Siderus Nuncius)* published in 1610, in which he described his discovery of the moons of Jupiter. The book was a sensation and brought him fame throughout Europe. These two books, with three others, were bound together with the *Arithmetica* of William Oughtred, inventor of the slide rule (still used by sixth-form scientists in the 1970s).

There were several books relating to the controversy that Galileo had aroused as to whether the sun or the earth was the centre of our planetary system. There was *Apologia Pro Galileo* by Campanella (Frankfurt 1622) and Kepler's *Epitome Astronomiae Copernicae* (1621), a comprehensive description of the new Copernican astronomy. On the other side of the argument were two works by the Jesuit Father Christopher Scheiner, a bitter opponent of Galileo who, it is alleged, was instrumental in bringing him to trial in 1633. The library also contained the complete works of Archimedes and the *Geometry* of Euclid (which was used in schools well into the 20th century). One of the great discoveries of the first half of the 17th-century was the circulation of the blood, discovered by William Harvey in 1628. The library had Roger Drake's *Vindiciae pro Sanguine Circulatione* (London 1641) which did much to publicise Harvey's discovery.

The alphabetical list of authors reads like a roll-call of the major writers from the 13th to the 17th centuries. There was Roger Bacon, Rene Descartes, Erasmus, the founder of modern humanism (especially well represented), Thomas Hobbes on political science and Hugo Grotius, the founder of international law. There was Mercator's *Atlas* and Sir Walter Raleigh's *History of the World,* written while he was imprisoned in the Tower of London. There were Bibles in Irish and Welsh (though few in English!) and books on witchcraft, astrology and the occult. Nor were more practical pursuits forgotten; there were classical authors on hunting, fishing and gardening. There were also several herbals – handbooks of botany with remedies for illness. But interestingly there was no drama – no Shakespeare, Milton or Marlowe.

The authorities we consulted are agreed that Adams' had an exceptional library, remarkable for the number of major works of scholarship and for its wide range of subjects.

The Wase School Collection

In 1673 Christopher Wase, a lecturer in Civil Law at Oxford University, sent a questionnaire to 700 grammar schools (there were around 2,000 in the country).[12] One of the questions concerned libraries. The reply of the Newport Master was clear and detailed. He stated: 'This school is furnished with a very fine library, wherein are many excellent and very choice books of all sorts especially for humanity.' This was in sharp contrast to the neighbouring schools. Shifnal said, 'Libraries none', Wroxeter replied it had no library but there was one at Shrewsbury three miles away and one at High Ercall four miles away. High Ercall itself replied that Sir Richard Newport gave several good books but did not appear to have a library! Wem, Ludlow and Oswestry gave no information, while the Whitchurch master replied, 'we have not any … Library but a few ordinary books'. It was reported of Wolverhampton Grammar School that 'it hath no Library belonging to it or any books of publicke use'. Bridgnorth had a sad story to tell: 'As for a Library wee have had one but lost in the late warres, only some reliques remain, manuscripts none.' Newport school was the exception in having such a large and excellent library and fortunate that it survived the Great Fire of Newport in 1665.

The Eighteenth Century

Most of the books of the 1657 catalogue also appear in a catalogue dated 7 May 1767 drawn up by Mr Forrester, Usher at the school. This is set out in a different way, in 11 cycles of folio-quarto-octavo-duodecimo, i.e. in order of size. It is unlikely that they correspond to bookcases because the number of books in a cycle varies from 39 to 368. There are no publication dates or details and no donors mentioned. They are not arranged by author or subject so locating a book would have been just as difficult as with the previous catalogue. However, we can calculate from it the number of books of each size and this shows that of 1489 titles, well over half were smaller than the book you are reading, so storing them in the library was not as difficult as we first thought.

The Nineteenth Century

In 1808 Edward Blakeway, writing about the school,[13] referred to the library where 'many ponderous volumes of the old classicks are secured by iron chains, some of them broke from their moorings … they seem to meet with little care or attention'. In 1818, the Haberdashers received a letter from William Liddle, proprietor of the principal inn in Newport, and a wine merchant. He wrote, 'it is credited that here is one of the finest libraries in England in that School, which the scholars are denied access to, and that for

want of proper care and cleanliness it is going
fast to decay and there are some valuable
books missing'.[14] In February 1822 the
Visitors asked for more coal for the
library because 'the books have formerly
suffered injury from want of proper
airing'.[15] In 1823 the Headmaster
Edward Meredith told the Governors
that he intended to have the library
cleaned and rearranged because it had
'got into great confusion and much
dirt by its many removals during the
progress of the late repairs'. Unfortunately his good intentions backfired. In

*Book sizes from Comenius' Orbis
Pictus (1659) including Folio(1),
Quarto(2), Octavo(3), Duodecimo(4).*

April 1824 the Visitors wrote, 'we are concerned to inform you that a considerable number of the Books (some of them valuable ones) of the School
Library have by an accident of Fire at the Stationers where they were sent for
the purpose of being bound and repaired, been destroyed'.[16] Meredith produced a list of 331 volumes lost in the fire and asked that the replacements
be Latin and Greek classics. He promised to provide a list for the Governors
to send to Chancery for payment.[17] The plan was later revised because it
would be too expensive to replace all the books at once. A sum of £25 a year
was suggested instead.[18] This is the only information we have about the fire.
However, the story does not end with a fire at the stationers for there were
still around 1,100 books left.

The deputation of 1827 found much local discontent with the school.
They were told that 'the Library is not open to the foundation boys, is in
a very dirty and disarranged state' and there was no catalogue.[19] They asked
the Headmaster whether the library and its room were being dusted and
kept clean and that foundation boys, 'under proper regulations to prevent
injury', were being allowed to use it.[20] Meredith replied that it was occasionally dusted by two of the foundation scholars but that little boys could not
do the job properly because of the height of the bookshelves and the
amount of hard work required. The Visitors suggested that a senior boy be
appointed as librarian at a salary of £10 a year (a large amount for those
days) to supervise scholars there as well as keep it clean, but the Governors
did not accept this. Meredith said he already allowed higher boys to use the
library, but not the younger ones for whom it 'would be quite useless'. The
library was from this time onwards used for Visitors' meetings.

The catalogue of 1839 contains 882 titles with an extra three pages of
'Books purchased by the Governors in 1839'.

The Catalogue of 1873

In 1873 'A Catalogue of the More Ancient Books in the Library of the
Grammar School at Newport, Salop' was made under the direction of the

Headmaster, Tom Collins. It fills 99 pages of an exercise book and gives us a clue as to the possible layout of the library. Seven sections are designated, labelled A to G, which we presume to be separate bookcases. For each letter there is a division into six shelves labelled I to VI and each book is given a number. There are 1,027 books in total. Only the 'more ancient books' are recorded, so many of those in the 1839 catalogue do not appear.

However, there are two intriguing facts about the catalogue that may explain why only seven books out of this whole library have survived into the 21st century. The first is that there are pencilled crosses against some of the books with a note at the beginning saying 'books marked with a cross are to be retained, the others disposed of'. Only 78 books were marked for retention, but none of these are the seven survivors in the library now. Who made the decision to dispose of the books and when? Where did they go? If they were sold, where did the money go? We have no records to answer any of these questions. Secondly we have a letter from a housemaster of Shrewsbury School dated 15 December 1914 returning the 1873 catalogue which had been found by one of his pupils. He gave no information as to where the boy found it. We can only surmise that the 'condemned' books and the catalogue were sent to a Shrewsbury bookseller at some time between 1880 and 1914. At least the boy was responsible enough to give it to his housemaster! The letter was presumably addressed to Mr Shuker, Headmaster at the time. Was Shuker seeing the catalogue for the first time or had he been the instigator of the library's dispersal? It was unlikely to have been Collins for he had been at some trouble to make a clear catalogue. As a new Head Shuker could have made the pencilled notes when he arrived in 1903. The school was short of money as it was growing in numbers and this would have been an opportunity to make some. Of course we are assuming that 'dispose of' meant sell. It could have meant throw them away or even burn them. The Shrewsbury schoolboy could have found the catalogue in a pile of rubbish.

In the school magazine, the *Novaportan*, of 1887 there is an article on 'Our School Library' which makes a plea for modern reference books to replace the 'old and useless ones'. These old books, the author says, are accumulating dust and are being 'literally eaten away by bookworms'. He suggests that the impending Queen's Jubilee would be an ideal occasion to restore the library. We do not know whether there was any response!

The alterations to the school building in 1901 included dividing the old library into two by a partition to form a classroom and a compartment in which the old books were deposited. A photograph in the *Novaportan* of July 1954 taken some fifty years previously shows this (plate 12). There are no books in the room, but through the door at the end is a glimpse of shelves on which books seem to be arranged in order of size, the largest at the bottom. We are looking at the last resting place of one of the finest libraries in England, containing the products of the greatest minds of the world, rarely read, often counted but never loved. This is the school's tragedy: to have had a priceless gift and not recognised it.

Four

THE KNIGHTON ESTATES:
HOW THE SCHOOL WAS FINANCED

The Manor of Knighton in the parish of Adbaston, seven miles north of Newport and just over the county boundary in Staffordshire, was to finance all William Adams' benefactions.

William Adams had first become involved with it in 1645, when the owner James Sawyer had mortgaged it to him for £1,200. William subsequently leased it to James Sawyer in 1647 and after his death bought it from his surviving brothers in February 1654 for £1,190. He was still owed £2,410 on the mortgage so the total value of the estate was £3,600.[1] William Adams conveyed it to the Master and Wardens of the Haberdashers' Company, as Governors of his Free Grammar School, on 26 November 1656 for the token sum of 20 shillings (one pound). The estate contained about 900 acres which included three large farms, the most important being Knighton Grange, which William let to his nephew Luke Justice, who then sublet the other farms and tenements. Out of the profits and rents he received Luke Justice was responsible for paying £175, in half-yearly instalments at Christmas and Midsummer, to all the recipients of William Adams' Charity set out in the First Deed of Uses (see pp.16-18). There was no intermediary; Luke Justice personally disbursed the money to everyone on the list and sent the residue to the Master and Wardens, together with yearly accounts.

William Adams reserved for himself, during his lifetime, control of the woods on the estate and the profits from the timber growing on it. In his will he bequeathed the woods to the Master and Wardens of the Company, the only constraint on their use of this being that at some time after the next three years, when a good profit could be had from the sale of timber, they should sell it and raise £400 to £500 to buy more lands near Knighton. These were to be added to the estate held by Luke Justice so as to provide more financial backing for the £175 due from it every year. This was done in May 1667, when the holding known as Duexhill, in Woodseaves, Shropshire, near Market Drayton, was conveyed to the Governors, with Luke Justice as principal tenant, the existing tenant Edward Piggott continuing to farm the land. William was making sure that his nephew need never suffer hardship in supplying the necessary money! A crisis came much later in the aftermath of the Napoleonic Wars, but not during the time that the Justice family was in charge.

The Justice family held these lands at the fixed rate of £175 for 127 years until 1784, even though the value of money altered radically during the period, thus making William Adams' provision for the school worth less and less in real terms.

Did William Adams envisage such an advantageous lease to his family? The wording in the will was that the lands at Knighton and elsewhere (to be purchased from the sale of timber) should be granted to Luke Justice, his Executors or Assigns for the residue of the term of years in the existing lease 'and for soe long time afterwards as the said Luke Justice his Executors or Administrators shall reasonably desire at and for the yearly Rent as are conseyned in the said lease...'. It all depends on the interpretation of 'shall reasonably desire'. The second lease was granted in May 1667 when the new farm at Woodseaves was added to the holding, so the whole thing was renewed. That this time it was for 70 years could be connected with the fact that Luke's brother William was an important member of the Haberdashers' Company at the time, but why yet another lease of 70 years should be granted in 1714 to Luke's grandson William before that of 1667 had fallen due is an enigma.

William Adams, and indeed all responsible Haberdashers, should have been aware of the problems caused at Bunbury School by a fixed sum being allocated to finance a charity which over the years decreased in real terms as the cost of living increased. In 1594 Haberdasher Thomas Aldersey had granted £122 out of the income from tithes to finance his charity, from which the Schoolmaster received £20 a year and the Usher £10. By the 1650s there were real problems in finding suitable schoolmasters for the small sum allocated.[2] Perhaps William Adams thought he had guarded against this by the original lease of 21 years, but the Justice family managed to turn it to their advantage by manipulating the words of his will.

As early as 1730 the Haberdashers were investigating whether they could legally grant such a long lease. Nothing seems to have come of this, and they had to wait over 50 years before they could let the lands at an economic rent. Mr Justice tried to get his lease renewed in the 1760s but the Company was in no mood to do so. This problem of uneconomic fixed rents inherited from the past was common in the 18th century and did not get fully sorted out until charity reforms in the early 19th century.

As owners of the woods and timber on the Knighton estate, the Haberdashers needed to keep an eye on it so as to fell the trees and sell the timber at the right time. They should also have inspected the whole estate to see that it was run properly. But the Company was in financial difficulties after the Great Fire of London in 1666 and their hold over all their charity possessions slackened. They had to rebuild after the Fire but were not allowed to increase rents, and high land taxes during the wars against Louis XIV made matters worse. Income from their other charities often fell below expenditure, though not in the case of Adams' charity.[3] The low esteem in which the Company was held, even among its members, can be seen from November 1711 to August 1712 when no fewer than 10 members chosen as Master in that period gave excuses and paid a fine of £20 rather than accept the office.[4] It was not until the 1750s that the Company took severe steps at retrenchment so that by about 1760 they were able to break even. The result as far as the Knighton estate was concerned was very little direct control from London. Informal local connections were used to assess the state of the property and so income from the sale of timber was not as much as it should have been, and the tenants took the opportunity to help themselves to whatever wood they wanted.

It is not until 1760 that the Report Books of Select Committees which include Adams' Charity give us an idea of what was going on, on the estates and at the school itself.[5]

The value of woodland

Meticulous care was taken to account for every tree in the woods and hedgerows. From the perspective of the 21st century this may seem strange, but it must be remembered that wood was the basic material of life at this time. Houses in this part of the country were half-timbered, with wattle and daub infill. Wood was constantly needed for new barn floors, pigsties, carts, wheels, barrels, gates and in fact for nearly everything that is now made of iron, steel or plastic. Although there were developments in producing wrought iron during the 18th century, this was not widespread until much later: it was expensive to produce and limited in use.

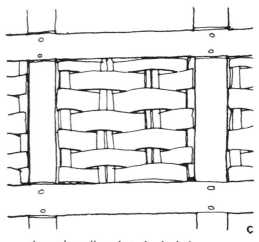

A wattle wall ready to be daubed.

Two types of saleable wood were produced from properly managed woodland. The majority of trees were cut down every few years (anything from four to 14 or more years) to produce underwood, for poles, lathes, wheel spokes etc, and making charcoal. The stumps left would sprout quickly to produce an infinite succession of further crops of underwood. Among these stumps or stools (called pollards if they were grown to eight feet or so before cutting, so that animals could graze beneath them), certain trees would be left to grow as timber trees, left standing for several rotations of underwood. They would eventually be felled for beams and planks. They were usually oak, but many other species could be grown for timber.

Although anyone now living near the Ironbridge Gorge should know that Abraham Darby first smelted iron using coke instead of charcoal in 1709, it was not until the time of his grandson, Abraham Darby III, in the 1760s that it was used in any quantity, even in Coalbrookdale. Other less adventurous iron masters would continue using charcoal for many decades. In Shropshire and Staffordshire a good price could be had for cordwood, cut lengths of wood sold by volume to make charcoal for furnaces.

The survey carried out by the Haberdashers' Company surveyor, John Dugleby, in 1782 was a very detailed one. It was very near the end of the Justice family lease, and the Company wanted a clear idea of their assets. Dugleby commented that underwood was now worth £5 an acre, 'at the rate the Woods are sold in this Country [County] for coaling the Ironwork'.[6] He advised that the underwood at Grange Farm should be cut that winter and that 'care should be taken that wood which should be made into charcoal should not be made in the wood but on the arable lands adjoining'. It is fascinating to think that charcoal burning would be done on the spot. Mr Dugleby went on to recommend that the sale of timber should be advertised in the Country [County] papers so that it may be sold while the Company is at Knighton. 'This may occasion more Buyers and the Timber sell better as many of the trees are very fit for planks and for Ship Building.' In fact, the Company found more difficulty in selling the timber than he had anticipated and in the end they settled for selling the timber to Thomas Parsons, timber merchant of Newport, for £570. The offers for the underwood were much below Mr Dugleby's estimate so they left it to their agent to sell off as best he could. Mr Dugleby's report of October 1782 includes a table of all timber standing on each farm on the Knighton estate and at Woodseaves, field by field, separating out Oak, Elm, Ash and Poplar, and the numbers of trees, pollarded trees and saplings. He also notes that there were 1,495 pieces of timber and young saplings in the hedgerows: each tree was a valuable asset.

By the 1840s the underwood was being sold for the Staffordshire Potteries instead of the ironworks, and the Company was advised in 1844 that it was a good time to sell timber as the Government might shortly be needing oak timber for shipbuilding. In 1862 it was noted that underwood was sold every seven years 'in this part of the country' for crates, baskets and firing for the Potteries.

Management of the estates
From the middle of the 18th century, as the Company took a more active interest in its Shropshire and Staffordshire possessions, they saw the need for a local agent to keep an eye on things and stop indiscriminate interference with their property. By 1750 a Mr Hammersley was the Company's agent at Newport, advising them when timber was ready for sale and carrying this out. Rather surprisingly the Master, Samuel Lea and later the Usher, his son John Lea, were actively involved in marking and measuring the trees, and in seeing to repairs to the school, using some of the timber. On Mr Hammersley's death in 1756 John Lea carried on alone until someone else was found for the job. It was later reported to the Haberdashers that Mr Hammersley 'had made a fortune out of Knighton Woods and at one sale

had received £500 from one Mr Allen for cordwood'.[7] This was never substantiated, but it illustrates how the Company could be at the mercy of its local agents. On the death of Mr Hammersley, Samuel Lea recommended a Mr George who is referred to as Steward and Woodreeve. He started off well for the Company, actively preventing the tenants from topping and lopping the trees in the woods and hedgerows and from using the roots and stumps for themselves, but he was unable to rectify the main problem, which was that the tenants had encroached on the Company's woodlands.

The 1762 Haberdashers' deputation found that the banks and hedges round the woods had been allowed to deteriorate, the tenants' animals grazed under the trees, destroying the underwood and young trees, and in several places the wood had been converted to pasture. This was known as depasturing. For instance, on Grange Farm, formerly lived in by the Justices themselves, four acres of Grange Wood were entirely open and crops were grown on some of its land, and the 47 acres of Knighton Wood had no underwood in it, having for years had animals grazing there. A fascinating light is thrown on the attitude of the Justice family by a small incident recorded at this point. The deputation asked an elderly cottager whether the tenants had been told not to depasture. He said they had been told not to many times, but they still did it. When the Haberdashers were passing two days later this Thomas Adeney came out and said he had been mistaken, and the tenants had always depastured. They asked him if anyone had been to see him since their visit and he said that a gentleman had done so the day before. They found out that the 'gentleman' had been Mr Felton, Mr Justice's agent, who had accompanied them two days previously![8]

Their Report concluded that Mr George, the Steward, was not up to the job. He lived too far from the site and his duties as a waggoner meant he was often away. The deputation recommended a completely different character to take his place: Mr Richard Whitworth, gentleman, of Batchacre Grange. For the next four years the Haberdashers, who happily accepted this recommendation, became increasingly frustrated by this gentleman.

Richard Whitworth[9] was a colourful character who threw himself into innumerable schemes on his estate in Staffordshire and in Shropshire – his lands virtually surrounded the Knighton estate. He was made a Visitor of William Adams' Free Grammar School in Newport in 1762 partly on the strength of the fact that he had been a pupil there under Samuel Lea. In his autobiography he states that he was at Newport between the ages of five and nine, going on from there to a school at Dunstable and thence to Eton and Trinity College, Cambridge.[10] He was High Sheriff of Staffordshire from the age of 21, a JP for Stafford and for Shropshire and Member of Parliament for Stafford 1774-1780. He was very interested in parochial matters, being instrumental in straightening out the roads between Shebdon and Forton and between Knighton and Puleston. He organised a Volunteer Militia based on Market Drayton in the 1790s, probably the earliest raised in

Shropshire in the French Revolutionary Wars. He had a house in Stafford and in 1765 he organised the setting up of the new Stafford Infirmary. He had even converted a building in Stafford into 'Castle Whitworth' with a martello tower and swivel guns. 'Though afflicted with an utterly impossible temperament he was without doubt a man of talent and learning ... a most persistent and implacable litigant,' says one writer. In the 1790s the Haberdashers' Company was at the receiving end of one of his lawsuits. The strangest story about him is that he flooded his Batchacre estate to create lakes on which he built a man-of-war and trained seamen to fight in the Napoleonic War. It was said he planned to sail the ship down a canal he was building to get to the open sea, and that the government heard of this and press-ganged nearly 200 men.

What we do know for certain is that at the time he became involved with the Haberdashers' Company he was planning to build a canal and needed to use part of the Knighton estate for this purpose. Could that have been why he was willing to take over as Woodreeve? In 1766 he published *The Advantages of Inland Navigation* which gave detailed plans for his canal. It was to go from the Severn via the Tern and the Strine to Newport and then north via Forton and Batchacre, skirting Knighton to Eccleshall, joining the proposed Mersey-Trent canal at Shallowford. He had worked out the cost of construction and the finances very thoroughly but it was never constructed as in 1776 another scheme, backed by Josiah Wedgwood, was adopted. However, several mapmakers thought it would be cut and showed it on their maps, in 1775, 1787 and 1817.

When Richard Whitworth was recommended to take over from Mr George in 1762 he seemed ideal. The Select Committee reported that they needed 'some proper person on the spot who is above the influence or threats of the Farmers'. They suggested Mr Whitworth as 'a Gentleman well qualified as he lives upon the Spot and is disliked by the Farmers because he looks into his own affairs'.[11] When the Company appointed Mr Whitworth they allowed him to take sandstone from the estate, as he had requested, but they were concerned that he had told the tenants they could continue to depasture until the timber was felled. Mr Knapp, the Clerk, was instructed to write insisting that the woods be fenced immediately and that no depasturing was to be allowed.

Some of the letters from Mr Knapp survive.[12] As Clerk to the Company 1754-1790, and a London solicitor he was used to associating with well-educated gentlemen. At first he seems to have been enchanted by Richard Whitworth's wit and classical erudition. But his tone changes as the Haberdashers become increasingly frustrated with Mr Whitworth. Although he had sold some timber on their behalf in February 1763, for which he was paid at Christmas of that year, it took nine letters from them, many unanswered, before at the end of October 1764 he actually sent them the whole of the money. Similarly, in June 1765 he received £200 for timber felled in Knighton Wood, but it took a terse letter from the

Company in January 1766, applying for immediate payment, with interest, to get any response.[13]

Mr Sloane, the Company's surveyor, on his visit in July 1765 found Mr Whitworth very uncooperative. Depasturing was continuing as no fencing or hedging had been done, and various trees marked for the Company had been used by Mr Whitworth and the tenants. He reported that a tree nursery where acorns and ash keys could be planted to provide replacements in the woods would be perfectly possible, but a waste of time and money if fencing and hedging were not done. His conversation with Mr Whitworth is illuminating: 'I told Mr Whitworth that the Woods would be very productive of underwood if proper care was taken, his answer was Gentlemen that live at so great a distance from their Estates seldom have much Underwood.'[14] A deputation the following year found that Mr Whitworth had done absolutely nothing that he had promised and allowed tenants to fell trees whenever they wished, so the Company appointed Mr William Hallen of Sambrook in his place. Richard Whitworth had no more direct connection with the estates but remained a very active Visitor of the School.

William Hallen was a landowner and ironmaster who worked forges at Sambrook, Caynton and Tibberton. He had already bought Knighton cordwood for his furnaces and therefore was interested in the upkeep of the woods. He proved to be a greater help to the Haberdashers than Richard Whitworth had ever been. He was officially made Gamekeeper (though his own gamekeeper did the everyday work). Poachers from Newport were a problem at this time, so action had to be taken. William Hallen accompanied the Haberdasher deputations and their surveyor when they inspected the estates and they often stayed with him at Sambrook rather than return to the *Red Lion* at Newport. In 1782 his son Richard Hallen took over as Woodreeve and Gamekeeper and the Company's agent, and was officially appointed Steward and Receiver of Rents of the Knighton Estates. This was confirmed by Chancery in 1797 and he continued in that office until his death in 1819.

In 1784 the Haberdashers' surveyor reported that there might be coal under the fields adjoining Knighton Wood. He had found the expense of boring for coal would not be very great as Mr William Hallen had offered to borrow the necessary equipment from Mr Reynolds of Coalbrookdale, 'being very well acquainted with him and knows he will not deny him the favour, if the Company should carry this into execution they will only have the labour to pay for'. If coal were found this would 'bring in a very great sum to the Company as there are no Coal pits nearer than 12 miles and the nighest place they are brought by Water Carrier is 2 miles beyond Newport'. (He must mean Pave Lane).[15] This Mr Reynolds must have been the Quaker Richard Reynolds (1735-1816), friend and son-in-law of Abraham Darby II, who ran the Ketley ironworks and managed all the Darby business after Abraham Darby II's death until his son took over in 1768.

William Reynolds, his son, took over the Ketley works in 1777 but he
remained influential and they both played a leading part in the industrial
revolution in the iron industry. Boring was carried out but, sadly, no coal
was found. The history of the school would have been very different if the
Knighton Estates could have produced more income. The Adams' charity
has always been small compared with, for instance, the William Jones'
charity at Monmouth or the Robert Aske foundation. In 1862 the Company
was asked to subscribe towards boring for coal, but remembered the previous occasion and concluded it was not worth it.

Under the Hallens the management of the estates was in good hands but
problems continued. 'Spring Cutters' came by night to cut young hazels to
sell for thatching rods. One guinea reward was offered for information on
this but, not surprisingly, no one came forward to claim it.[16]

Legal action

The Company decided to make an example of one of the tenants, to deter
others from tampering with their property. Mr Harford (or Heaford) of
Grange Farm had already in 1766 been threatened with action for letting his
cattle into Grange Wood. The Woodreeve described him as 'a man of
wicked disposition' who keeps promising not to let his cattle into the woods
but always does so. It was decided to sue for damages at Stafford County
Court. The case came up in September 1769. Mr Sloane and another representative of the Company, Mr Rutherford, came on horseback, taking
three days to travel the 135 miles from London. Witnesses for the Company
included 'Mr Lea the Schoolmaster at Newport, for whom we had provided
a Post Chaise and Private Lodgings, he being very old and infirm, his
Daughter attending him.' The Company was awarded £50 damages and
costs.[17]

About the same time there was trouble with a certain Mr Parton of West
End. He was not a tenant, but he insisted that he had the right to drive his
cart through Knighton Wood to his land the other side. He left gates open
and broke down fences hastily put up to secure the wood from cattle. In fact
the 1771 delegation (including the Master of the Haberdashers and the First
Warden) happened to meet Mr Parton in his cart when they were inspecting
the wood. He was very truculent when threatened with prosecution.[18] Eventually a compromise was reached: the undoubted bridleway through
Knighton Wood was widened to take carts but diverted round the woods so
as to cause minimum destruction.

1784 and its consequences

The detailed report of the lands belonging to the William Adams' Charity
made in 1782 by John Dugleby, Surveyor, of Deptford, and the accompanying map, can still be seen in the Guildhall archives in the City of London
(plate 69).[19] It revealed that the land was worth múch more than the tenants
were currently paying. The existing rents totalled £294, but Mr Dugleby

reckoned that it was now worth over £441. So when the Justice family's lease as principal tenant expired in 1784 the tenants were asked to tender for new leases. In the event the leases agreed totalled £476 14s. This was an enormous leap in income for the charity from £175 (because of course the Justices had pocketed the surplus). How to use the extra money led to arguments and considerable acrimony between the local Visitors and the Haberdasher Governors.

Before leaving the tenants at this point it is worth noting an unusual clause in their new leases. They were required to deliver one wagonload of good Shropshire coal from the pits to the school at their own expense. It had been discovered that Mr Justice had insisted, as lord of the manor, that his tenants should supply him with coal (and lime), so this was continued for the use of the school and the almspeople. The obligation was not abolished until the 1920s, after which a fund was set up to provide coal for the almspeople.

In September 1784 Humphrey Felton, Attorney, of Market Drayton, agent of the Justice family, wrote to the Haberdashers' Company asking for 'pecuniary reward for his services during the last 30 years during the lease of Mr Justice'.[20] He had done a great balancing act, maintaining his client's interests as against those of the Company. He had manoeuvred to get another lease in 1764, which they refused, and had defended the tenants' rights to depasture and use the Company's woods on the estate as if their own. But he had been 'very gentleman like' and extremely helpful in other matters, such as the enclosure of Woodseaves and demands on the tenants for payment of Poor Rate. The Company agreed to give him a piece of plate worth 40 guineas. By chance this same 'piece of plate', an elegant two-handled cup with a cover, came up for sale at Christie's in 1995 (plate 13). Past Master of the Company Christopher Bostock was able to buy it and present it back to them. It was made by Thomas Chawner of London and bears the coats of arms of the Haberdashers' Company and Humphrey Felton. The inscription reads: 'Presented by the Worshipful Company of HABERDASHERS LONDON, to Mr Humphrey Felton of Drayton, Salop. For his Integrity & Services rendered them during his Receivership of their Estates in Staffordshire and Shropshire for them and their Late Tenant Philip Justice Esq.'

At first the Governors acted on the recommendation of the Visitors and used some of the extra money to appoint a part-time Writing Master, Mr Horton, in April 1784. But they were not happy when the Visitors asked for the salaries of the Master and Usher to be increased. The Visitors saw this as a way of improving the status of the school, which would lead to recruitment of masters of a higher standard in the future. But the Haberdashers' reply was that there were too few pupils to warrant this, and suggested a scheme whereby the salaries of the Master and Usher increased as the numbers in the school rose. They all agreed that the occupants of the almshouses should get more. The Visitors at this point seem to have been led by Mr John Cotes of Woodcote, Tory MP for Wigan 1782-1802, and

NEWPORT SCHOOL.
AUGUST 23, 1786.

AT a Meeting held this Day, of the Vifitors of the Free Grammar School in this Town, founded by the late WILLIAM ADAMS, Efq; for the Benefit of the County of Salop;

It appeared to them, that the Eftates, left for the Support of the faid School, and other Charities, are increafed in Value from the Sum of One Hundred and Seventy-five Pounds, to nearly Five Hundred Pounds per Annum. And that feveral other confiderable Sums have arifen from the fame, which have never been accounted for by the Truftees.

It was therefore Refolved, to inftitute a Suit in the Court of Chancery, againft the Company of Haberdafhers, (the Truftees appointed by the faid William Adams, Efq;) in order to obtain an Account of the Rents, Iffues, and Profits of the Eftates, and to procure a proper Application of the fame.

They are encouraged to this Undertaking by the Opinion of able Counfel upon the Cafe.

Relying on the Juftice of their Caufe, the Vifitors take the Liberty of foliciting the Affiftance of every Perfon in the County, who may be interefted in the fuccefs of their Endeavours : And they are hereby requefted to fend their Addrefs, and fpecify the Sum, in Writing, they intend to contribute, to Thomas Marfhall, Efq; at Newport, that Application may be made to them, in cafe it fhould be found neceffary to call on them for their Subfcriptions.

A Subfcription is already begun by the Vifitors, and the Inhabitants of Newport.

RICHARD WHITWORTH, Efq;
JOHN COTES, Efq;
The Rev. WILLIAM PIGOTT,
The Rev. CHARLES COTES,
The Rev. CRESWELL TAYLEUR,
The Rev. ROBERT OUTLAW,
The Rev. SAMUEL DICKENSON,
The Rev. RICHARD RYDER SHORT,
                                        VISITORS.

The Visitors' advertisement in the Shrewsbury Chronicle, *1786.*

Whig MP for Shropshire from 1806 until his death in 1821. His brother, Washington Cotes, had Chambers at Lincoln's Inn, London, and advised the Visitors on legal matters. Richard Whitworth was certainly an important member, but he was often away in London on business.

Although the Governors seem to have granted some increase in salary to the Master and Usher they did not respond when the Visitors wrote asking for even more. In February 1785 they adopted a fairly sharp tone in refusing any further increase and inquired whether boys attended Divine

Service and were being catechised as required by the statutes. They also wanted to know whether Mr Scott the Master held an ecclesiastical preferment incompatible with his duty in the school and contrary to the statutes. (Mr Scott had in fact been curate-in-charge of Forton until 1776, but we don't know if he held any other living.) This letter was handed personally to Mr Washington Cotes at his Chambers at Lincoln's Inn, to make sure his brother received it.

The Visitors eventually decided to make a stand against the Haberdashers. They issued a public statement which was printed in the *Shrewsbury Chronicle* (and in Staffordshire and Cheshire as well) on four consecutive weeks in September and October 1786. This announced their intention of proceeding against the Haberdashers' Company in the Court of Chancery to obtain an exact account of the revenues of the Knighton estates and to ensure that they were spent in a suitable way. They asked for subscriptions to support this action. When the Haberdasher Court of Assistants was shown this advertisement they decided there was no need for them to respond to it!

In the summer of 1787, Richard Whitworth initiated a lawsuit in Chancery against the Haberdasher Governors of William Adams' Charity, by making complaint to the Attorney-General who then took action. Since the reign of Elizabeth I the Court of Chancery had had overall supervision of all charities, but did not intervene unless its attention was drawn to misuse of funds. Action in Chancery was usually avoided as it was costly and slow. This case took 10 years to resolve.

The Visitors' two main complaints in this lawsuit were that the Haberdasher Governors were keeping the increased rents from the charity's estates for themselves and that they had always kept the profit from the timber on the property for their own purposes instead of for the good of the School. Both Visitors and Haberdashers consulted several legal counsels (barristers) to test the legality of their position. The advice given to the Company was that any surplus money must be used for the purposes of William Adams' Charity, not for any other charitable uses, and that they as Governors must submit to the directions of the Court of Chancery.

The Haberdashers' final answer to the Information (complaint) in February 1788 made much of the fact that the Justice family had always received in rents more than they were obliged to pass on to the Charity – from about £220 in 1656 to over £294 in 1783. They submitted that they could use the surplus for 'other pious purposes' as well as for Adams' Newport Charity. They pointed out they had done a lot since 1784, for example appointed a Writing Master, increased payments to the poor, increased the Master's and Usher's salaries, repaired buildings including the Master's and Usher's houses even though by bond they should have done it themselves, and provided coals, 'by which means the school was now advanced from 15 to 40 pupils'. They argued that the excess over £175 should be entirely within the control of the Governors, that the Company must keep a reserve of money for building repairs and that it would not be prudent to extend the charity further.

They ended with a fine display of injured righteousness: 'That the Haberdashers' Company's prudence and moderation is well known having formerly sustained very great losses in the Reign of Charles I and the Usurpation. They sold their Barge laid aside all their Entertainment not even going out on Lord Mayor's Day nor ever treating their Livery or having dinner for the Court of Assistants for 33 years. By which good Management they have supported and regularly paid all their Charities with Credit Justice and Honor. Therefore cant help thinking themselves ill treated by the Authors of this Information who being only appointed Visitors of the school by the Company have most ungraciously presumed to advertise in the Country papers soliciting subscriptions to carry on this unjust Information against them.'[21]

Chancery's first action was to take steps to find whether there was any Heir-at-Law who could have a claim on William Adams' estate. Advertisements were placed in the papers and a certain Randle Tonna came forward, whose ancestor we have seen married William Adams' niece. He was accepted as Heir-at-Law, but was not considered entitled to any of the excess money from the charity. The £2,430 belonging to the charity was taken over by the Accountant-General and invested in 3 per cent stocks.

After that proposals as to what should be done with the money went to and fro between the Company and the Visitors through the Court of Chancery. The Visitors suggested that eminent local gentlemen (including the bishop of the diocese and several baronets) should be made Trustees to advise the Governors who were at such a distance from the school. Richard Whitworth even wanted to petition Parliament to abolish the Haberdashers as Governors and let local Trustees have complete control, but Washington Cotes advised him that this would be impossible: 'If they are to be removed from their trust it must be upon the ground of Misconduct and I never was furnished with any evidence to support that charge.'[22] The Haberdashers never heard of that revolutionary plan, but their indignation at the idea of local Trustees led them into a completely distorted view of William Adams' intentions. 'We are of opinion that the poor in the Almshouses were intended by Mr Adams as almost the first Objects of his Attention' and therefore it was more important to increase their pay than that of the Master or Usher.[23] Even a quick glance at the statutes we have printed in Appendices B and C shows that this is completely untrue!

Eventually, after a great deal of ill-feeling was aired, the two sides agreed to a scheme put forward in 1797 by the Master in Chancery. This produced increased payments to everyone involved and still left a good sum to be added to reserves each year. The minister of Newport received £40 a year, the Schoolmaster £100 and the Usher £50; these were increased in 1808 to £60, £150 and £75 respectively.

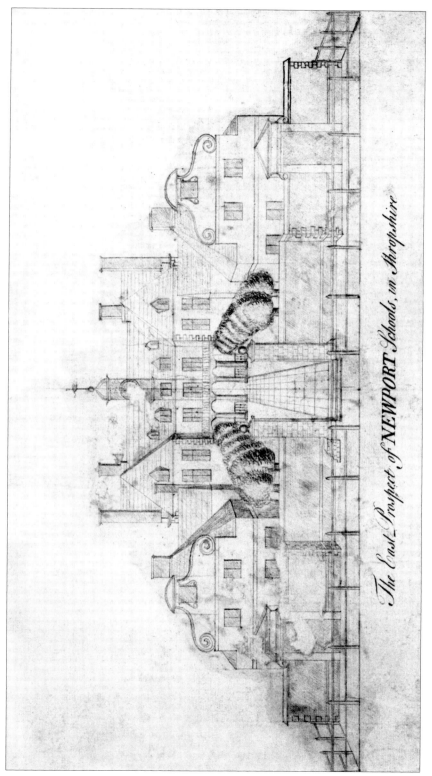

1 *The earliest representation of the school by Francis Perry, who died in 1765.*

2   *The school after the rebuilding of 1802 to 1804.*

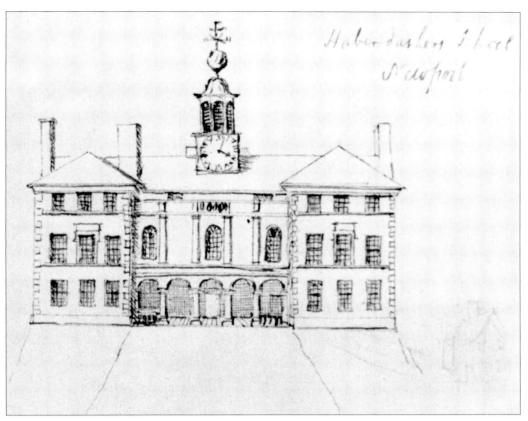

3 *Sketch of the school in 1827 (artist unknown).*

4 *Sketch of Newport Church, 1827 (from the same note book).*

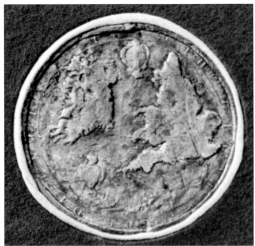

5   *Seal of Oliver Cromwell's Letters Patent showing Parliament instead of the monarch's head and the Union of England and Ireland without Scotland.*

6   *The initial O of the Letters Patent of Oliver Cromwell showing his portrait.*

7 *Title page of sermon preached at William Adams' funeral by Dr Thomas Horton in 1661.*

THE
VNRIGHTEOVS MAMMON
EXCHANGED FOR THE
TRUE RICHES·
OR A
SERMON,

Preached at the Funeral of *William Adams* Efq;
In the Parifh Church of St. *Lawrence Iury* on
Tuefday. Septemb. 3. 1 6 6 1.

By THOMAS HORTON. **D. D.**

Pfal. 112. 5. 9.
A *Good Man* fheweth mercy, and lendeth: He wil guide his
affaires with *Difcretion.*
He hath difperfed abroad, He hath given to the poor, his righte-
oufneffe remaineth for ever.

L O N D O N

Printed by *I. R.* fot *John Clark,* and are to be fold at
the Entrance into *Mercers Chappel.*
1 6 6 1.

8 *List of contents on the inside lid of an oak box on which is carved 'For Newport W A'. The box contained documents relating to William Adams' endowments for the school and the town and was for many centuries kept in the Parish Church. Now in the school archive.*

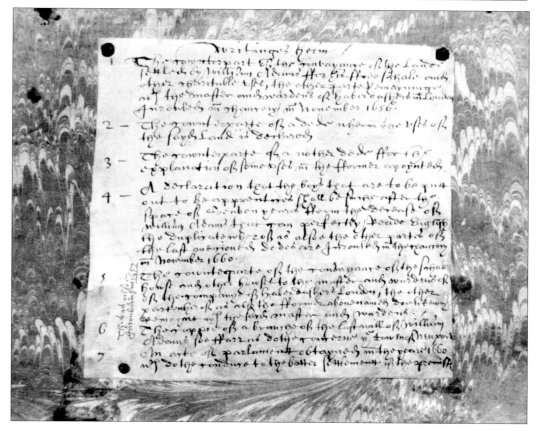

9 The initial letter of an indenture dated 30 April 1657, conveying to William Adams Iscoyd Hall, Flintshire, the site of the Angel Inn, Newport (on which the school had already been built) and other smaller pieces of land from a consortium of London businessmen.

10 Title page of the oldest surviving book in the school library, published in 1593 at Treviso, near Venice. It examines classical views on the rituals involved with food and drink.

11   *Chained books in Shrewsbury School library showing that books were originally displayed with their fore edges facing outwards. The Adams' library would have been similar.*

12   *The library after reorganisation in 1901. The ancient books can be seen on shelves behind the partition. The main part of the room was used for teaching and for sixth-form study. The partition was later removed.*

13 *Silver cup presented by the Haberdashers' Company in 1784 to Mr Humphrey Felton, Attorney of Market Drayton, in recognition of his services as Receiver of their estates during the tenure of the Justice family.*

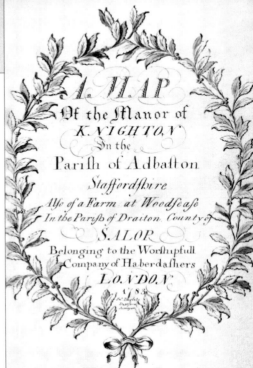

14 *Title page of 1783 Knighton estates map.*

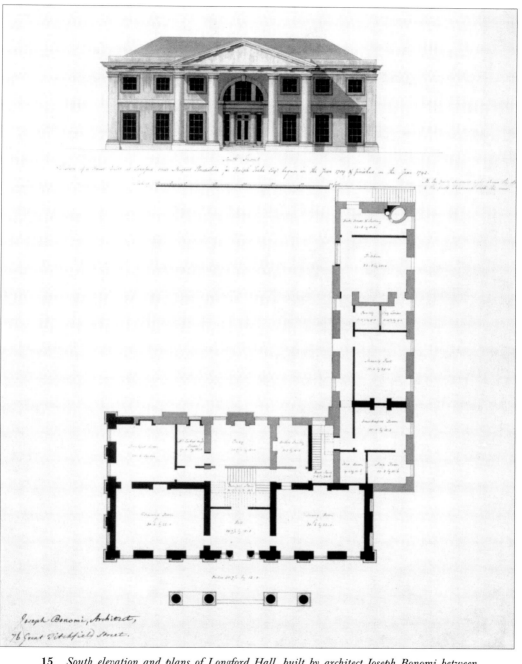

15 *South elevation and plans of Longford Hall, built by architect Joseph Bonomi between 1789 and 1792 for Ralph Leeke Esq.*

16 Thomas Percy, Bishop of Dromore, old boy of Newport Grammar School, whose Reliques of Ancient Poetry *published in 1765 was a basis for the Romantic Movement in literature.*

17 *The Revd William Sandford, Usher of Newport Grammar School 1820-1853 and Rector of Newport 1827-64.*

18 *Professor Oliver Lodge (ON) at the age of 43 in 1894, the year in which he gave the world's first demonstration of signalling by radio waves.*

19 *Remnant of a letter written by John Langley, Usher, in 1817 to Richard Hallen asking for an advance of salary. Discovered in the Headmaster's House in 1980.*

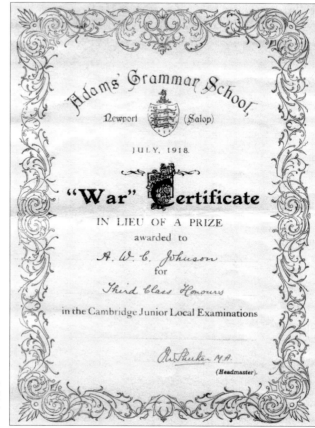

20 *War Certificate awarded to A.W.C. Johnson in July 1918. These were awarded throughout the First World War, with National Savings Certificates instead of book prizes.*

21 *Newport Grammar School boys Claude and Allan Perry with their brother Frank pose by the Buttercross in 1908. Elkes' Bakery is in the background.*

22 *William and Sydney Preston (ONs) in their Sunday uniform ready for 'Church Parade', 1939. The 'bumfreezer' jacket and Eton collar were discontinued shortly afterwards.*

23 *Newport Grammar School football team 1906-1907 in front of the open colonnade. Note the door through to the back at the right-hand side.*

24 *The School Cadet Corps led by Mr Shuker and Mr Gill parade in June 1916 for the funeral of Lance Corporal Patrick Kilcoyne, the first in Newport for a serving soldier in the First World War.*

25 *Big School with the glass partition added in 1901 fully open. Note the blackboard, the gas lighting and the bell rope hanging through the centre of the ceiling attached behind the stairs.*

26 *The back of the school soon after the Manual Room (the right-hand building) was built in 1926. The small buildings were probably the boys' privies.*

27 *The dining hall* c.*1930 lit by gas (electricity was not installed until 1931). Known as Room D for many years, it is now an Upper Sixth Common Room.*

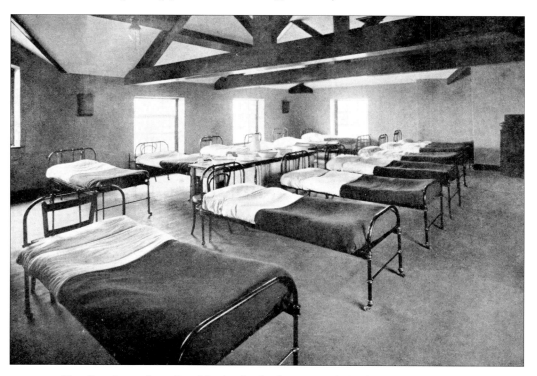

28 *Dormitory above Big School, also lit by gas. Did the boys have no personal possessions?*

29   *The physics laboratory in the Annexe set up in 1919.*

30   *The chemistry laboratory on the first floor of the 1929 Building, later the art room.*

The result of all this was that the Adams' Charity was closely tied to Chancery and its funds held by the Accountant-General. Any expenditure of money, except for very small sums, had in future to go through Chancery, which could take a very long time. So, for the future, it was a recipe for inaction.

The Knighton Estates in the Nineteenth and Twentieth Centuries

On the death of Richard Hallen in 1819, after 36 years' service, there were five suitable applicants for the position of Receiver of the Rents, far more than applied for the Headship of the School that year! William Evans of Calvington was appointed, 'a good practical Farmer and a man of integrity'.[24] By 1840 Robert Fisher, Esq, of Chetwynd Lodge was a very active agent, obviously a gentleman of some status as he is always referred to as Esquire and the Haberdasher deputation in 1842 recommended that he be allowed to shoot on the estate as the tenants were, otherwise his prestige would suffer. After him Mr John Cobb (died 1863) and his son John Francis Cobb took over. John Cobb had been the builder who carried out extensive repairs and rebuilding to the school in 1801-4 and 1819-22, and had built Longford Church in 1804. Father and son (described as architects) were responsible for rebuilding Newport Parish Church in 1837 and for building completely new farmhouses on the Charity's estates from 1841.

Detailed critical surveys were made of the estates by surveyors sent from London in 1804, 1808 and 1818. These led to increased rents being charged.

In the 1820s there were real problems because of the agricultural depression after the end of the Napoleonic Wars. All five tenants wrote to the Company in November 1821 asking for help. They stated that the prices of grain and all kinds of livestock were in a depressed state. Their rents had been increased in 1805, when wheat was 13s. to 14s. a measure, and again in 1819 when it was only 9s. to 10s. It was now reduced to 5s. 6d. a measure. They pointed out that many gentlemen had reduced rents by anything from 10 per cent to 30 per cent and they asked the Worshipful Company either not to impose new rents, or to give a rebate. (This was the time when conditions were so bad on the Duke of Sutherland's estates that he got his tenants to drain the Weald Moors to provide some employment.) The Governors agreed to a rebate of 15 per cent on the rents from March 1820 to March 1821, and would do so the following year if necessary.[25] This, of course, had to go through Chancery and would take some time to be approved.

Meanwhile these problems filtered through to the school. As the tenants could not pay their rents Mr Evans had no money to pay salaries. He did not manage to pay the Headmaster and Usher their half year's salary to Midsummer 1822 until January 1823, by which time they were due to receive their pay for the second half of the year. Mr Sandford, the Usher, had been promised £50 towards his rent as he was unable to occupy the Usher's house while it was being repaired, but this had not been paid. There was no money to pay the Exhibitions or Mr Evans' own salary. On 28 January 1823 Mr Meredith, the Headmaster, wrote to the Company saying he had had to borrow money at 5 per cent because his salary had not been paid, and could they do something about regular payment in the future![26] Despite this the Governors kept putting off asking Chancery to pay out of reserves until Mr Evans had pressed the tenants once more. He wrote that if he pressed too hard it would ruin them. He managed to pay the Head's and Usher's salaries to Christmas 1822 by the end of February 1823, so it was decided not to bother Chancery at that point. The Governors told him he need not make payments to the Company's poor or its officers. The Visitors appeared to have little sympathy with the tenants, pointing out that their rents were lower than most in the area, and recommending legal measures against them (which were never taken). Gradually the crisis passed and Mr Cobb was also paid for his work on the school building.

Things were never so bad again, but rents were occasionally lowered in times of hardship, for instance in the 1880s, before the First World War, and in the 1930s. The Company refused to help in 1863, however, when the tenants had to sell their cattle at low prices because of cattle plague (foot and mouth disease). In 1827 the Birmingham and Liverpool Junction Canal was cut through part of the Knighton Estate and the tenants whose lands were diminished by it had their rents reduced. This Shropshire Union Canal became an important link between the Black Country and Birmingham to the south and the Trent and Mersey canal and Chester to the north.

A radical reorganisation was made of the farms at Knighton at the expiration of the 21-year leases in 1840. Clay on the estate, and at Woodseaves, was used to make bricks and tiles for new buildings, and drainage tiles to improve the land. The four Knighton farms were now amalgamated into the three that still exist today – that is, Knighton Grange Farm, Knighton Mount Farm and Knighton Hall Farm. This arrangement freed more land for cultivation. The *Haberdashers' Arms* public house now appears for the first time, kept by the blacksmith. The Cobbs (father and son) were employed to build completely new farms and farm buildings – the end of the half-timbered constructions which had traditionally served. The Haberdasher deputation of 1842, met by numerous officials involved in the work, thought the houses unnecessarily extensive for farms of this size, but well built.[27] These are basically the houses that exist today.

In 1856 the Company bought Palins Farm, a small farm on the edge of the existing estate. Part of this was owned by the Jones Charity of Monmouth, but the Newport Receiver administered it and was paid accordingly.

An important change came with the new Adams' school scheme of 1878 which abolished the local Visitors and replaced them with 13 Managers. The Haberdashers still had control of the estates and the local Managers lost little time in criticising their management. At a meeting in April 1879 Mr Liddle and Mr Cotes MP (both of whose forebears had been active in school matters at the beginning of the century) resolved that the Surveyor and Woodreeve were either inefficient or overpaid and that the only benefit of

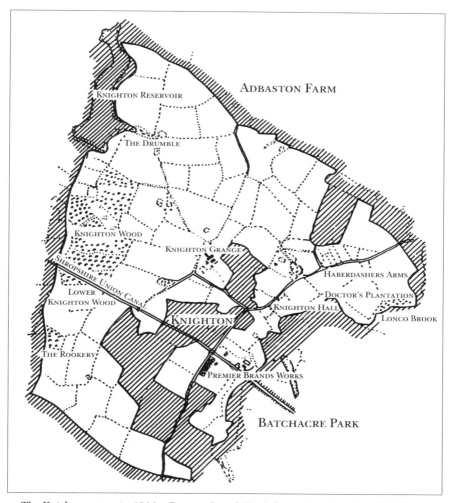

The Knighton estate in 1988, Premier Brand Foods have taken the place of Cadburys.
The rate-free area is shown white.

the woods was occasional sale of timber. They concluded that the cost of management was a drain on the charity income. They estimated that by selling the estates and investing the sum in government Consolidated Annuities (Consols) the income available to the charity would rise from the current £1,188 to £1,971 per year.[28] Nothing was done. The Managers complained again in 1884 and 1890, when the London Governors insisted there were not enough funds to build a new school. In 1892 the Charity Commissioners wrote to the Company asking whether the farm income could be increased, but were told that this was not possible. The financial position by now was worsened by the payment of pensions. The first, of £50 a year, had been to William Sandford, to get him to give up his post as Usher in 1853. He received it till his death in 1868. Dr Saxton, the Master, had a pension of £95 a year from 1870 till his death in 1890 and Mr Crowther, the Writing Master, received £75 a year from 1882 to 1892. It seems tragic that the financial position in 1903, on the retirement of Tom Collins as Headmaster, was so bad that the only payment the Company could make to him was a gift of £134 15s., instead of the pension that he surely deserved.

In 1911 the Haberdashers rented out 22 acres of Knighton Hall Farm by the canal to Cadbury Brothers of Bournville. They built a large milk condensing factory there, which could process milk from the surrounding farms, mix it with ground-up cocoa brought by canal from Bournville and sugar brought by canal from Bristol to make 'crumb' which was then transported back to Bournville to be made into milk chocolate. This factory was of great benefit to local farmers who now had a useful outlet for milk which would otherwise go sour during a long journey, and it was a good source of local employment. The Company was able to charge a rent for 22 acres which was equivalent to that of a whole farm of over 200 acres, so the Charity benefited.

It was half-way through the 20th century before the estates ceased to be the source of Adams' Newport Charity income. In 1920 the farm at Woodseaves was sold for £5,200 to the existing tenant, in 1954 Cadbury's bought their holding for £21,000. The rest of the Knighton Estate was sold in 1957 as a complete unit to Lord Sackville (Sackville Settled Estates) for £85,000 and the money was invested in Government stock.

One benefit which was passed on to Cadbury's and retained by the tenants even though the estate was no longer owned by the Charity was the freedom from rates and taxes which was granted by the Act of 1660. Over the centuries attempts were made by the parishes of Newport, Adbaston and Woodseaves to get poor rate contributions from the school and the tenants. Sometimes the tenants paid without realising they need not do so. The Haberdashers took legal advice on their behalf and, often with the help of local JPs, such as Richard Whitworth, they were able to claim exemption. Similar problems arose with the Window Tax during the Napoleonic Wars when the tax authorities claimed that the exemption only applied to taxes existing in 1660. Eventually the principle of complete exemption was upheld.

Sadly this was finally ignored in 1990, with the introduction of the Community Charge (Poll Tax). Since then both estates and school have paid taxes. The Company appealed to the local authority on the school's behalf to no avail. They took legal opinion, as on so many previous occasions, but this time the advice led to their acceptance of the inevitable, and the end of 330 years of a unique status.

Five

LATE SEVENTEENTH
AND EIGHTEENTH CENTURY

The school ran into trouble soon after Thomas Chaloner's departure. He left in March 1663 and the next Master was appointed in July. He was John Wickens, High Master of Manchester Grammar School, a leading Puritan, a 'cultured scholarly man and a fine teacher'. He would have set the school firmly on the road to excellence, but unfortunately for Newport the people of Manchester valued Mr Wickens too highly to let him go. After a large public meeting and a lot of activity among the feoffees (governors) of the school, he was persuaded to remain in Manchester, with an increase in salary (that brought him up to Newport's standard) and a larger house in which he could accommodate paying boarders.[1] In the meantime, until Francis Potts was appointed in November, the school was run entirely by the Usher. This was Thomas Millington, minister of Newport since the Puritan John Malden had been ejected in 1662. Millington had been minister of Cheswardine during the Interregnum. Whether he disliked having a Master appointed over his head after this we do not know, but we do know that less than three years later the 'divisions and animosities between the Schoolmaster and Usher'[2] led to three Haberdashers, including William Justice, being sent to Newport to investigate the problem with the help of six learned ministers or schoolmasters, chosen by the Schoolmaster and Usher. The result was that Mr Potts was asked to leave, and Mr Millington was to take over the school till a new Master was found. However, soon after Francis Potts was replaced by Timothy Wood the Haberdashers realised that Mr Millington had been a cause of conflict and in March 1667 they ordered him to vacate his post as Usher by midsummer, otherwise his salary would not be paid. The reason given was that he was minister of Newport, and no one was capable of holding the post of Master or Usher if he held an ecclesiastical post. Their minutes note that 'The quarrels between Potts and Millington are likely to deter and hinder any worthy person to attempt of the said Master's place while the said Usher continues that employment'. It is interesting that the Governors must have known all along that Millington was minister of Newport and only made the school statutes an excuse when they wanted to get rid of him.

The Haberdashers were determined that no more quarrels between Master and Usher should spoil the school and allowed Mr Wood to choose his own Usher, so his son Thomas came from Whitchurch School to join his father. The Visitors wrote that they were delighted with the new Master, and

An 18th-century classroom (note the birch on the table).

asked for some extra money for his removal expenses. The Governors had
already given him £5 but readily agreed to this. They pointed out it was not
to be taken as a precedent, but in practice they appear to have made a
contribution to furniture removal at every new appointment. Unfortunately,
all these high hopes came to nothing as Timothy Wood had to resign two
years later because of ill health.

The school was luckier with the next Master, Samuel Edwards, who
served it for 36 years. From what little we can piece together about him, he
seems to have been an excellent Head. He had been Head of Whitchurch
Grammar School for four years and while he was there he sent at least six
boys to university. His brother Jonathan Edwards was Vice-Principal of
Jesus College, Oxford.

We have no record of curriculum and activities at Newport at this time,
but as Latin plays were performed at Whitchurch under Samuel Edwards,
and Latin and Greek plays at Wem under Francis Williams, who moved
there in 1681 having been Usher at Newport since 1678, it seems highly
likely that such plays were performed at William Adams' school. This
Francis Williams, born at Lilleshall and educated at Newport from where he
went on to Trinity College, Cambridge, took two ex-Newport pupils with
him to be Ushers at Wem. The Reverend Samuel Garbett in his *History of
Wem* describes him as 'a jolly personable man, had a pleasant way of discourse, and brought up a great number of scholars ... I saw them perform
in a handsome manner, and before a great audience, the Plutus of
Aristophanes.' One hopes he was as great an asset to Newport before he
moved on.

There seems to have been only one London deputation sent to Newport in Edwards' 36 years. This visited Adams and Monmouth in 1673. We know no details but it was obviously complimentary about the Head because, as a result, the Court of Assistants allowed him to choose his own Usher a few months later when the current Usher left to return to university. This was 'to prevent all clashings and dissents between Master and Usher' but the Court was careful to state that this should not be taken as a precedent. There are references to several other inspections carried out at the request of Mr Edwards by the local Visitors – substantial landowners such as Mr Thomas Wilbraham, John Cotes Esq, Thomas Corbett Esq and local clergymen. These all gave satisfactory reports, even towards the end of Mr Edwards' long tenure of office. Less than a year before he died the Court of Assistants noted its 'great satisfaction upon the visitation both as to the care and application of the School Master and his Usher and also the great proficiency of the scholars at Newport'. The Court thanked Mr Edwards 'for his great care and good management in his employment hitherto and did not question but he would continue the same both in respect to his own and the Company's reputation and honour'.[3]

Tom Brown 1663-1704
One of Newport Grammar School's most well-known old boys was educated under Samuel Edwards. Tom Brown was the son of William Brown, tanner, who was one of the burgesses of Newport. Tom went on to Christ Church, Oxford, where he was said to be proficient in Latin, Greek, French, Italian and Spanish. Where had he learnt all these languages? He must have had an excellent grounding at the school. At Christ Church he came up against the Dean, Dr John Fell and wrote the verse known to generations of schoolchildren:

> I do not love thee, Doctor Fell
> The reason why I cannot tell
> But this I know, and know full well
> I do not love thee, Doctor Fell.

The story is that Dr Fell had offered to cancel a punishment due to Tom if he could do an extempore translation of words by the Roman poet, Martial, and this is what he came up with. Whether this actually happened is uncertain, but certainly Dr Fell has been immortalised by this ditty. He was in fact an eminent university administrator after the Restoration and founder of the Oxford University Press.

After getting his degree in 1684 Tom went to London to enjoy society there and support himself by writing, without much success. He did a spell of teaching, but soon gave it up. He lived a precarious life, lodging in Grub Street, the centre for impoverished writers who would write anything at the command of booksellers. In *The Poet's Condition* he describes his life:

> Without formal petition
> Thus stands my condition
> I am closely blocked up in a garret,
> Where I scribble and smoke,
> And sadly invoke
> The powerful assistance of claret.

The style is reminiscent of a Gilbert and Sullivan patter song.

He wrote some serious works, such as his *History of the World*, his life of William III and *Satyr upon the French King on the Peace of Ryswick*, for which he served a spell in prison. He was well known in literary circles, but his attacks on others such as the poet John Dryden made him unpopular. He translated many works from foreign languages, but he was chiefly known for his irrepressible wit and sarcasm, laced with a crude humour which offended many. He died in poverty and was buried in the cloisters of Westminster Abbey. Various editions of his works appeared throughout the century, but he has since faded from memory.

Thomas Parker 1667–1732
Thomas Parker, of Leek, Staffordshire, was educated at Newport School for some years and made his career in the law. In 1710 he became Lord Chief Justice and a member of the Privy Council, and on the death of Queen Anne in 1714 he was one of the Lords Justices ruling the country until the arrival of George I. He quickly became a favourite of his, reading the King's Speech at the opening of Parliament in 1718 because the King could not speak English. He became Lord Chancellor that year, and was made Earl of Macclesfield and Viscount Parker of Ewelme in 1721. However his fortunes then declined. He was accused of misuse of funds and in 1725 was impeached for corruption as Lord Chancellor and imprisoned in the Tower until he paid his fine of £30,000. (The King privately promised to pay this for him but died after paying the first instalment of £1,000.) As a result an Accountant-General of the Court of Chancery was established to prevent further abuse of funds, and stamp duties were imposed for the relief of distressed suitors. Parker retired to private life at Shirburn Castle, Oxfordshire.[4]

The Eighteenth Century

Samuel Edward's death brings us to the beginning of the 18th century, which is often said to have been a period of decline in grammar schools. It is worth looking at education as a whole at this time, so that we can see William Adams' grammar school against this background. In many ways the Restoration of the Monarchy in 1660 was the turning point. Certainly the great impetus for founding grammar schools in the 16th and 17th centuries petered out after this and virtually none were founded after George I came to the throne in 1714. Eighteenth-century benefactors turned their attention to founding new hospitals, reforming prisons and other good works. Their interest in education turned to providing elementary schools for the poor. The Society for the Promotion of Christian Knowledge, founded in 1698, took the lead in this movement, which aimed to provide religious education for boys and girls and to teach them the discipline that would be necessary for them to carry out their duties in life. There was always the fear that they would educate the children beyond their station, and many schools faded out in the latter part of the century. The Sunday School movement of the 1780s revived this type of school for children who were at work during the week. Even adults attended to learn to read. Robert Raikes of Gloucester is usually taken as the founder of this movement, but he was not the first to teach on a Sunday, and such schools were started by both Anglicans and Nonconformists. There was a flourishing Sunday School in Newport at this time.

Numbers of pupils in grammar schools were low throughout the century and into the 19th century. Many examples can be cited: Edward VI Grammar School, Birmingham had no pupils in 1734; Monmouth had three at one point in the 1740s; Ashbourne Grammar School had one in 1790; even Winchester, the oldest grammar school foundation, had only eight in 1751. In Shropshire, Whitchurch had five pupils in 1681, Shrewsbury seems to have had only one boy in 1798, Bridgnorth only 11 in 1819. The smallest number that we know of at Newport was 17 in 1782, but records are not complete.

Why was there such a decline in grammar schools and where did parents send their children if not to grammar schools? It must be realised that a school was only as good as its Headmaster. If he was an attractive character and an effective teacher, numbers could rise as quickly as they had declined. Records of pupils attending Oxford and Cambridge frequently mention the name of the Schoolmaster who sent them up, rather than the school. But Heads often stayed too long in their posts for the simple reason that there were no pensions, so a Schoolmaster could not afford to retire. He continued in his post, and in his church living if he was lucky enough to have one, until he died. No wonder the fortunes of schools varied enormously. Newport School affords good examples of this. It had only four Heads in 150 years, from 1668 to 1818. Samuel Edwards was Head for 36 years, John Greenwood served Newport for 41 years as Usher and Head, Samuel Lea was Head for 48 and Joseph Scott was Usher and Head for 46 years. When Joseph Scott resigned in 1818 because of ill health the Visitors asked the Governors for a pension of £50 for him, as he had done the honourable thing by resigning. The Haberdashers replied that only Chancery could grant this. There is no record that it was ever paid, but they need not have worried about the expense as he died within a year.

More important than the longevity of individual Headmasters, however, were the broad changes within society which meant that the 18th-century grammar schools appealed neither to the higher classes nor to the middle classes and those wishing to better themselves. Society was beginning to polarise. Whereas in the 17th century there had been much inter-marriage between families of differing status, this now became unthinkable. The gentry and nobility became disinclined to send their sons to endowed schools where they would mix with the lower classes. They sent them instead to a few chosen schools – the beginnings of the public school system. Shrewsbury was the 'public school' in Shropshire.

At the same time, the curriculum taught in the grammar schools no longer met middle-class needs. Before the Civil War a good classical education had been perceived as the way to advancement in life, whatever one's background. But in the second half of the 17th century, while a knowledge of classical culture was still expected in polite society, it was becoming irrelevant to tradesmen. It was also less possible for a poor boy to raise himself through a career in the church, as sons of clergy replaced bright boys from poor backgrounds at the universities and in church benefices. Towards the end of the century the cost of attending university increased to such an extent that it became impossible for poor families.

The middle and lower classes did not want their boys to spend their time learning Latin and Greek – they wanted subjects that would be useful in later life. They wanted English and writing (the elementary schools like the English School in Newport only taught reading), and commercial subjects like arithmetic and accounting.

Some endowed schools met this problem by altering their curriculum even though it was contrary to the founder's intention. In the 18th century 16 grammar schools actually dropped Latin in favour of English. Some became elementary schools, such as the Haberdasher school at Bunbury, Cheshire. In large towns many schools developed a commercial side along with the classical. Manchester Grammar School was very successful at this. Between 1740 and 1765 it admitted 196 boarders and 477 day boys, of whom only 100 went on to university. The other pupils went on to industry and commerce well-equipped for it. Numbers at Rugby School rose from 66 in 1778 to 245 in 1794 when the school modified its classical curriculum to include history, modern geography and mathematics as well as writing, arithmetic and French.

Some pioneer grammar schools had offered more relevant subjects even in the 17th century. The Royal Mathematical School of Christ's Hospital, founded in 1676, started a trend that was taken up by others. Dartmouth Grammar School from its foundation in 1679 had one master who taught Latin and one who taught English, navigation and mathematics.

Newport Grammar School seemed immune to all these changes. It plodded on steadily as a classical school until in 1784 the Visitors insisted that a Writing Master be employed out of the increased revenue. He also taught arithmetic and, according to the Charity Commissioners report of 1820, mathematics to those desiring it. But his teaching was only part-time.

Where did pupils go for their education if not to grammar schools? The answer must be private schools, but it is very difficult to trace such schools. Many private schools taught classical and non-classical subjects in a way far removed from the flogging traditionally associated with grammar schools. Private tutoring was increasingly used by the rich and privileged. Clergy often taught their own sons and took in a few others at the same time, to prepare them for university; this would have been a classical education.

A group of schools that have often been quoted as alternatives to endowed grammar schools at this period were the Dissenting Schools and Academies. Dissenters, another name for the Nonconformists, whose forms of worship were severely limited after the restoration of the prayer book in 1662, gained freedom of worship by the Toleration Act of 1689. They were not, however, allowed to attend endowed Anglican schools, nor take degrees at the universities. It was not until University College was founded in London in 1828 that any university education was open to them and they could not take a full part in Oxford and Cambridge universities until 1871. Dissenters therefore provided their own education up to university standard, where their teaching methods were more enlightened and the subjects covered a much wider range than in the traditional schools and universities. Sheriffhales Academy, Shropshire, was run by the Reverend John Woodhouse as a university for Roman Catholic and Protestant Nonconformists. Eminent pupils included Robert Harley from Brampton Bryan, Shropshire, who as Earl of Oxford became leading minister to Queen Anne, and Henry St John, Viscount Bolingbroke, who became his political opponent. Subjects taught included logic, anatomy, mathematics, physics, ethics and rhetoric; teaching methods emphasised practical skills, so the pupils would prepare sermons, write English compositions, dissect animals, or perform land surveys. There was a similar academy at Shrewsbury.

One of the most well-known was Warrington Academy which flourished between 1757 and 1783, having 393 students at one point. Joseph Priestley, the discoverer of oxygen, taught there from 1761 to 1767. This was the sort of broad-ranging education suited to pioneers in industry such as the Quaker Darby family of Coalbrookdale.

With this background we turn to William Adams' Grammar School at Newport in the 18th century. There were basically three headmasters during this period, and eight ushers. Their details are given in Appendix D.

John Greenwood
Headmaster 1704–1722

John Greenwood was appointed Usher in 1681 and became Head in 1704, continuing until his death in 1722. He was the only applicant for the Headship when Samuel Edwards died, and was obviously well prepared with recommendations from the Bishop, nobility, gentry and clergy, as well as the inhabitants of Newport and all the scholars.

We have already seen in Chapter Two that the Company allowed John Greenwood to become minister of Newport at the same time as being Usher (and later Head) and that the people of Newport subscribed together to buy back the tithes, which had been in other people's hands since the dissolution of St Mary's College, so that he had a much better income than his predecessors. They also bought back the Parsonage in St Mary Street, originally the College House, and this remained the Parsonage until 1866. Whether he lived in the Parsonage or the school we do not know. He had complained in 1688 that the Usher's house was decayed and in want of repair because his predecessors had not lived in it, and this only just over thirty years since it was built. At his request the Governors ordered Mr Justice to repair it, contrary to the statutes. The full £175 from the estates was already allocated – did Mr Justice have to pay out extra that year?[5]

That the two did not get on was shown in 1697 when Mr Justice complained of 'the usher's severe and rigorous correction of the children under his care'. The Governors had had similar complaints before, so they summoned Mr Greenwood to appear at their next meeting. When the charges were read out to him 'he gave distinct and particular answer to each of them'. He was also able to produce 'divers Gentlemen of very great reputation on his behalf, some of which were Parliament men who had … been his scholars' who spoke on his behalf, saying he was a man 'of unquestionable reputation both in life and conversation and that he was a very great Instrument of the now so flourishing condition the School is in …'. The Governors decided that the complaints against him were caused by 'private and personal pique and animosity rather than any just cause'.[6] This incident shows that the schoolboys at this time were of at least gentry class or even nobility.

In 1705 the Haberdashers asked John Greenwood for his help in finding a suitable Schoolmaster and Usher for Bunbury School, as they were having trouble with the current Head, Mr Hoole, who had turned out the Usher with no warning. He recommended Matthew Birch, an old boy of Newport Grammar School, son of a farmer at Stockton, who had gone to Sidney Sussex College, Cambridge as a sizar. He became Headmaster at Bunbury until 1721. John Greenwood was also very helpful to the Haberdashers in overseeing the English School in Newport and reporting to them about it. Later on he asked permission to build apartments for two poor widows next to William Adams' almshouses. This was granted, but it seems nothing was actually done.

Sadly, as in so many cases, he continued as Head when he was no longer capable of doing the job. In July 1722 a letter from the Visitors told of the ill state and condition of the school by reason of the Master's indisposition. They recommended James Onions (curate of Chetwynd and curate-in-charge of Forton) to help. The Court ordered that if no account was received of the death of Mr Greenwood by the next post, a letter was to go to the Visitors to recommend Mr Onions to be assistant to the Usher, 'till this Court shall further order'. John Greenwood died in September, but there is no indication that Mr Onions was called upon, the Usher being charged with the running of the school until a successor could be found. As a result of the 'improper management of the late schoolmaster' it was resolved that in future all appointments to the schools under the care of the Haberdashers' Company should be for one year only, renewable on application. This had been done for some Haberdasher charity appointments but not previously for Adams, Monmouth or Bunbury. They continued with this for many years but there is no evidence that the practice was ever used to get rid of unsatisfactory teachers.

There were only four applicants for the post of Head when John Greenwood died. James Onions, who had been recommended by the Visitors, tried in 1722 and again in 1725, but he was not successful. He became Rector of Boston, Lincolnshire soon after. Robert Symonds was appointed in 1722, but died eighteen months later. In 1725, out of three applicants, Samuel Lea was made Head.

Samuel Lea
Headmaster 1725–1773

Samuel Lea, born in Staffordshire, brought a new vigour to the school. Richard Whitworth, writing in 1801, lamented the poor state of the school for the previous 30 or 40 years, and added, 'I remember being at this school with 80 scholars and many of them of the first families of Shropshire, Staffordshire and Cheshire'.[7] We know that he was only five when he went to the school for four years in 1742, but even allowing for nostalgic exaggeration this must mean the school was flourishing. The earliest report on the School we have in the Haberdasher archives is that of 1762.[8] By this time there were only 27 pupils. When the London deputation asked why there was such a great decrease in numbers since 1730 they were told: 'As to the Decrease of the School, apprehended it was owing to Infirmities which it had pleased Almighty God to inflict upon Mr Lea in his Old Age and therefore was to be pitied rather than blamed Especially as the Great Increase of the Scholars in the year 1730 appeared to the then Visitors to be intirely owing to Mr Lea's Ability and Care.' There was obviously a lot of support for him. He was 73 or 74 by this time, but he continued as Master until his death at 84. In 1771 there were 'not 20 pupils', chiefly under the Usher, Mr Forrester. The deputation was told that parents preferred to put their children out apprentice rather than give them a liberal education, but they thought the poor numbers were 'due to the advanced age of Mr Lea and the inattention of Mr Forrester'.[9] They did not see the need for altering the classical curriculum. When the new Master, Joseph Scott, reported in 1774 that there were 24 scholars, he was congratulated by the Company on the much-increased numbers, so one wonders how low they had dipped!

The 1762 report gives a glimpse into the duties of a Haberdasher deputation. It is signed by William Cracroft and Nathaniel Hedges, the Master and the Fourth Warden. They set off from London on Monday 13 September and arrived at Newport on Tuesday about seven in the evening. Two miles out they were met by Messrs Lea and Forrester, the Schoolmaster and Usher. They spent the evening with them, seeing to the arrangements for the visit, and lodged at the sign of the *White Bear*. On Wednesday morning they read the statutes, Mr Justice's lease and the Company's reports about the school. They surveyed the school buildings and the almshouses. The lead gutters at the front of the school needed repair as did chimneys at the almshouses which were smoking and likely to fall. They got these repaired during the visit. In the afternoon Mr Lea showed them the books in the library, which were well preserved. They asked Mr Forrester to make a catalogue, which had not been done since 1657.

On Thursday morning at 11a.m. they met the Visitors 'under the Piazzas' and adjourned to Mr Lea's parlour. The Visitors were Robert Piggott Esq of Chetwynd and the Reverend Messrs Piggott of Edgmond, Haynes of Longford, Binnell of Newport and Dickenson of Blymhill. Col. Cotes of Woodcote, Charles Baldwin Esq of Aqualate, the Reverend Mr Sanders of Chetwynd and the Reverend Mr Holbrook of Church Aston were unable to attend because of illness or business. William Jourdain Esq had died. They proceeded to the school where the 27 boys were ranged according to their classes. When the Visitors were seated the two Senior boys, Sampson Webb and Joseph Scott, each spoke a Latin oration in praise of the Founder, Governors and Visitors. Afterwards the boys were examined in Greek and Latin authors by the Master and Usher, which they construed and parsed to the satisfaction of all present. The statutes should now have been read, but as there had been no complaints and they were up in the school anyway, this was dispensed with. At this point the Haberdashers raised the question of small pupil numbers, which we have already quoted. Back in the parlour they appointed Richard Whitworth Esq of Batchacre Grange to succeed William Jourdain as Visitor. Two William Adams' Exhibitions were vacant since William Church and John Forrester had finished their studies (incidentally both returned as Ushers to the school). They elected the two senior boys – one of them, Joseph Scott, later returned as Usher and Headmaster. They then went to the Town Hall, built by William Adams, to discuss the English School with the Steward and the Bailiff. They visited the school and checked the lands left to it by William Adams. In the evening they entertained to dinner everyone connected with the Charity.

On the Friday they started their lengthy survey of the Knighton estates, accompanied by Mr George the Woodreeve and Mr Felton, agent to Mr Justice, which took 10 days. This resulted in their appointing Mr Whitworth as their local agent in place of Mr George. After the survey was completed they dined with Mr Felton at Drayton. Although they differed with him on the tenants' right to depasture, he expressed the hope that all would be amicably adjusted. They observed that he behaved 'in a very gentlemanlike fashion'.

Although his teaching ability may have tailed off with advancing age, Samuel Lea was always actively involved in the affairs of the Knighton estate. It was he, not the Justice family, who by now was responsible for dispensing the Charity's money, and the Haberdashers refused to let him give this up even to the last. Mr Scott continued with this responsibility until Richard Hallen took over as Receiver.

Richard Whitworth remembered that 'an old schoolmaster, Mr Lea, rode out every day till he was 90 years of age, he used always to take his horse through the school …'.[10] This was an exaggeration; we know Samuel Lea died at 84, but it is an evocative picture of an old schoolmaster completely at home in 'his' school. In fact his route through the school would have been simply under the portico and out to the back, which saved him having to go right round to the Beaumaris road entrance. He was Rector of Bucknall, Staffordshire, from about 1718 to 1773. He must have had a curate there to do the work. His brass memorial tablet is in Newport Parish Church.

A Celebrated Old Boy: Thomas Percy 1729–1811

James Boswell, in his life of Dr Samuel Johnson, the great lexicographer and man of letters, states that at the age of 15 his father 'applied to have him admitted as a scholar and assistant to the Rev Samuel Lee, M.A., headmaster of Newport school in Shropshire (a very diligent good teacher, at that time in high reputation …).' This application to Mr Lee was not successful; but Johnson had afterwards the gratification to hear that the old gentleman, who lived to a very advanced age, mentioned it as one of the most memorable events of his life, that he was '*very near* having that great man for his scholar'. Johnson went to school at Stourbridge instead, for little more than a year.

This information was given to Boswell by Thomas Percy, a friend of Johnson's and one of Newport's outstanding Old Boys. Born in Bridgnorth, in the house still called Bishop Percy's house, he went to the grammar school there until, at the age of 12, his father sent him to Newport School, as he wrote, 'then in great repute, under the Rev Samuel Lea, M.A. who had at that time near 40 boarders in his house. Mr Lea had no great depth of learning, but an excellent method, and therefore as he kept the boys closely to their business, though they did not learn much from him, they generally acquired a good deal of knowledge in his School.'[11] Mr Lea put him in for one of the first Careswell Exhibitions (see below) and he went to Christ Church College, Oxford in 1746. There he gained a further Exhibition that had been endowed by Dean Fell. The College presented him to the living of Easton Maudit, Northamptonshire and it was while he was there, until he was made Dean of Carlisle in 1778, that he did his most effective literary work. His *Reliques of Ancient English Poetry* in three volumes, published in 1765, was a collection of nearly 200 ballads inspired by his finding a tattered manuscript in the house of his friend Humphrey Pitt at Priorslee near Shifnal, with which the maids were lighting the fire. Friends and scholars from all over the country, including Oliver Goldsmith and David Garrick, searched in attics and libraries to find old songs and romances for him. He was also able to use several existing collections, such as those at the Bodleian Library, the British Museum and the Society of Antiquaries.

There was obviously widespread interest in preserving old songs, and Percy's *Reliques*, annotated in a meticulous scholarly fashion, became immensely popular. They were reprinted three more times by the end of the century and repeatedly before the mid-20th century. The Romantic movement in England and Germany was inspired by these ballads. Wordsworth and Coleridge in their *Lyrical Ballads* owed much to them. Walter Scott in his autobiography remembers how as a schoolboy in about 1782, 'The first time I could scrape a few shillings together I bought unto myself a copy of these beloved volumes; nor do I believe I ever read a book half so frequently or with half the enthusiasm'. In Germany the reaction against the rationalistic outlook of the Age of Enlightenment owed much to his romantic ballads: the young men of the *Sturm und Drang* movement (Storm and Stress) which included Goethe and Schiller wrote imaginative dramas set in the Middle Ages, about great men in revolt against society. Percy could never have anticipated that his collection would foster such a movement. Johnson praised his 'minute accuracy of information' and remarked 'he was a man out of whose company he never went without learning something'.[12] After he was made Bishop of Dromore, Co Down, in 1782, he lived in his diocese and worked ceaselessly there, so he withdrew somewhat from the English literary scene.

The Careswell Exhibitions

Edward Careswell established 18 Exhibitions for Shropshire boys to be held at Christ Church, Oxford. They were to be shared among six grammar schools: Shrewsbury and Newport with four Exhibitions, Bridgnorth and Shifnal with three, Wem and Donnington with two, making 18 in total, not 18 every year. Each scholar had £18 a year for four years as an undergraduate, £21 for three years as a BA, and £27 for three years as an MA, ten years in all. The Exhibitioners were chosen by the Master of the College and local Justices of the Peace. The first Careswell Exhibitioners were chosen in 1746, the three from Newport being Thomas Percy, John Lea, son of the headmaster, and Jonathan Stubbs, son of the Receiver of the Rents of the Careswell estate.

The scheme has been altered over the years, but has always been of great benefit to Newport pupils going on to university. Since 1900 the Exhibitions have not been restricted to Oxford University but can be held at any institution of higher learning. Currently pupils from Shrewsbury School, Adams' Grammar School, Thomas Adams' School Wem, Bridgnorth Endowed School and Idsall School are eligible for these exhibitions, which are of £150 per year for three years.

Joseph Scott
Headmaster 1773–1818

Joseph Scott, aged 27, was the only candidate for the Headship in 1773. He was the son of Robert Scott of Newport, gent.; his brother, Mr Samuel Scott, grocer, had been appointed Master of the Free English School by the Lord Chancellor in 1771. Joseph Scott became Usher in 1772 at the same time as being curate-in-charge of Forton (to 1776). He could not take up the Headship immediately on the death of Samuel Lea as, although a BA, he had not obtained his MA. This he did as soon as he could and became Head in December 1773. He was in sole charge of the school until a new Usher was appointed in 1775.

It would appear that Mr Scott was not a very effective schoolmaster. From 24 scholars in 1774 the number dropped to 17 in 1782. There were eight under Mr Scott in the Upper School and nine under Mr Hughes the Usher in the Lower. These had always been treated as distinct schools, but this is the first time we have specific numbers for each. In 1788 the Haberdashers, in their official reply to Richard Whitworth's Information against them in the Court of Chancery, claimed that since their reforms, and the appointment of a Writing Master, the numbers had risen from 15 to 40. The reasons they gave for the low numbers support the general conclusions of later historians. This lack 'appears to arise from the different mode of Education adopted of late years, persons in low and middling life finding Writing and Arithmetic more useful than the languages and persons in higher life adopting a more polite education for their Sons than sending them to a free School.'[13] By 1790 only 28 pupils were reported, in 1814 there were 33, and in 1818, 41 pupils. In 1803 Mr Scott had only three boarders and only one in 1817. Despite this we have one example that shows the continuing attraction of a free classical education (and incidentally the state of the Anglican Church). The Archdeacon of Salop noted in his Visitation of 1799 that the Vicar of Wrockwardine had moved to Newport, ten miles away, on account of his son's education. He took services at Wrockwardine on Sundays but left the occasional duties to neighbouring clergy.[14]

Scott was caught up in the crossfire between the Visitors and the Governors over the extra income from the estates and the lawsuit that followed (see pp.48-53). There had been no Haberdasher deputation to the school since 1771 but the Governors seemed determined not to cooperate with the Visitors. Three times (1795, 1798, 1807) they refused the Visitors' request to add the money from a vacant Exhibition to help an existing Exhibitioner even though, as the Visitors pointed out, this was in accordance with William Adams' Deed of Uses. When the Usher resigned in 1801 Richard Whitworth wrote expressing their concern about the state of the school and suggesting that the vacancy 'should be filled by a Person (qualified certainly as the Statutes direct) of a respectable family well known in this Country, likely to induce parents to send their children to be under him'.[15] All ten Visitors had considered much on the subject and recommended Mr Henry Dickenson 'of whom I most heartily approve'. The Haberdashers ignored this plea (they had no reason to love Mr Whitworth) and chose instead, out of three applicants, John Langley, for ten years officiating minister at Newport Church. We shall deal with Mr Langley and the troubles he caused in the next chapter.

Mr Scott's had problems with demands for Poor Rate and Window Tax, which the Company helped to resolve, and with the newly formed Sunday School's use of the Grammar School's gallery in the church. He first complained to the Company about the Sunday School in September 1787,[16] and they ordered investigations by him, Mr Hallen and the Clerk. They found that the gallery had been built in 1658 by the Town for the use of the Scholars, and repaired by the Governors. The Visitors were then consulted as to why the boys should be deprived of the sole use of the gallery after so long a time. The reply of the four clergy Visitors was not sympathetic. They found the gallery had not originally been put up for the exclusive use of the school, though the Parish had not repaired it until 1787. They said the Parish was only putting Sunday School boys there while there were few Grammar School scholars and they would withdraw them when necessary, so Mr Scott must accept this.[17] There had been trouble over the school gallery back in 1687 when Samuel Edwards had objected to the Churchwardens' plan to move the school's gallery 'so far from the pulpit that neither he nor his scholars can hear divine service nor the Word of God preached there'.[18] Mr Scott returned to his complaints in 1802. This time the Visitors had changed their tune. They said the Sunday School could use the chancel but the gallery belonged to the Haberdasher Governors. The whole matter was put off till later and we find no mention of it again until the 1830s.

In 1800 Mr Scott asked the Governors whether a boy of Roman Catholic religion could be accepted as a pupil. They consulted the deeds and decided 'looking to the period of time and the nature of the Government of the Country when this Charity was founded' that children of Roman Catholics should not have the benefit of this institution.[19] They were content to ignore the statutes about amalgamating Exhibitions but would not take a new stand on admissions. But maybe that would have been too far from the religious climate of the time.

A letter from the Visitors to the Governors in 1817, when Mr Scott was about to retire, gives a sorry account of the school. 'It is unnecessary to enter into detail of Causes which have reduced an Establishment liberally endowed and happily situated to a state of comparative decay.' They go on to state that there is only one boarder at the Headmaster's house, none at the Usher's, and only seven boys in the Upper School. No gentleman of the neighbourhood has a son at the school. There have been no candidates for the university since 1813, and two Exhibitions have been vacant since then. 'It is our firm conviction that nothing can revive the Credit of the School and restore it to its due rank and influence but the Appointment of an Able active and learned Master upon the present Vacancy.'[20] The school's lack of prestige was confirmed when Scott retired in 1818. There were only three applicants for the post, one of whom was the curate-in-charge of Newport, whereas at Atherstone Grammar School in 1817, there were 22! The difference could be that Atherstone had a number of boarders, many of them from titled families, whereas Joseph Scott had only one.

The English School in the Eighteenth Century

The Haberdashers took seriously the instructions in William Adams' will that they should keep an eye on the English School and the lands that he gave for its upkeep. William Adams had intended it to teach English to boys before they went on to the Grammar School but for most of the 18th century it taught far more boys (and girls) than ever went on to the Latin School. In common with other 'petty' schools it taught reading only, not writing. The Haberdashers from time to time made suggestions for its improvement but there was no one on the spot answerable to them to carry these out.

In 1673 the schoolmaster was Thomas Munck, gentleman,[21] who we know as the Parish Clerk from 1658 to 1691. In 1691 Peter Greene of Newport, gentleman, was recommended as schoolmaster and promised if he was appointed to give £10 in trust to repair the Booth Hall where it was held, as it was very ruinous.[22] Is this an indication that the official schoolmaster was a man of some means who would employ others to do the actual teaching? £10 was a quarter of the Grammar School Headmaster's annual salary.

In 1705 the Haberdashers had been alerted to 'the great abuse and neglect of the English school' and asked John Greenwood to report. He consulted the deeds in William Adams' box which was kept in the Church (now in the school

Carving on the top of William Adams' box, in which documents relevant to the Charity were kept.

archive), and reported that since the Governors' last visit new leases had been made. 'As for a place to teach in, I have consented that he have a good square room over the Church porch. It will hold at least 50 children and hath a fireplace in it. I sometimes go into the Schoole and often make enquiry and I cannot find but Mr Raven the Master is very diligent and applies himself wholly to his business and hath a greater number of Schollers than when our Governors last visited.'[23]

We know no more until the 1762 Haberdasher deputation, by which time the schoolmaster and his assistant were both shoemakers. Between 50 and 60 boys and girls attended, but very few had lately gone on to the Grammar School. 'And the reason assigned was the Parents preferred binding their Children Apprentices to trades (being chiefly the children of poor Persons).'[24] The school was kept in a 'low inconvenient cottage' in what is now Salters Lane, for which the schoolmaster paid 40 shillings a year. The deputation recommended that the school be held in the Town Hall, as they had already suggested in 1730 and were to again in 1771 and 1782. The town authorities agreed but there were no funds for adapting it. It was a long room and the only end where there was a fireplace was currently 'parted off' and rented by a Writing Master who taught there. So nothing was done.

In 1771 the school was being held in a house that was too small, and in 1782 in an 'inconvenient little house' rented by the Master 'below the bar'. The Master on these occasions was Mr Samuel Scott, grocer, brother of the Revd Mr Scott. He was assisted by Walter Crutchley (yet another shoemaker).

In 1783 the Haberdasher deputation found the boys in the English School had a 'disagreeable tone in their manner of reading'. They recommended the Master and Assistant should use some method to prevent this in future.[25] At every visit the deputation was careful to examine in person the lands left for the school's benefit by William Adams. We shall revisit it in the 19th century.

Six

THE EARLY NINETEENTH CENTURY

The School Buildings

The problem of repairs to the school buildings came to a head in Joseph Scott's time. Small repairs earlier had been financed by the sale of timber from the estate. A new brewhouse was built for Mr Lea in 1727 and a washhouse and brewhouse for the Usher, Mr Dickenson, in 1751. In 1755 considerable repairs (we do not know the details) were recommended by the Visitors as the school and almshouses were 'much decayed'. These were left to Mr Hammersley, the Company's agent, and Mr Lea to carry out.[1]

The London deputations after 1762 dealt with small repairs and problems on the spot, but in 1774 the purchase of a new clock worth £20 was referred back to the Company. The earlier one had fallen from 'the top of the school' in 1771. It was noted that the Town had usually borne the expense of cleaning and winding it. This must mean that it was an important public clock in the town. But by 1852 this clock was not working properly and was said to be 'of little use to the neighbourhood as it is so close to the Church clock which is a most excellent one'.[2]

By 1784 extensive work worth £275 7s. 6d. was recommended by the Company's surveyor, Mr Dugleby. This included putting fireplaces in the schoolroom. He recommended using existing chimneys in the garrets above the Head's and Usher's houses and building two fireplaces, one at each end of the room. 'It may be better to have 2 fireplaces as School is very large, 60 feet 6 inches long, 25 feet 2 inches wide, 19 feet 6 inches high, and must be very cold in winter. One of these fireplaces would serve for the Latin scholars and the other for the Writing scholars.'[3] Traces of one of the chimney breasts can still be seen in Big School library.

He also reported that the chestnut trees in front of the school were old and rotten and a threat to the roofs of the almshouses. Were these the trees that appear in neat rows in the Francis Perry drawing? The Master and Usher were told to see to this and to the planting of 12 other trees further from the almshouses. Looking at the space today, remembering that there were several walls across the area, one wonders where these trees could have been fitted in. The 19th-century drawings of the school show no trees in front of the school itself, only behind the almshouses.

In 1789 Mr Dugleby made an estimate for the Company's presentation to the Court of Chancery. He predicted that in 40 years it would be necessary to take down and rebuild the school, Master's and Usher's houses and

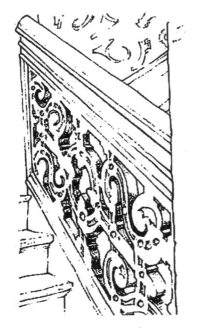

Seventeenth-century strapwork on the staircase in the Headmaster's house.

almshouses. The cost would be in the region of £5,000. Up to that time about £50 a year would be needed for running repairs, which should be increased to £100 when the leases on the Knighton estate could next be renegotiated in 1805. He estimated fairly accurately the amount of money needed but overestimated the length of time the buildings could stand without major help. A lot of work was done in the early 1800s at a cost of just over £1,000 and the thorough rebuilding of 1820-1822 cost well over £3,500.

The rapid price rises at the end of the 18th century, caused mainly by the Revolutionary Wars against France, led to problems. An estimate for repairs submitted in 1798 could not be carried out for the price by the time Chancery had agreed to it three years later. Mr John Cobb took some time to put together his estimate of 24 August 1801 owing to the unsettled state of the price of iron. This estimate is recorded in the Select Committee Report Book and gives us some idea of the buildings at this time.[4] All the windows seemed to need repair. The school and cloisters were to have seven new cast-iron sashes in frames (for casements), whereas the Headmaster's house was to have four pairs of new oak sashes and frames with shutters (presumably at the back), with a further 12 oak pairs for the front of the Masters' houses. There were also new attic windows and the almshouses were to have slide casements. The school was to have a new Gothic nailed door. The roof of the main building (the school and the two houses) was to be stripped and re-tiled, with new lead where necessary. There were to be new lath and plaster ceilings throughout, four new doors in the Head's house and eight in the Usher's. Both houses were to have part of their gable ends taken down and rebuilt. Other basic work was to floors, chimneys, hearths, with repainting throughout. The Head's kitchen was to be paved with Donnington Wood bricks.

The fronts of the school and the almshouses were to be painted in oil and drawn to represent stone. New improvements were to include 20 yards of iron palisades in front of the school with large double gates, and lowering the pavement in the street in front of the building with new posts and chains on its far side. New privies behind the almshouses would cost £20. There was to be a new wall for the Usher's garden, seven feet high.

Richard Whitworth thought the external alterations misguided and sent an impassioned letter to the Haberdashers in January 1803.[5] It is worth printing in full.

I do not write in the name of the Visitors of the School at Newport but in my own name only as a part of them, for our meetings are held but once a year in February. I write as a Neighbouring Gentleman who go to Newport most days in the week and as the School is now repairing to the order of which as far as relates to the repairs of the Schoolhouse and Masters' Houses I may have given my hand but as to any Improvement Tastes or Convenience Out of Doors I have no hand. I must observe that every Inconvenience of old time and late complained of as to the Court before the Schoolhouse being shut up with large High old Walls ten or twelve feet high inclosing little courts of about 20ft square in particular the two Courts before the Masters' Houses as well as the Small Gardens much of the same size with large Old Walls 12ft high or 15, thus immured like or worse than a Prison to the prejudice of the health of the boys. The Walls of no possible Use upon earth but to harbour Damps and putrid matter. There are also nearly the same Kind of old Walls but not so high on each side the length of the Court as you go up to the School, the Contents are Filth and Nastiness dead Dogs Cats and old green Mossed Brick Ends that perhaps may have lain there ever since the Founder's time. The Old Court before the School is above 100 yards long to go to the School and you are going to Flag it all the Way up with two steps out of the Street when a Handsome Gravel walk would have been done for One Tenth part of the Expence and infinite better to all purposes; it may happen that in some future Age the School may flourish and Gentlemen and Ladies come in their Carriage to bring their children to School, if it is flagged and the steps there, they must get out in the Middle of the street and walk in Wet weather to get to the School, besides the Masters, flagged in the Court Yard, have no way up to their houses either for Carriage or Horse or to get to their stable; I remember an Old schoolmaster [Mr Lee] who rode out every day until he was 90 years of age, he used always to take his horse through the School; this wou'd not be thought right now a days surely. There was next the street at end of the Courtyard two immense old Brick Pillars they are down now, thank God and you are going to erect them again, for no possible purpose at a useless expense. I think that the Pillars, the steps, Flaggs and Walls; and 12 New Posts which I forgot to mention set 12 feet into the middle of the Street (not the least possible use) but certainly wou'd be deemed a great Public Nuisance, would be better Omitted in the Repairs I am also of opinion that effecting the above wou'd be a most wanton Expenditure of public money, through a want of common Taste and Judgement in laying it out. I wou'd advise a Revision of the Articles complained of for the Credit of the School.

I am Sir your obedn. Rd Whitworth.

To Thos. Geo. Knapp Esq. Clerk and Agent to the Master and Four Wardens of the Haberdashers Company Governors of the School at Newport.

We do not know whether the letter was sent, as no evidence of it appears in the Haberdasher records, but a close examination of the drawing of the school in the early 19th century (plate 2) shows no indication that Richard Whitworth's pleas were heeded. There is no evidence of high walls but the lowered walls between the almshouses and the school 'court' are visible. The other 'improvements' have been carried out, that is the flagged pathway (still there today), wrought iron gates with pillars and iron fencing to replace the original high walls and doors to the almshouses and the posts and rails on the far side of the pavement. The façades and the (presumably brick) pillars are painted to resemble stone. The building between the almshouse and the Headmaster's house must be his brewhouse. The writing on the cartouche on the Almshouse gable reads:

> *These Almshouses for the benefit of two single Women were founded by William Adams Esqre. of which the worshipful Company of Haberdashers London are Governors. Built A.D. 1657 Repaired and Beautified 1802*

By early 1803 there were complaints that the rebuilding work was very slow and causing great inconvenience and Mr Scott wrote a very critical letter to the Haberdashers. For his part Mr Cobb said that Mr and Mrs Scott kept asking for work to be done that was not in the estimate and would cause further expense. They 'do all they can to perplex and interrupt his plan.'[6] He added that Mr Scott also objected to the workmen. He had carried out the work so as to give minimum inconvenience to Mr Scott, who had a small family and only three boarders. The main job of redoing the gable end had taken a fortnight. The Haberdashers' Committee asked the Visitors to inspect the work but they declined as they were not qualified. One suspects that they wanted to keep out of it. The Committee decided that Mr Scott was being unreasonable and accepted Mr Cobb's offer of a surveyor to inspect the work and report back to them.

But in January 1804 the surveyor sent by Mr Cobb had 'received such improper treatment from Mr Scott that he would not continue'. The Visitors again would not be drawn in personally but recommended Mr Bromfield of Shrewsbury as fit to do the inspection. He made repeated visits to the school and observed that Mr Cobb should have kept the workmen to their contracts only, because when they did more on request they were unwilling to do more again in case it was not paid. It sounds as if 'request' was not a strong enough word to describe the pressure Mr Scott had put on them. In a letter of May 1805 Mr Bromfield hoped all would now be settled 'as this has been a very troublesome business, as it is more so than anything of the magnitude I have ever met with'.[7] It was not until October that everything was finally paid for, the last problem being new doors for the Master's and Usher's houses. As it stood the two doors did not match, but Mr Scott and Mr Langley did not want them altered, and the two Visitors, Messrs Outlaw and Piggott, agreed. So they were not done, even though some might think this spoiled the appearance of the building. We should very much like to know where these doors were.

Major rebuilding by Mr Cobb transformed the appearance of the school in 1820-22. Few details of the work have been preserved. We only know that his first estimate was for a total of £259 0s. 8½d. on the Usher's house and £70 11s. 5½d. for work on the Master's side. He reported that the whole of the buildings were in a bad state, not having been repainted since 1802. The Company decided that as the money had to be obtained through Chancery Mr Cobb should do a thorough estimate of all that was needed. The result was two estimates, one for £3,564 12s. 5d. and the other for £2,464 10s. 9d. The former, larger one, was recommended by the Visitors. This was agreed and sent to the Court of Chancery for approval and the provision of the money from the £11,937 which was currently in the Accountant-General's account for the Charity.[8]

Unfortunately, no written record exists of the rebuilding of the school which followed but an examination of the sketch of the school which was done soon afterwards (plate 3), and indeed of the school as it appears today, can give us some idea of what was done. The main change was the raising of the walls so that the second-floor windows are no longer dormer windows but an integral part of the façade. How many people nowadays, walking up the front path, realise that some of the windows on both sides are blanks, inserted for symmetry? One of the authors as a new Headmaster's wife in 1973, having measured up for curtains, had a shock when she saw two extra windows – only to realise on closer inspection that they were dummies! The roof was rebuilt at a much shallower angle, but the cupola and the clock remain the same. The two houses are unashamedly made of brick with stone finishing off the edges, and the central portion, the school itself, now has flat pilasters reaching through two floors surmounted by a stone balustrade. The open arcade on the ground floor with rounded arches is echoed in the three round-headed windows of the library. All that is now faced in stone. The sketch (plate 3) does not manage to show the pilasters extending the full length of the two floors, but what it does show, interestingly, is that there are no doors at the front. As the sketch book in which this was drawn contains meticulous drawings of churches it is unlikely to be a mistake. No other drawing shows where the front doors might be because of the walls and the almshouses in front, but it seems unlikely that in 1805 there was concern about spoiling the appearance of the building by having two doors that did not match if they were not visible from the front. No later record of adding new front doors has yet been found. Inside we know that the Usher's staircase was rebuilt, the way up to Big School, but nothing else is certain. Presumably the elegant frieze incorporating sphinxes in the Headmaster's drawing room dates from this time. The wording on the almshouses, now showing the brick of which they were made, was similar to before, but 'Repaired and Beautified 1821'.

Early 19th-century frieze in the Headmaster's drawing room.

What was it like to live and work in these buildings? We have a few references that throw some light on this. The Master and Usher shared the water pump at the back of the Master's house. The Usher had to limit the times he used it so as not to disturb the Master and his family. This continued until at least 1843 when the Governors reluctantly agreed that the Charity should pay up to £12 for laying pipes to supply water to the Masters' houses. The Masters were to pay the annual expense of the water supply themselves. In 1848 Mr Cobb was authorised to install a water closet in the Headmaster's house.[9] We have no idea when the brewhouses ceased to exist, but the Charity paid for repairs to Mr Meredith's cowshed and the construction of two new pigsties in 1823. It may surprise us, in the 21st century, that the Headmaster should keep cows and pigs (and brew his own beer), but it is a useful reminder that everyone had to be much more self-sufficient in the days before reliable food shops, let alone supermarkets. By 1860 the deputation found that the Headmaster's pigs were causing 'much inconvenience' (presumably smelly as well as noisy) so they suggested that it would be a good idea if the Company 'intimated to the Headmaster [Dr Saxton by this time] that pigs should not be kept.'[10] They were obviously trying to be very tactful about this.

Conditions in the two houses cannot have been healthy, or even hygienic. In 1831 the Company hesitated to put in a sewer which was needed to avoid cholera, in case Chancery would disallow it. In March and April 1837 the *Shrewsbury Chronicle* noted the deaths of Mr Meredith's only son, aged ten, and an infant daughter. In 1854 Dr Saxton reported that two daughters of Mr Sandford had died of consumption, and one of his boarders had just left with the same disease. His own wife had been diagnosed with consumption three months previously and was unlikely to recover. He blamed the dampness of the house. He and his wife had to have fires constantly in their bedrooms, his son had had to be moved out of his room because it was so wet, and certain rooms had to have their windows permanently open, otherwise the paper peeled off the walls. He asked for a stove to be installed so that its pipe would run through the stairwell from the ground floor up through the roof. Mr Cobb was asked to investigate and drain the pigsties properly. We know no more. As for the school itself: the schoolroom had become stuffy and smelly when numbers rose, and openings in the windows had to be made to improve ventilation. In 1842 the deputation reported that the new system was working well.[11] The boys' outside privies must have been smelly too; in 1868 they were in a 'disgusting state'. In 1860 it was noted that the stove in the centre of the schoolroom had been removed to the side, which minimised annoyance from the smoke. When this had been put in to replace the two fireplaces we do not know. Gas lighting was put in during the summer holidays of 1862.

The John Langley Scandal

John Langley had been officiating minister of Newport Parish Church for ten years before he was appointed Usher in 1801. His name is not on the list of incumbents in the church because the Revd Dr Charles Buckeridge was Rector at the time, although resident in Lichfield because he was also Deputy Registrar of the Diocese of Lichfield. John Langley was in effect curate-in-charge.

John Langley's controversial character can be inferred from his surviving letters to Richard Whitworth in 1805 asking for support over a 'breach' between him and Mr Scott about the Usher's rights.[12] He had consulted the previous Usher, Mr Hughes, about his rights and privileges, complaining that he had not received the amount of coal due to him from the Knighton tenants. He queried the limits to his use of the water pump and claimed the right to half the field, half the stable and hay on his side. He complained that he had no key to the gate at the bottom of the schoolyard so had 'no road to carry manure etc to his garden'. Mr Hughes' reply had not been reassuring: he had never had the use of a stall in Mr Scott's stable. 'As to the Yard Mr Adams designed and appropriated it as a play ground for the use of the Boys. If I was a Visitor I should consider it very improper to turn horses at all into it.' John Langley passed all this on to Richard Whitworth and nevertheless asserted that Mr Hughes had 'occupied part of the schoolyard for potato ground and was used to put his horse into the Field'.

Langley felt it necessary to tell Richard Whitworth that he had been 'most cruelly persecuted for 13 years, but from motives of delicacy and a fear of appearing troublesome' had not appealed to anyone. He refers to 'two persons in this town who I believe make it their constant Business to asperse the characters of those who profess rather more feeling than themselves'. He also said he had become an object of envy because he had lately sold an advowson (the right to appoint a clergyman to a living) that he had purchased four years previously and great pains had been taken to ruin his character 'to our worthy Bishop but so far without success'. It is somewhat surprising that an ordinary curate could buy and sell an advowson and treat it as a piece of property.

Despite these indications that he may have been a troublesome figure, in 1814 the Visitors gave him their full support. They awarded an Exhibition to his son, William, and asked the Haberdashers whether extra money could

> # NEWPORT, SALOP.
> ## THE Office Head Master of Mr. WILLIAM ADAMS's Free Grammar School at Newport will become Vacant at Midsummer. next—The particulars of the duties and emoluments of the appointment, may be known by applying at the CLERK'S OFFICE, Haberdashers' Hall, Maiden Lane, London. All Candidates must have taken the degree of Master of Arts at one of the Universities.
> ### Haberdashers' Hall, 30th Jan. 1818.

Advertisement for a new Headmaster in the Shrewsbury Chronicle, *1818.*

be added to it from the other Exhibitions which were currently not in use. They said he was particularly worthy 'being the son of a laborious and unbeneficed Clergyman of the Church of England who without great assistance is utterly unable to defray the usual expenses of a College Education'. The Company refused this. The Rector, Dr Buckeridge, who was one of the School Visitors, also always supported Langley. Twice, in 1797 and 1808, when increased income made it possible to increase allowances paid by William Adams' Charity, Dr Buckeridge insisted that the minister should be allocated more than the Haberdashers and Visitors had intended, so that the minister's grant rose to £40 and then £60 a year. In 1808 Dr Buckeridge pointed out that Langley had been assiduous in instructing 40 or 50 poor children and youths in the catechism, in accordance with William Adams' instructions, which was more than his predecessors had done.

It seems, therefore, that when Joseph Scott gave notice of retirement in December 1817 the London Governors were not aware of any personal criticism of John Langley. As we have seen (p.71) the Visitors stressed that 'an Able and learned Master' was essential to restore the fortunes of the school but despite advertising widely there were only three serious applicants – the Revd Edward Meredith of Christ Church, Oxford, the Revd Matthew Davies of Brasenose College, Oxford and the Revd John Langley.

The first intimation that there might be problems had come in a letter to the Haberdashers from their agent Richard Hallen in September 1817, saying Mr Scott wished to resign and Mr Langley intended to offer himself for the post but was not considered suitable by the town of Newport. Just how unsuitable they considered him to be was made very clear to the Governors over the course of the next few months. In January 1818, after Mr Scott had given notice but before the post had been advertised, 14 inhabitants of Newport wrote to the Haberdashers asserting that 'the present

Usher of the school and his Domestic Establishment' was not suitable for the situation of Headmaster. They recommended the Revd Matthew Davies. The Company sent copies of this letter to the Visitors and Langley for comment.[13]

The Visitors' reply was, 'Although we have abstained from any personal Allusion we do not hesitate to express our opinion that Mr Langley the present Usher is not calculated as Head Master to advance the Interests or to uphold the Dignity of the School.' But they would give no opinion on Mr Davies, leaving it to the Governors, who they were pleased to see had advertised the post. They obviously hoped at this point that there would be many suitable applicants.

In his reply John Langley produced testimonials from many eminent people, including the Bishop of Lichfield and Coventry, the Revd Dr Buckeridge, the Master of the Free Grammar School in Wolverhampton and ten other clergy, many of whom had known him nearly all his life. In addition 148 inhabitants of Newport vouched for his suitability to be Head-master. He was 'totally at a loss to account for the ungrateful and cruel conduct of some of his Parishioners … As for his Domestic Establishment', he explained, 'the temporary absence of part of his family was because of illness, necessitating recourse to Leamington Waters.'

This satisfied the Haberdashers. They summoned the three applicants to meet them at the Court of Assistants on 4 May 1818. The Master of the Haberdashers and the four Wardens with 32 members of the Court of Assist-ants were present. Before they interviewed the applicants they were presented with four more letters against John Langley. The two churchwardens accused him of misappropriating funds while 17 leading inhabitants of Newport wrote reiterating complaints about his domestic situation: 'During his long resi-dency here he and his wife have lived together and separately on so bad terms and in a way so obnoxious to the Inhabitants that common intercourse among other families has long ceased … . Their disputes have been of so riotous and public a nature both by day and night as to have called for frequent interference of neighbours.' They went on to say that Mrs Langley had had to call magistrates for protection against Mr Langley and he and his wife had lived apart for several months. He had ample money resources but had used them so wastefully as well as using charity money in his care, that creditors had had to resort to an attorney to get their money. All he had was now under assignment for his creditors. 'These circumstances and others too delicate and improper to mention in writing render him in our opinion an unfit person to be placed at the head of a seminary for whose character the Pupils can feel little reverence or respect.' A third letter signed by 14 leading Newport citizens, which included many who had signed the other letter, stated that Mr Langley had gained their signatures to a certificate saying he was fit to be a Headmaster by a trick. What they had signed was to support him against a criticism of his actions as curate, which they did not consider serious enough to deprive him of that post. It was never intended to support his application to be Headmaster. The fourth letter was from one Mr Thomas Parsons to an individual member of the Haberdashers' Company objecting to Langley's appointment and recommending Mr Davies.

All three applicants were now interviewed and John Langley refuted all the allegations against him. A motion to postpone the appointment was made, but defeated, and the Governors duly appointed John Langley as Headmaster from Midsummer 1818. A later insertion in the minutes gives the voting figures: 'J Langley 25, E Meredith 10, M Davies 1'. At the next meeting Edward Meredith was appointed Usher. The Visitors confirmed that appointment in December, according to the statutes, but they categorically refused to accept John Langley as Head.

This appointment of John Langley was indeed a difficult one for the Governors to make. The four lay Visitors who were against Langley were gentlemen of considerable standing: Lord Bradford of Weston, John Cotes of Woodcote, Ralph Leeke of Longford (who was High Steward of Newport), and Sir John Fenton Boughey of Aqualate. They were backed by the clerical Visitors: the Reverends Robert Outlaw of Longford (also a Burgess of Newport), Thomas Lloyd of Albrighton (a Haberdasher appointment), J. D. Piggott of Edgmond, a member of a leading local family, J. S. Bright of Forton and William Otter of Chetwynd. But relationships between the Governors and Visitors had been strained ever since the lawsuit in Chancery of the 1790s and, although Richard Whitworth had died in 1813, John Cotes was still an active Visitor. Also Dr Buckeridge, a clerical Visitor who should have known John Langley well as his curate, consistently supported him. The Visitors had not previously made any unfavourable comments on Langley, and they had not backed up their disapproval with specific charges. They probably thought their simple stated opinion was weighty enough to sway the decision. Many leading citizens of Newport had signed letters against him but on the other hand 148 respectable inhabitants had expressed their support for him.

A letter written by John Langley on 16 August 1817 might have influenced the Company against him – if they could have seen it – but it lay undiscovered for 173 years! It was found, when major repairs were being made in 1980, under the floorboards of a cupboard in a bedroom in the Headmaster's house (plate 19). Quite why it should have been in that house when Langley at the time was still Usher is not clear. It is addressed to 'Rich'd Hallen Esq', the Company's agent responsible for paying the salaries, and is asking for money. Mice have eaten away much of the paper, but what can still be deciphered backs up the complaints of the townspeople.

> ... you for an advance of ... (for there is more due yet it is not payable) This is to discharge a Bill for Flour and to pay the wages of a Servant who lately lived with Me. For the former I am threatened with an Action and on this account trust your [good]ness will excuse [me] [for] [tro]ub [ling] you...which has occasioned this deficiency in pecuniary supply. In the hope I shall obtain pardon for the liberty I have taken I remain, Dr Sir, your obliged & faithful servant, John Langley'.

Small wonder that Richard Hallen had advised the Haberdashers in September that John Langley was not suitable to be Head!

Further information on John Langley's spendthrift ways has recently come to light in a ledger belonging to William Liddle, landlord of the *Union Inn* (later renamed the *Royal Victoria*), general dealer and churchwarden.[14] In 1811 he supplied Langley with wine, brandy, port and sherry costing a total of £23 14s. 2d. By 1819 it was £46 17s. 0d. And he was borrowing small amounts of cash. Langley's total income was £135 (£75 as usher and £60 as minister of Newport). Although Langley paid £10 10s. towards this in 1812, by 1818 the debt was again over £23. As late as 1824 and 1828, long after he left the school, his debts were still being paid off.

The Visitors sent a very stiff letter to the Haberdasher Governors in July 1818 expressing their dismay at the appointment of Langley. 'Presuming upon the unfeigned respect which the Governors profess to entertain for all the Visitors ...' they expected an unobjectionable person to be appointed ' ... But truly astonished and concerned we all are to find that no attention has been paid by the Governors to ... the Visitors and to the memorial of a considerable number of principal inhabitants of Newport ... .'

Whatever their worries, the Visitors were obliged to accept the appointment of John Langley, but in the course of normal communications about the running of the school they frequently reminded the Governors that they would not grant the necessary certificate of approval when his six months' probation was up. Langley sent a circular letter at that point to all Visitors, listing his faithful services as Usher for 17 years and minister of Newport for 26 years. More letters on his behalf were sent to the Governors from Dr Buckeridge and many inhabitants of Newport, including, oddly, William Liddle (churchwarden) and two senior boys at the school. But the Visitors would not be moved and when the Governors sought legal advice they were assured that, according to William Adams' statutes, the Visitors were within their rights to refuse a certificate. Accordingly the Court of Assistants on 28 January 1819 resolved that the post of Headmaster was vacant, authorised advertisements in the newspapers as before, and asked Langley to continue with his duties until another Head was appointed. This last horrified the Visitors – they would not recognise Langley 'in any shape as attached to the Establishment'. Meanwhile Langley employed a Wolverhampton solicitor to prepare a petition to Chancery against his rejection, querying whether this could be done without specific reasons. The Company postponed the appointment of a new Head until the result of this action was known.

Things dragged on until at a meeting in June the Haberdashers received three affidavits in answer to Langley's petition. Two were in favour of Langley, one by Mr Richard Till, a member of the Court of Assistants, and one from five others. But the decisive affidavit was signed by all nine Visitors (Dr Buckeridge excepted) and various others, such as magistrates and the Constable of Newport.

The following facts were proved:

Most violent indecent private and public quarrels between Mr Langley and his wife from 1810 to the end of 1817, so violent as to render the frequent interference of the Constables and Magistrates absolutely necessary.

Absolute proof by a Surgeon of Venereal Complaints in 1810 and 1817.

Obscene and Indecent Conduct and the Use of improper and blasphemous Expressions by Mr Langley.

A loss of respect and Obedience of the Scholars and a Consequent want of Subordination in the School so far as related to Mr Langley as Usher.[15]

As a result the Haberdashers asked the Lord Chancellor for permission to proceed with a new appointment. Langley announced he would appeal but, when his own solicitor refused to sign his appeal, the Company was at last free to act.

On 6 October 1819 they wrote to Langley to instruct him to cease being Master, not to enter the school again and to quit the Headmaster's house. In November they appointed the Revd Edward Meredith as the new Head, he and the Revd William Sandford being the only applicants. Sandford was appointed Usher but not until July 1820 so Meredith had to carry on alone until then. There were about 35 boys in the school. There were no other applicants for the post of Usher.

Smarting because they had been persuaded to support so unsuitable a candidate for the Headship, the Court of Assistants passed four resolutions criticising the Visitors. Luckily the Company's Clerk realised these could widen the breach between Governors and Visitors, so wisely did not send them.

One would think that this was the end of the matter, but John Langley refused to accept defeat. He would not vacate the Headmaster's house and continued to go into the school. Anguished letters from Edward Meredith to the Clerk of the Haberdashers revealed the extent of the problem. Langley would go into the school in the morning before Meredith arrived from his lodging elsewhere, say Prayers at 7a.m. and refuse to hand over the School Prayer Book. He told the boys to ignore Meredith and say their lessons to him alone. He said Prayers again at 4p.m. Meredith reported that the boys obeyed and responded to him alone, but it must have been a tricky situation for them. At one point Meredith hit on the stratagem of getting the Senior Boy to sit on the Headmaster's chair until he arrived, to stop Langley doing so. At another he locked the public door of the school and let the boys in through the Usher's house. Langley had to resort to threatening language as he was barred from entry – it seems there was no way through from the Headmaster's house. Meredith was always careful to keep his temper and behave in a manner befitting a clergyman. The Haberdashers praised him for this, and agreed that he and the Visitors must not be seen to be in the wrong, or give any excuse for riotous behaviour to Langley and his supporters. They passed on their legal Counsel's opinion that it would be better to wait for a legal Notice of Ejection rather than to try to take over the house from Langley if he were temporarily absent. The matter was made even more complicated because Langley insisted in signing as Headmaster as well as minister in appointing new almspeople and apprentices while Meredith was away during the Christmas holiday. Eventually a Notice of Ejection was obtained by the Company at the Shrewsbury Assizes in March 1820. No more is heard of John Langley. We do not know what future he had or where he went. He could only have been in his mid-fifties. The Revd Colin Campbell took his place as curate-in-charge.

Seven

THE NINETEENTH CENTURY
TO THE 1860s

Edward Meredith
Headmaster 1819-1846

In this chapter we follow the fortunes of the school under two Headmasters, the Revd Edward Meredith, 1819 to 1846, and the Revd Doctor Charles Waring Saxton, 1846 to 1870.

When Edward Meredith finally took control the school's prestige increased. Numbers rose, briefly reaching 85 in 1824, but for the next thirty years they were between fifty and seventy. Meredith took boarders but his successor, Saxton, would not, so by 1860 numbers were again down in the thirties. The Governors asked questions, and so did the townspeople, their opinion being that boarders raised the tone of the school.

The school was in effect two schools, Upper and Lower, until a Middle School was added with the appointment of a full-time Writing Master in 1834. Although they were in the one schoolroom they operated separately, each composed of several classes. The Headmaster taught the Upper School and was supposed to keep a watching brief on the others. In practice he rarely did so and it was left mainly to the clerical Visitors to decide by oral examination which boys should be promoted from one school to the next.

What type of boy attended the school?

As the school was free to those living in Newport and Chetwynd End, within five miles in Staffordshire, and in effect to anyone living in Shropshire because the maximum of 80 foundation boys was never reached, boys from many places and backgrounds came to the school. As well as Newport and Chetwynd End, they came from Church Aston, Edgmond, Lilleshall, and a wide circle of other settlements such as Pave Lane, Brockton, Woodcote, Cheswell, Heath Hill, Hatton, Caynton and Pickstock. They also came from villages further afield: Meeson, Bolas, High Ercall, Donnington Wood, Preston, Snedshill and Wellington. Staffordshire boys came from Forton, High Offley, Sutton, Knightley and Gnosall.

A register kept from 1834 to 1879 shows an interesting mixture of parental occupations.[1] They included shoemaker, sawyer, lawyer's clerk, nurseryman, upholsterer, book-keeper, labourer, innkeeper, chemist, collier, servant, joiner, coal carrier, wood ranger, gardener, surgeon, china painter, groom, maltster, clergyman, gentleman, decayed gentleman, pig dealer, tailor, bricklayer, butcher, attorney, schoolmaster, excise officer, dissenting minister, farmer – the list seems endless. A number stayed with relatives or friends in Newport to take advantage of the free education.

Boys came at all ages, some as young as six and others as old as 16, but most started when they were nine to 12 years old. The only test they had to pass was to show they could read English; the Headmaster's selection was confirmed by the Visitors at their next meeting. If they refused to ratify this, the boy had to leave. Most stayed for only two or three years and never got beyond the Lower School. This was partly due to Mr Sandford's poor teaching but also because many parents thought the classical curriculum in the Middle and Upper Schools was irrelevant. The result was that the Lower School was always the largest: in 1847 it had 44 pupils, while the Middle School had 21 and the Upper School had three. The Headmaster had an easy time!

Of those who reached the Upper School a small number went to university, usually Christ Church, Oxford, helped by Careswell Exhibitions and Adams' Exhibitions. Among those who went to Oxford were sons of gentlemen, clergymen, a surgeon and a schoolmaster, but also sons of a Lilleshall publican, a Madeley grocer and a Newport excise officer.

What did boys do when they left school?
Out of some 400 boys who left the school between 1828 and 1850, 100 left without telling the Headmaster, 36 left when their parents left the district and 68 went to English schools. A quarter of these went to Mr Lees at the Free English School but 31 other local schools are named, some private, such as Mr Pickins', Mr Sillitoe's and Mr Collins' at Pave Lane, but many of them National Schools in surrounding villages such as Aston, Chetwynd, Sheriffhales and Gnosall. There was clearly a demand for a curriculum more suited to their way of life than that at the grammar school. The largest number of leavers, 116, became apprentices to various trades, 44 of them with their fathers. Only eight went into farming, mostly with their fathers and three were apprenticed to surgeons. 17 went into service and 17 to clerical work. 19 boys were expelled (mostly 'for irregularity'), seven left through ill-health and six died. Ten went to university in this period.

A few entries illustrate the diversity of the pupils and their later life. In 1829 William Scott Underhill, 12-year-old son of William, ironmonger and clockmaker, went on to an English school. He became one of Newport's most successful businessmen, founding an agricultural and bicycle manufactory at St Mary's Works in 1869 (the site of which became Serck Audco, the biggest employer in Newport for much of the 20th century). Nearly twenty years later Sam Tipping, ten-year-old son of a gunmaker, went as a clerk to Underhill's. He later became manager of a coffee plantation in India. Others were not such high-fliers. Sam Lowe, son of a draper, was sent to jail in 1847 for robbing his grandfather of £7 10s. and clothes. Jas Davies, a blacksmith's son, who left in 1850 aged 12 after four years at school 'cleans knives at Mr Sandford's'. Josh Hudson, a stonemason's son, left aged 12 and 'minds cows for Mr Lindop' (a surgeon whose sons were also at the school). Another boy left after two years, aged about 11, because his mother, a widow, 'could not make him come to school'.

The School Curriculum

It is not until the 19th century that we have any accurate idea of what was actually being taught at William Adams' Grammar School. In the 18th century the Haberdasher Governors had been chiefly concerned with finance and the Knighton estates, but they now began to take an active interest in education. Not only were they influenced by local pressure and a change in society's attitude to education, but also by Parliamentary investigations into the management of charities nationwide. Charity Commissioners visited Newport in 1820 and published their report on Shropshire in 1829. There were several government attempts to improve the management of charities between 1835 and 1860 which the Haberdashers and other London Companies opposed. They saw these reforms as an attack on their independence. But as a result the Haberdashers' Company became more active in running its schools, sending regular deputations from London.

Changes came slowly, partly because they had to be ratified by Chancery, which could often take several years, and partly because of the innate conservatism of Governors, Visitors and schoolmasters in Newport, and their inability to agree among themselves. Sometimes the townspeople urged reform, but they were rarely heeded. The Taunton Commission of 1864 enquiring into endowed schools gave a much-needed impetus to a school that was gradually changing. We deal with this in the next chapter.

The earliest information we have on the school curriculum is in Joseph Scott's report to the Governors in 1816.[2] There were 25 boys in four classes in the Lower School. The youngest, in the fourth and third classes, were doing Latin Grammar (sometimes called Accidence), learning parrot-fashion the declension of nouns and the conjugation of verbs, without any examples of how they were used in sentences. The second and first classes had progressed to constructing sentences and reading selected passages in Latin. They used *Selectae Sententiae* ('a selection of sayings'), *Selectae e Prophanis* (profane, i.e. non-biblical authors) as well as *Bailey's Latin and English Exercises*, already in its third edition by 1706.

In the Upper School under the Headmaster's direction five boys in the fourth class were using the same text books as the Lower School but were also reading a classical Latin author for the first time, Ovid's *Metamorphoses* – a collection of tales from classical myth and legend, each of which describes a change of shape. The only boy in the third class had Caesar's *Commentaries* and Ovid, and also used Ellis' *Exercises*, a collection already in its second edition in 1782. The two boys in the second class were reading Homer in Greek and more Latin authors, Virgil and Terence in addition to Caesar. They also used Willimot's *Particles*, a collection originally published at Eton in 1703. The one boy in the first class was reading Homer, Horace and Terence. The three boys in the top classes were intended to go to university.

It is interesting that this report to the Company makes no mention of the part-time Writing Master.

Whatever its use for those intending to go to university, this syllabus was hardly relevant to the tradesmen and lower classes of Newport and in 1827 a Company deputation heard from 'many of the respectable Inhabitants of Newport ... that this noble Establishment of Mr Adams produced scarcely any benefit to Newport and its Neighbourhood, that many of the inhabitants send their Children to distant Schools because they could not get them adequately Educated there without paying for such instruction as they wished for their Children.' A thorough investigation into the workings of the school followed and some changes were made.[3] Mr Meredith and the Usher, Mr Sandford, were well-respected members of the community, but nevertheless there was implicit criticism of the Usher's teaching.

The 1827 survey shows some enlargement of the curriculum since 1816. Arithmetic is now mentioned, taught by the Writing Master. All boys were doing vulgar and decimal fractions, but only some paying boys were on algebra and Euclid. The Head taught geography to all boys in the Upper School, on Thursdays after breakfast. (This was not in the statutes!) He supplied his own globes, as the school had none, but each boy had a set of maps. Presumably each boy had to buy his own, probably from Silvester's the Newport booksellers and stationers. £10 a year was set aside to provide books for the foundation scholars and the accounts show money paid out to Silvester, so one hopes the poorer boys had their maps paid for. The Visitors recommended that a pair of globes, terrestrial and celestial, and two sets of maps, one ancient and one modern, be bought for the school and kept in the library. The Headmaster was also teaching mathematics in his own time to those boys who would benefit, either because they were going on to university or to work in an attorney's office. He had tried teaching foundation and boarding boys together in his house in the evening, but because of 'undesirable habits of some poorer boys' he now separated the two groups, the foundation boys being taught during the day. He also taught some background to the classical authors, including chronology (dates of Greek and Roman history) and Roman antiquities.[4]

The Writing Master taught for three hours every morning, but this was considered to interfere too much with 'general learning' so his hours were cut to 10a.m. to 11a.m. and 4p.m. to 5p.m. every day.

A major change in the curriculum did not come until 1834, when, after several years of discussion, the Haberdasher Governors increased the role of the Writing Master to a full-time post. The Visitors were not very keen but this move had the strong support of the townspeople and Edward Meredith who considered that proper English teaching was good preparation for the classics. Advanced mathematics tuition was also introduced. Samuel Cobb, part-time Writing Master since 1795, accepted the full-time

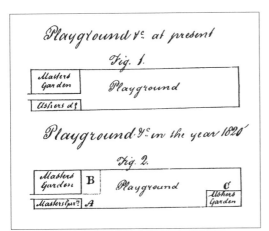

Fig 1 Playground in 1827.
Fig 2 Playground in 1820.
Joseph Scott had added section A to his garden. Edward Meredith gave it to the Usher in exchange for C. He then opened C to the playground, enclosing B instead, but some Visitors objected, so he also gave up B.

post at a salary of £100. On his death in 1837 his son-in-law Richard Crowther took over and taught, very effectively, for over forty years until his retirement in 1882.

Aspects of the School in 1827

The 1827 enquiry covered many other aspects of school life, not just the curriculum. The school day still started with Prayers and a Bible reading, and ended with Prayers as in the statutes, but no Psalms were sung. Tuesday and Saturday were half-days, and the year was split into two, with six weeks' holiday each at Christmas and Easter. This was customary by now at all the endowed schools in the county, and seems to have been in place by 1819, but it was completely different from the holidays laid down in the statutes. In 1827 the Governors insisted that they should be cut down to four weeks each. Everyone agreed that numerous Saints' Days kept as holidays disrupted work and should be discontinued. Mr Meredith had already stopped the Upper School having them but had not wanted to deprive the Usher of his customary days off. Complaints about some boys paying for extra tuition were dealt with. Mr Meredith was being paid ten guineas a year (at that point only for three boys) for extra tuition to enable them to reach the first class of the Upper School, after which they would be on the foundation and therefore pay nothing. Despite his arguments that William Adams had envisaged this, and set a limit of 50 paying boys, he agreed to take on no more. So from then all day boys had free foundation places. There was no objection to his having fee-paying boarders – 27 at that time, the highest number since the early days of Samuel Lea. William Adams had stipulated that an extra Usher should be employed by the Head at his own expense if the numbers at the school rose above 130 boys. Mr Meredith told the Governors that he had employed one since 1824, when the numbers were far less, which showed his concern for the pupils. This Usher was an old pupil, John Lees, whom Meredith paid £45 a year plus board, washing and lodging. He was commended as an excellent teacher by both the Head and the Visitors. In 1838 he left to become Head of the Free English School.

Entry fees which by now varied between 2s. 6d. and £1, although the original 2s. 6d. in the statutes was still in force, were to be increased to £1. But in 1834 the Governors had still not cleared this with Chancery.

The Head assured the Governors that, contrary to some complaints, the foundation scholars had free use of the playground during and after school. He even sketched two plans to show how he had lost some land after he had handed over part of his garden to the Usher in 1820. He stated that for four years his boarders had 'a convenient field of three acres' for their playground. We have no idea where that could have been. The Governors made no answer to the Visitors' suggestion, which had originally been made two decades earlier, that a Fives Court should be erected on the playground. This was brought up again later but the Governors never authorised it. In 1859 the Usher wrote to the Governors to say that the school 'playground is more deficient in any means of athletic exercises than most other schools of the same or indeed inferior standing'. He suggested 'a Gymnastic pole or leaping bar or something of this nature' which would 'tend both to the moral and physical improvement of the boys'. The Governors granted £10 towards this.[5] It was in place by 1865.

The Visitors were from now on to be more actively involved in the school. They were to have meetings once a quarter in the library, with a Secretary to keep the minutes and a permanent Chairman chosen by their number. It is probably at this time that the oak chairs with the Adams' coat of arms on the back were introduced (plate 80). In 1842 four new chairs were added 'for the Visitors'.[6] Mr Meredith volunteered to act as minute secretary until another could be found. The Visitors were to examine the progress of the boys in their studies (a custom which recently had been neglected), and prizes of books bound with the arms of William Adams and the Haberdashers' Company and inscribed 'Honoris Causa' ('as an honour') were to be distributed to encourage hard work. Admissions of new boys was now to take place only at the quarterly meetings of the Visitors.

The Governors were very concerned that the boys should attend church, as required in the statutes. There were too many boys to be easily seated on the three benches reserved for them so some boarders sat in the Headmaster's pew and day boys sat with their parents. Mr Meredith observed that 'a boy is no where more likely to behave well than under a parent's eye'. In 1837, when substantial repairs and alterations were carried out at the parish church under John Cobb's direction, the Visitors were keen to ensure that there would be sufficient seating for the school. Services were held in the Grammar School while the work was being done.

The School in 1846
The Reverend Edward Meredith resigned in 1846 after 27 years as Headmaster and the Governors asked him for a full account of the organisation and timetable of the School in readiness for the appointment of his successor.[7]

The school day was from 7a.m. – 5p.m. with breaks from 8.30a.m. – 9.30a.m. for breakfast and 12p.m. – 2p.m. for dinner. Mr Meredith reported that there had originally been only half an hour for breakfast, 'but I found that between 9 and 12 we were liable to so much interruption from boys asking leave to go down for necessary purposes and it was so difficult, nay so impossible to discover when the occasion was pretended only, that I determined to give another half hour before the bell ringing and then to require each boy so to manage as to be able to remain in school without interruption till 12 o/clock'. Similarly, the dinner break had been extended from one and a half to two hours. Dinner time would have been long enough for most boys to return home, but they must have brought their breakfast with them. We do not know where they ate it. In winter lack of daylight meant school started later, sometimes not until 8a.m., and finished occasionally as early as 4p.m. On Tuesdays and Saturdays school closed at 1p.m., and there was a 15-minute break at about 11a.m. Vacations of about four weeks started on 22 December and 22 June and ended the Monday after four weeks later. Occasional holidays occurred about once a month on a Monday afternoon, but double Latin and Greek exercises were given. The Visitors generally gave a half-holiday at their meetings, except for the boys being examined.

The syllabus was now slightly wider. Scripture history had appeared in the Upper School and English history in the Middle. The Writing Master taught writing and arithmetic to all boys in the Middle and Lower Schools from 11am to 12 noon on all full days and from 11a.m. to 1p.m. on half days. The Upper School was taught writing, arithmetic and algebra on Thursday afternoons by the Head and, sometimes, the Writing Master. The Head gave an evening lecture on Euclid (geometry) from 7p.m. to 9p.m. four nights a week. This was in his private room for foundation boys and boarders with no distinction between them (suggesting the day boys were now better behaved!). The criterion for moving from the Middle to the Upper School remained the ability to read Ovid. Boys were also supposed to have begun Greek grammar, but Mr Meredith said in practice he taught them Greek from the beginning. He said that he no longer required such an advanced ability to read the Bible in English for new entrants as formerly as 'they now have so good an opportunity of improving under my excellent Third Master, Mr Crowther'. The Head's salary was now £200 a year with house rent-free and a small annual sum instead of coals from the tenants of the Knighton estate. The Second Master received £100 with a house and a similar sum. The Third Master had £100 but no extras.

The Governors also decreed that the Head should see that the boys throughout the school should have 'a sound and useful Education in the English language in accordance with the advanced state of Education of the present age'.

Some of the prizes given to boys about this time are fairly wide-ranging: Latin and Greek Grammars are predictable, but there were also Milton's *Poetical Works*, Goldsmith's *Rome*, Goldsmith's *Greece*, Keightley's *England* and Turner's *Arts and Sciences*.

When Edward Meredith retired he took the living of Longdon on Tern. We know he held a living while Head as, in 1827, he refers to taking boys with him to 'the Church which I serve' but we do not know where that was. He was only 25 when he became Head, having been Usher for 18 months previously, and had raised the profile of the school after the slackness of Joseph Scott's last years and the John Langley scandal. The fact that he resigned at 52 and was still on top of his job may account for the glowing tribute the Visitors paid to the 'ability diligence and efficiency with which he has for so long a period filled that office'.[8] Meredith could afford to retire because he had a church living. He became a Visitor, and a very active one, until 1865 when he was made Rector of Ightfield and gave up being a Visitor because Ightfield was too far from Newport. He died in 1873 and his memorial is in Ightfield church. His son George, born in 1841 and a pupil at Newport from 1856-7, had a daughter who under her married name of Mary Webb became famous in the 1920s for her romantic novels about the Shropshire countryside. *Gone to Earth* and *Precious Bane* were the most popular and they remain in print in 2002.

William Sandford
Usher 1820-1854

Both Meredith and Saxton were hampered by the inadequacy of William Sandford as a teacher. He came from a wealthy and influential Shrewsbury family, was educated at Shrewsbury School, and was a priest for ten years before being appointed Usher at Newport in 1820. He took over from Dr Buckeridge as Rector of Newport from 1827 to 1864. He seems to have been an intellectual who was entirely out of touch with the local boys he was required to teach. There was implicit criticism of his teaching in 1827 but in 1834 the Haberdasher delegation in their report to the Company went much further. On examining Mr Sandford's boys they 'felt disappointed and mortified at their extraordinary and grievous inefficiency and with regret they declare their firm conviction ... that Mr Sandford from some natural eccentricity or unfortunate but irremediable unskilfulness is disqualified from pursuing a proper method of instruction.'[9] They noted that boys under his tuition will continue to be 'perpetually defeated'. Progress to the Upper School was so slow that many parents took their boys away before they had a chance to get there. They did not question Mr Sandford's classical and general knowledge, nor his kind intentions and moral conduct, but they felt that with no curate to assist him all his time should be devoted to his parish and it would be of great benefit to the school if he were to resign. They quoted the second statute by which a Master or Usher could be removed from office if he took employment which hindered the performance of his duties. Despite these very definite statements no Visitors spoke out against him and no action was taken, so this unsatisfactory state of affairs continued for another 19 years!

In 1842 the deputation was highly satisfied with Mr Meredith's teaching and very satisfied with that of Mr Crowther, but not with Mr Sandford's. On several occasions it was noted that no boys were suitable for promotion to the Upper School. When there were only three boys in the Upper School in 1847 the Governors asked for an explanation.[10] Dr Saxton replied that it was not his wish to have so few boys. He had suggested promoting some before they reached the usual standard, but Lord Bradford, Chairman of the Visitors, had not allowed this, saying it would degrade the character of the school and be a bad precedent. Dr Saxton had then tried to make a private arrangement with Mr Sandford that he should teach the boys while they were still in the Middle School, but Mr Sandford had refused this. It must have been frustrating for the Head, who went on to suggest what Mr Meredith had been condemned for twenty years earlier, that certain boys might be willing to pay for the privilege of being taught by the Headmaster, until they were of sufficient standard to be taught free on the foundation. He thought such a system would raise the respectability of the school and attract more families to the town. Sandford said the scarcity of boys ready for the Upper School was mainly because of the short time he had them in his school. He said parents could not afford to keep them at school long enough to go into the Middle or Upper Schools. When they were old enough for that they left to go into 'common trade or servile employment'. The majority never even reached the Middle School.

It was not until 1851 that the Governors resorted to positive action about Mr Sandford. He was asked to resign but refused to do so, demanding a personal hearing. This was granted by the Company, but settled nothing. In 1852 the Governors dismissed him and ordered him to leave the Usher's house. He enlisted the help of his brother, Foliot Sandford, a Shrewsbury solicitor, and said he would petition Chancery to be reinstated. In fact he did not do so and there was no repeat of the squalid tussles when John Langley refused to leave. But he still refused to vacate the Usher's house or share it with the new Usher, appointed in October 1852. The new man, the Revd J. S. Benifold, accepted the Governors' requirement for annual re-election and no house until Sandford left, but the Visitors disagreed with both these conditions. Negotiations continued until January 1854 when Sandford indicated that he would vacate the house in return for an annual pension of £50. This was finally agreed and by Midsummer 1854 Sandford had left the school, the possessor of the first pension to be paid from the William Adams' Charity.

Charles Saxton
Headmaster 1846–1870

Charles Saxton was 40 when he became Head. He was the eldest son of Charles Saxton, gentleman, of Whitchurch, Shropshire. An uncle founded Christchurch College, New Zealand, and Charles had spent some time there. He took his Doctorate of Divinity soon after he came to Newport, and was the author of several classical texts. He started off very well but, as with so many others, his energy waned.

The removal of William Sandford did not settle the school's problems. The syllabus and teaching methods were still not attracting enough pupils even though the new Usher taught several new subjects. In addition to Greek and Latin he also taught 'the elementary branches of sound English education' comprising Scripture instruction and history, grammar, composition, general history, geography and map-drawing, physical science (the first mention of science!), mathematics and arithmetic. He also helped with French.[11] But when Mr Benifold left in 1857 to found his own school in Carmarthen, taking at least one boy with him (probably more),[12] there were only seven boys in the Middle School (11 in the Upper and 14 in the Lower). The Governors asked Dr Saxton to take them over, for an extra £50 a year, instead of appointing another Usher. Dr Saxton refused, suggesting that he should have the whole of the Usher's salary and Mr Crowther should move into the Usher's house, so that he would no longer feel it necessary 'to eke out his income by taking private pupils'. He added that Mr Crowther 'often appears to me fagged' (over tired).[13] The Governors changed their minds after they received a 'memorial' signed by 29 inhabitants of Newport about the appointment of a Second Master, which begged 'respectfully to suggest the propriety of giving the pupils an opportunity of being instructed in the elements of a good sound English Commercial Education, in addition to the instruction provided by Mr Adams which we by no means wish to be lost sight of'.[14] They also thought it absolutely necessary that French and drawing should be taught. The Governors felt that, since reforms the previous year, a good sound English Commercial Education was already being provided. They would now pay the Head and Second Master an extra £10 each a year to teach French, but as adequate instruction in drawing was available in the town on moderate terms they did not need to provide it. In 1863 a separate French master was appointed, but the Charity Commissioners refused to approve this until a complete new scheme was established, so French teaching reverted to the Head and Second Master. When in 1857 the Governors asked why there were so few pupils Saxton did not mention the curriculum, but blamed a private school in Newport that had 22 boys and good National Schools in neighbouring villages which were diverting boys from the Grammar School.

A new departure which showed the Governors' determination to improve standards at the school came with the appointment of a professional examiner. This had first been suggested in 1833 but did not occur until 1861. The examiner visited Newport at Midsummer and Christmas while the local Visitors continued their inspections in March and September. The first examiner was J. R. Seeley, Fellow of Christ's College, Cambridge and Composition Master in the City of London School. He later became widely known for his controversial life of Christ, *Ecce Homo*. His brother, L.B. Seeley, took over in 1862 until 1871. Their recommendations were acted upon by the Headmaster, as successive reports show. The teaching of French, neglected in many schools, was much improved by the second visit and the Head was congratulated on the style and spirit of the boys' Latin Prose Composition. The Middle School's knowledge of Euclid was praised and every report was extremely complimentary about the teaching of Mr Crowther, the Third Master.

In his second report Mr Seeley commented that examining another school of nearly the same character had made him more respectful of Classics at the top and arithmetic at the bottom of Newport School. However he commented on a 'certain despondency among the boys' and a lack of competitive spirit. Eighteen months later L. B. Seeley found 'apathy ... is the most unfavourable symptom in the condition of the School' and recommended that the pupils be made more aware of what prizes they could compete for. It is pleasing to record that in 1864 Mr Seeley noticed 'a decided improvement in the general tone of the pupils.' The examiners always named the boys who were to have prizes.[15] Both examiners pinpointed the main problem at this time: the conflict of aims between a classical and a commercial education, over which there was enormous public interest in the town. J. R. Seeley commented that it was extremely difficult for the Middle School master to teach Latin at the same time to boys who wanted to go on to university and those who wanted to go into commerce, and advised that the Governors should make up their minds which type of education the school should provide. At Monmouth the classical and commercial schools had been separated for seven years and this worked well. (Monmouth at this time was flourishing with numbers limited to 100, and a waiting list.) If this system were to be introduced at Newport it should be done 'entire rather than by stealth'. The School 'should go further or go back'.

But this was a problem the Governors and Visitors were not prepared to solve, still less the Head. Dr Saxton was keen on the classical status of the school but allowed into the Lower School boys who were inadequately prepared for it. This made Mr Crowther's task very difficult and the Visitors frequently had to reject boys already admitted. But at least the School could pride itself on accepting boys free of tuition fees, according to the Founder's instructions, which the Taunton Commissioners found was not true of any other endowed school in Shropshire (see chapter 8). With the Free English School in decline by this time, suitable elementary education for the poor was not provided until the building of the National School in 1872.

In 1860 Dr Saxton's teaching methods were criticised by the Visitors, but he pointed out that he had gained three Careswell Exhibitions in 14 years, whereas the previous Head had obtained only three in 25 years. Others of his boys had gained entry and scholarships to the universities. He claimed that he seldom had to rebuke boys for idleness and used the cane very infrequently.[16] Perhaps his mind was on higher things because, when a later deputation reported that the school privies were in a disgusting state, the boys having cut up one seat and several doors, he said it was impossible to stop boys vandalising them. The Governors became very annoyed when they found he had not told them that the school gallery in church had been taken down when the new organ was installed in the West End in 1861. The boys had been squashed to one side on benches intended for the poor, although the Headmaster's own stall had not been affected.[17] By 1866 the whole neighbourhood was complaining of 'want of energy' in the Headmaster's teaching, which gave the school a bad name.[18] When he became really ill we do not know, but by 1870 he was so paralysed he was unable to do his school duties, which were being carried out by a Mr Rupert St Leger, and he could not even hold a pen.[19] He formally resigned that Christmas, aged 64, with a pension of £95 a year. He lived for another 20 years.

Some memories of Dr Saxton's time can be gleaned from the school magazine, the *Novaportan*. Whatever Dr Saxton had told the Governors, it was common knowledge that he used the cane frequently. Canon Irton Smith (1864-7) recalled his habit of beckoning with his finger at the empty air 'and any boy looking up naturally supposed himself to be the object required. After walking to the table and receiving a cut for his pains, he returned somewhat the wiser for his experience.'[20] Dr H. W. Pooler (1876-82) said Dr Saxton was noted for his swishings, but his successor Tom Collins based his discipline on trust. Canon W. J. Oldfield (1868-75) in 1911 recalled Saxton's frequent doses of the cane, but in 1928 he was 'most anxious to rescue Dr Saxton's name from the credit he got as being a thrashing master. The cane was always going, admittedly, but Dr Saxton had had an operation and used to sit in a specially made wire chair from which he never rose. His hand was so tender that whenever he was going to use the cane he had to have his hand wrapped up. The result was that they only got a cut. There was never a real thrashing. Dr Saxton was very kind-hearted and always entered into the boys' lives.'[21]

The schooldays of Oliver Lodge

We have a record of what life was like at Newport Grammar School in the 1860s from Sir Oliver Lodge, an eminent physicist who was a pupil from 1859 to 1863.

He was born near Stoke-on-Trent, the eldest of eight children of a prosperous businessman who acted as an agent selling clay and other materials to the china and pottery industries. His aunt was married to a young clergyman, John Heawood, who was appointed Second Master at Newport in 1859. It seemed a good opportunity to send Oliver to board with his uncle: he was just eight years old. The following four years were the most miserable of his life. He recalls this in his autobiography *Past Years*, published in 1931. Although 80 years old by then, he appears to have had very good recall of his childhood experiences and feelings. A schoolboy's life at Newport was no doubt similar to that in many other schools at the time.

Oliver Lodge describes how all the boys had to be in place before the school bell stopped ringing, on pain of receiving a blow on the head from the Headmaster's walking stick. The room was extraordinarily dirty and, although two day boys called monitors were paid to clean it, the dust lay thick everywhere. There was a large stove in the middle of the room but, he said, the instructions of the Founder were still observed and it was not lit until 5 November. As a result the boys were often very cold, even though they were allowed to wear overcoats. They often caught colds and Oliver had several periods in the sick room, where he was well looked after. He believed he had more illnesses at Newport than in the rest of his life. Gas lighting was introduced a year or two later but presumably in Oliver's time the original rule of no candles was still in force, so the room must have been very dark on a dull day. Boys in the Upper School would sit on long forms (benches) at the far end of the room with the Headmaster, Dr Saxton; Middle School boys were at the other end, with the boys under the Third Master in the middle, by the steps to the Library. Lodge says that Crowther was a kindly man, who could write beautifully but had no special knowledge or instinct for teaching. (This rather contradicts the opinion of the examiners and Headmasters which we have noted!)

On his first day at school Oliver was given a copy of the Eton Latin Grammar, every word in Latin, and told to learn the first page with no explanation of what it meant. He sat over it all morning and gradually dissolved into tears. We may well ask how it was possible for him to spend several hours unsupervised? Eventually Mr Crowther 'found him', took pity on him and explained what he ought to learn. However it was still gibberish! That Latin Grammar was a nightmare for he had no instinct for languages, had to learn a lot of rules by heart and, according to him, no one explained what they were for. The only text book he found interesting was his geography book, but the part that interested him – the chapter that dealt with the shape of the earth, the phases of the moon, latitude, longitude and the solar system – was the part they were told to skip over. If we are looking for early signs of scientific interest, they can be found here. Geography and history were, however, minor subjects only taught once or twice a week.

After about a year Oliver was promoted to the Middle School under the charge of his uncle, the Revd Heawood. He felt it was an honour to be promoted so young and wanted to make the most of it. However, the discipline not only became harsher but his uncle was determined that he should not receive any special treatment; in fact, he seemed to take a pride in being especially severe. Mr Crowther, whom the boys called Dicky Larrup, carried a short cane in his boot which he plucked out when required 'either smiting a boy with it or throwing it at him and telling him to bring it back again'. His method of caning was also 'jocular'. You held out your hand, the cane came down and missed it but then came up again and hit your knuckles from below. At least Dicky Larrup had some sense of humour and would occasionally tell them things of interest. His uncle's method was different and his full-length cane with a curved handle was a more formidable instrument. 'He brought it down on your hand with some vigour so that a weal across the hand instantly appeared, and the tears started to your eyes.

After one or two blows of this kind the smart was unendurable; your hand curled up and writing was impossible. I don't think he could have known how much it hurt. In after life I once offered to show him, but he declined, and would not hold out his hand.' The older boys showed Oliver how to keep his thumb well out of the way otherwise it might be broken. Sometimes caning was on the head or shoulders or on the back of the legs. He was given a bath by the housemaid every Saturday night (remember he was only nine years old at the time) and the kindly girl cried when she saw the scars. Very few boys escaped the cane, because it was an inherent part of the method of instruction, used to punish mistakes, even minor grammatical ones. It was not only the use of the cane that disheartened Oliver, it was also what he described as 'instruction by crossness', whereby the master was in a perpetual state of annoyance with his pupils. There was no notion of education as a process of inspiring or stimulating a pupil nor helping him to reach his potential. Education was a form of training that could equally be applied to dogs, boys and horses. The end product in many cases was no more than a set of tricks which relied on memory rather than thought.

Although Latin grammar was learnt most thoroughly, Lodge does not recall learning any English grammar. 'I think it must have been despised,' he said. We know it was being taught; maybe he was considered too superior, or even too advanced, to benefit from it.

At the age of ten he was allowed to begin Greek. This clearly pleased him for there was a new alphabet to learn and he enjoyed trying to copy the master's expert calligraphy. At this stage he sometimes came top of the class 'though there were louts of sixteen near the bottom'. Even at his age he realised that the subjects taught were most inappropriate to the majority of the day boys. Every boy had to have a copy of *The Oxford Pocket Classics* but it had no explanatory notes and the master concentrated on the language and grammar without explaining the content. The result was that they read exciting accounts by famous authors of various military campaigns but gained no joy from them. 'We neither knew nor cared where the places were nor what the expeditions were for.'

Despite the canings Oliver Lodge remembered his uncle as '... not altogether an unkindly man. I never really had any real dislike for him, I had indeed a sort of veneration, as for one who knew a terrible lot more than ever I could know.' But 'he was not really learned enough to be the sole educator of youth. He knew his classical grammar thoroughly but of nearly all the rest of life he was ignorant.' However, he did encourage Oliver in his love of geometry and took his boarders on excursions several times a year. Lodge remembers visits to the Wrekin, Cannock Chase and once to Coalbrookdale.

Heawood must have been entirely unaware of the unhappiness Oliver endured at the hands of some of the other boarders. He remembers the three Ashburnham boys as 'very decent fellows', but they slept together in another room. (Their father, Lord Ashburnham, promoted John Heawood to a living at Combs in Suffolk a few years later and Oliver went with him.) There were four boys in Oliver's room. At first an older boy, John Mountfield, saw there was no unfairness, but he moved on and, when a boy arrived from Rossall School, having been expelled, Oliver as the youngest and smallest was at his mercy. Oliver was sent to bed earlier than the others, but was always woken up to put out the candle when they were in bed. On one occasion towards the end of term he refused to do this. The result was a black ear, which lasted through the holidays. This produced 'some remonstrance from my parents', but he does not say whether any action was taken against the bully. Thrashings were frequent amongst the boys: two examples will suffice. One Sunday afternoon Oliver and some others had gone to a service at Chetwynd Church. Some servants were in the same pew and he opened the door of the pew to allow them out first. His punishment by the older boys for this was 50 lashes! Another boy, 'whose guardian had been foolish enough to make him promise never to fight', was tied to an upturned chair and given one hundred lashes with a rope end, the onlookers counting the strokes as they were delivered. 'The result was not so much that blood was drawn, but that his skin went like a rotten apple and before the torment was over he had to be given a glass of water to revive him … . There were other things, of which I do not care to speak, which I am sure would have led to expulsion if they had been discovered.' He made some mention of what was going on to the Ashburnham brothers, after which things were better.

Oliver was a fairly quiet boy and accepted whatever punishment he received. His younger brother, Alfred, was not so docile. Three years after Oliver came to Newport, Alfred was sent to join him. He was keen on algebra and on one occasion, having spent three days working on a problem, he turned to the answers at the back of the book to confirm his solution. The master (presumably his uncle) saw him looking, rushed over and soundly thrashed him. Alfred made such a fuss at the injustice of this that he was taken away from the school and sent to another, less repressive uncle, who was Headmaster of Horncastle School. Alfred in later life became a Professor of Mathematics.

Despite frequent physical assaults by the schoolmaster during the day and his fellow pupils at night, Oliver still managed to look back with affection on some of his time at Newport. He remembered days of skating and sliding, the Fair day in the town, the rejoicings to celebrate the wedding of the Prince of Wales in 1863 and invitations to tea with an aunt of one of his friends. On the occasional holidays he remembered expeditions to the country and 'gambolling like dogs that have been long chained up'. Although he left at the age of 12 when his uncle moved on and Newport can take little credit for his later success, he retained some affection for the place and returned to Newport to present prizes at Speech Day in 1904 and again in 1936 when he was 85. The Oliver Lodge athletics trophy provides an annual reminder of the school's most famous Old Boy.

Eight

THE TAUNTON COMMISSION
AND REVIVAL UNDER TOM COLLINS

The Taunton Commission

The Taunton Commission of 1864 was set up to investigate endowed secondary schools in England and Wales and to suggest ways of improving them.

This was the first time the government had concerned itself with secondary education. In 1861 the Newcastle Commission had reported on elementary education in the country, finding the distribution of schools was extremely uneven. This had led to the Forster Education Act of 1870, which set up schools in areas where none existed. They were available to all, though not necessarily free, and Christian though strictly non-denominational. They were run by locally elected boards (hence 'Board' schools), and took their place alongside the already existing National and British schools.

The nine leading public (i.e. independent) schools, which included Shrewsbury School, had been the subject of a report in 1864 by the Clarendon Commission. There was little this Commission needed to recommend as these schools had already been influenced by the reforms introduced in the first half of the 19th century by such Headmasters as Samuel Butler of Shrewsbury and Thomas Arnold of Rugby.

The report of the Taunton Commission completed the picture of education in the country, its 20 volumes being published between 1867 and 1870. However, endowed schools were reluctant to change their ways, and it was not until the turn of the century, when the new County Councils became responsible for secondary education, that the 1902 Educational Act did for secondary education what the Forster Act had done for elementary.

In 1865 and 1866 Assistant Commissioner James Bryce visited Shropshire and reported on its 12 endowed schools.[1] Almost the first thing he noted when he visited Newport was the large annual income from the Knighton estates (over £1,700) and the small amount of it that was spent on teachers (£420) and educational purposes (£500). Most of the rest went on management expenses. However his impression from consulting the townspeople was that the Haberdashers' Company managed the school 'with as much diligence ... as can be expected from a body quite unconnected with the place. They occasionally visit it and have usually shown themselves anxious to promote its welfare.' But the double system of government, with 10 local Visitors overseeing the school itself and reporting back to the Governors when necessary, had not worked very well. He commented that the Visitors had limited powers and, possibly as a result, had not been very active, while the Haberdashers, though well intentioned, 'have been too far away and known too little of the place to exercise an efficient control'.

Bryce described Newport Grammar School's buildings as spacious, with an excellent residence for the Headmaster, but the playground was small and a cricket ground much needed. The boys were taught in a single room which was not large enough for their number. He was critical of the curriculum and the way the school was organised, a view shared by the townspeople. His main criticism was that the school was operated as three separate schools, managed entirely without reference to one another. Because promotion from one school to another depended on proficiency in Latin there were boys in all three schools at the same stage in other subjects who were being taught separately. 'Such a waste of teaching power is as needless as it is intolerable; and no one who sees the school can doubt that the three departments ought to be fused in one, and the boys reclassified for arithmetic according to their proficiency in it.' He was clearly surprised that the Headmaster refused to take boarders.

Other complaints made to him were that the instruction was too classical, not sufficiently commercial and not as vigorous as it should be.

The overall impression gained from the report is that, whatever the curriculum and the financial resources of the endowment, it was still the character and energy of the Headmaster that made a successful school. A good Headmaster could attract boarders, thereby improving the social status of the school. Newport's endowment salary of £210 for the Headmaster was among the highest in the county but he was not supplementing it with boarders' fees. The two schools Bryce commended most in Shropshire benefited considerably from their boarders: Oswestry had 55 boarders among its 78 pupils and Whitchurch had 26 in a total of 58 pupils. As a result both Heads had much larger incomes than Dr Saxton. The Headmaster of Whitchurch for instance received £450 extra to his £235 from the endowment, making the Headship there a very attractive post.

Unfortunately Saxton did not accept or understand these criticisms. He believed the 'chief obstacle to the welfare of the school is the agitation that has been got up about it', pointing to the recent increase in numbers as proof of efficient teaching. In Saxton's defence Bryce said that, although his teaching was criticised, no one accused him of neglect, and everyone professed a sincere respect for him.

Bryce suggested seven main changes for Newport Grammar School:
1. The Visitors should have more power and be more active.
2. The school should be reorganised, the three distinct departments abolished, a new arrangement of subjects made, and the Headmaster to control the whole school.
3. Provision should be made for the teaching of drawing.

4. Fees should be imposed of from £4 to £6 a year, and the Second Master, whose salary is too small, should be allowed a percentage of the fees paid. The Visitors and many of the leading inhabitants of Newport are strongly in favour of the imposition of fees.

5. A better playground should be procured.

6. A boarding house or hostel should be established, and steps made to attract the sons of Shropshire farmers. Many of these could well pay £25 or £30 a year for board and instruction for their children, who are now for the most part very poorly taught in private commercial academies.

7. When this has been done and the school, under an energetic master, has become popular with the local farmers, it may be appropriate to teach natural science and especially agricultural chemistry. 'There is no part of England where the need of such teaching is greater than in Shropshire.'

Bryce's recommendations for Newport reflected the Commission's philosophy in two important respects. First it believed that schools founded for the lower classes could only survive with any standard of classical scholarship by also attracting pupils of a higher social status. These would bring some enthusiasm for classical learning as well as fees to keep the school financially afloat. The Commission also believed that most parents should pay fees, so they would appreciate the education given. 'The characteristics of free schools are slovenly management, irregular attendance, scholars unfit for the instruction, and contempt from the parents.' Free education should 'be confined to those who are most capable of profiting by it', by open competitive examination for boys over 13 and for boys under that age through observation 'of their industry and progress for the year preceding'. (This was in line with current thinking; in 1870 the Civil Service was opened to competitive examination for the first time, instead of entry by private recommendation.) Restriction of free entry by area (as at Newport) was 'unwise and the mere fact of living on one side of a line ought not to entitle one boy to a privilege from which another is excluded'.[2] This sentiment was echoed by parents in the 1970s whose boys were excluded from Adams' by living outside the LEA catchment area. Incidentally, Tom Collins entirely agreed with charging fees. In a letter to the Endowed Schools Commission in 1872 he wrote, 'several people look upon the school as the cheapest place they can send their children to, in order to get them out of the way, and accordingly use it as a species of cloakroom'.[3]

Bryce summed up his report by commenting, 'it seems a paradox that, with this superb grammar school foundation, Newport should be no better off for education than many another town where there is not a penny of endowment'. He concluded, 'William Adams' foundation has already more money than it knows what to do with; certainly far more than it uses well'. This acid comment seems rather unfair when one looks at the efforts made by the Company to maintain the Knighton estates, and raise enough money to enlarge the school buildings. Newport was in a very different position from Monmouth which in 1868 had an income of £4,288 and expenditure of £2,274.[4]

Changes at Newport
The 1869 Endowed Schools Act established the Endowed Schools Commission to put the recommendations of the Taunton Commission into practice. This body was short-lived, City opposition causing the Conservative government of 1874 to transfer its powers back to the Charity Commissioners who continued its work in a slightly more cautious way.

The Haberdashers' Company, like other London livery companies, saw all this as interference and a threat to its independence but nevertheless attempted to reform its charities before the government did. At Monmouth new buildings were put up in 1864-5, and a new scheme for the school was approved in 1868. In 1891 another more extensive scheme established a girls' school and an elementary school in Monmouth, and another mixed secondary school in West Monmouthshire under the same wealthy foundation. Similarly great plans and discussions between the mid-1860s and 1873 led to the setting up of four new schools under Robert Aske's charity: two at Hatcham (one for boys and one for girls), a boys' school at Hampstead and a girls' school at Acton (both of which moved to Elstree in the 1960s).[5]

For Newport, after discussion with the Visitors, the townspeople and the Charity Commissioners, the Haberdashers finally printed a scheme in 1868 which took notice of Mr Bryce's recommendations. One of the most urgent – specialist teaching across the whole school rather than one master teaching every subject to his group of boys – had already been adopted.[6] The school was to be divided into an Upper Classical school and a Lower Commercial school with natural philosophy and physical sciences added to existing subjects. All boys were to pay a capitation fee, though this could be remitted on grounds of poverty or merit, and masters were to take boarders.

This scheme was never formally adopted; indeed the Endowed Schools Commissioners immediately proposed several alterations, such as abolition of the apprenticeships and payments to boys for sweeping the school and ringing the bell, but the Governors would not accept them. They also proposed a model farm for boys to have practical instruction, but their own Commissioner, Mr Stanton, visiting Newport in 1871, advised against it. He wrote that boys 'will have their necessary elementary instruction gravely interrupted by having to attend the practice of agricultural operations, and the practical instruction could hardly go farther than what they witness at their father's farm'.[7] In 1874 the Company printed more suggestions which included agricultural chemistry and modern languages in the Commercial school.[8]

In 1871 the local Congregational minister caused the authorities some confusion by arguing that the minister in William Adams' day (John Malden) was a Protestant Dissenter and therefore it was he who should receive the salary from William Adams' Charity, not the Anglican minister.

But this claim was quietly ignored. The townspeople at public meetings changed their minds; they agreed with school fees in the Haberdashers' scheme, but were firmly against them in the Endowed Schools Commission proposals. By 1878, largely because of the energetic reforms of the new Headmaster Tom Collins, appointed in 1871, they were happy with the school and wanted no new scheme at all.

The 1878 Scheme

The scheme that was finally adopted was put forward in 1878 by the Charity Commissioners, and approved by the Queen in Privy Council on 27 November 1878; it made important changes and is worth quoting fully.

The Haberdashers' Company as Governors were to continue to administer the funds and property of the Charity – now for the first time called Adams' Grammar School Foundation – but they were no longer to govern the school itself. This was to be done by 13 Managers (the term Visitor now disappears). The Master and First Warden of the Company were to be Managers *ex officio*, the others being chosen by various bodies: five by the Court of Assistants for seven years, of whom four were to be resident within ten miles of Newport Parish Church; two by local Justices of the Peace for six years; two by Newport, Salop, Local Board (the equivalent of the Town Council) for five years; and two by the ratepayers of Newport and Chetwynd End for five years. Chetwynd End was defined as that part of Chetwynd within a mile of Newport Church. Managers were to meet at least twice a year and failure to attend for a year entailed dismissal. Accounts were to be published annually.

A major new proposal was for a girls' school to be called, with the boys', the Adams' Grammar Schools. However this was to be 'if and so soon as the funds of the foundation will admit', and enough funds never were available. The boys' school was to be for 100 day boys and 50 boarders, while the girls' school was for day girls only. The Governors were to supply the money for altering existing buildings or erecting new ones 'on a convenient site', out of capital or by selling property or otherwise, subject to the consent of the Charity Commissioners. 'Or otherwise' presumably envisaged borrowing to finance new buildings but the Haberdasher Governors were never happy with this.

Religious instruction was to be in accordance with the principles of the Christian faith. A pupil could be exempt from attending religious worship or lessons on written notice from parent or guardian. The Head was not required to be in Holy Orders. He was to live in the school residence and, as in William Adams' statutes, was not to hold any other employment which might interfere with his duties as Head.

The Managers, in consultation with the Head, were responsible for the subjects to be taught and their relative importance, arrangements for school terms, holidays, payments of day boys and number and payments of boarders, supervision of sanitary arrangements and provision of school 'plant or apparatus'. The Headmaster was responsible for the day-to-day running of the school, including discipline. If he expelled anyone he should report the case to the Managers. The Managers were to determine the number of Assistant Masters and their pay but the Head was to have sole power to appoint or dismiss them, and had a say in how the money for them was allocated.

The Headmaster's salary was to be £150 a year plus a capitation payment for each scholar, to be fixed at between £2 and £5 a year. The Managers were to make arrangements for boarding either in any master's house or in hostels. Tuition fees were to be between £6 and £12 a year, with (as in the original statutes) certain categories being privileged, paying only £3 a year. These were, in order of priority, those living in Newport or Chetwynd End, those within three miles of Newport Church, and those within five miles. Numbers at such reduced rates should never be more than eighty. Boarding fees were set at £35 in a hostel and £50 in a master's house, these payments to be passed on to the foundation. Incidentally we have no evidence that a hostel was ever set up. Pupils were to be between the ages of eight and 17, needing special permission to stay beyond their 17th birthday. Entrance was by examination, the minimum standard to be in reading, writing from dictation, sums in the first four simple rules of arithmetic and the multiplication table.

The subjects taught were to be: religious instruction, reading, writing and arithmetic, geography and history, English grammar, composition and literature, mathematics, Latin, at least one foreign European language, natural science, drawing and vocal music. Greek might be taught for an additional fee of not less than £3 a year for each boy.

An annual examination was to be held by an outside examiner (as it had been since 1861), who was to report to the Managers each year. The Headmaster was also to produce an annual report.

Regulations for the girls' school were similar though the Headmistress' salary would be only £80 and the girls were to be taught domestic economy and the laws of health and needlework instead of mathematics and Greek.

Foundation scholarships (exemption from all payments) were to be available to boys and girls who had been for three years at any of the public elementary schools in Newport or Chetwynd End and had passed an examination in the highest class. £1,666 13s. 4d. was to be set aside for a Repairs and Improvements Fund. Until this was available £50 a year could be spent on repairs. There never was enough money to set up such a fund. A Pension Fund for the Headmaster was described, with the Head and Managers each contributing. It seems unlikely that this was done.

Lastly, the Charity Commissioners were to be the final authority on any matter relating to the scheme or the two schools.

There was fierce criticism of the Haberdashers for accepting this scheme. They pointed out that they had managed to modify it but had had to give in to the inevitable. In the event lack of money curtailed the scheme, no girls' school was set up and there were constant wrangles about

money between Managment, Governors and the Charity Commissioners. Details of this are in Chapter Four, pp.54-6. We do not know exactly how many of the financial provisions had to be left unfulfilled, but a section of the townspeople was soon complaining loudly at the loss of its 'free' education. The scheme came into operation in the summer term, 1879.

John Lees and the end of the Free English School

The English School had two good Headmasters in the 19th century, Samuel Cobb and John Lees, but it came to an end in 1878.

In 1829 Samuel Cobb, who since 1795 had run his own school at the same time as being part-time Writing Master at the Grammar School, became also Headmaster of the English School. He was an effective teacher who, by 1833, had nearly trebled the number of pupils – to about ninety. Despite being called the Free English School the pupils were at this time paying 8s. a year. The Visitors used this flourishing school as an excuse not to increase the English teaching at the Grammar School, but were overruled in 1834.[9] After some hesitation Samuel Cobb accepted the full-time post at the Grammar School. How he managed both schools is not clear. He made enough money from this and his private schoolmastering for his widow to be described in 1841 as of independent means.[10] At his death in 1837 his son-in-law, Richard Crowther, took his place at the Grammar School and John Lees became officially Master of the Free English School.

We have already met John Lees, aged 20, as a valuable extra teacher at the Grammar School from 1824 to 1837. He was admitted to St John's College, Cambridge in 1828, but seems not to have taken his place. A charming letter written by an old pupil in 1847 shows how he inspired his pupils.[11] It is from John Moffit, Seaman, aboard HMS *Rodney* in Athens, who must have been a pupil at the grammar school as no Greek would have been taught at the English School. We can find no reference to him in the school register, but a shipmate he mentions, Charles Griffiths, the youngest son of a shoemaker, was entered at Newport Grammar School in 1830 and left to be apprenticed to a blacksmith.[12] It shows how teaching Greek to the sons of artisans might not be entirely useless!

Moffit begins, [punctuation unaltered]

> Dear Sir, From the ancient seat of learning and wisdom a whim entered my head to address one under whose tuition I first learned to comprehend their ancient language. It may be deemed strange that I should now after so long a distance of time and perhaps an insult to you knowing the opinion many people and perhaps you sir amongst the rest entertained of me but still sir what ever opinion you or anyone else may have had of me yet sir Your memory has always been held in respect by me and it is in gratitude for your kindness and attention to my education which I can never sufficiently repay.

He mentions that amongst the marines on board is

> Charles Griffiths son of Mr Griffiths the shoemaker. I told him I was writing to you and he desired me to give you his kind respects and likewise if you would be kind enough to remember him to his Father and friends. ... You must be prepared to find quite a different sort of character from the slovenly apprentice who left so long ago. I forget the exact time now. I am I hope rather reformed and perhaps better informed than I was when I was at school with you I have had some rough wear and tear since then twice cast away twice in action with pirates and in gales of wind without end or number. I have not been home to Liverpool these 5 years and perhaps never may again ... .

It would be nice to find that John did manage to visit his old schoolmaster, but we shall never know.

John Lees established a thriving school for girls as well as boys. The school register notes many boys who left the Grammar School to 'finish their education' at the English School in the 1840s and '50s. This of course was not the way round that William Adams had intended when he left money to provide free English education for the poorer inhabitants, but is a telling commentary on local attitudes to classical education by this time. The Haberdasher deputation of 1842 commented that Lees was 'very efficient and doing great service to the younger children of the Town'. The following year a new brick building was erected to house the school just off Wellington Road, near the new Infant School and Sunday School connected with the Independent Chapel (now Trinity Church). John Lees was active in getting subscriptions for this. The Haberdashers were asked to contribute but regretted they had no funds for the purpose and could not divert Mr Adams' funds under the Court of Chancery.[13] Lees served as churchwarden of St Nicholas' Church in the 1850s. By 1865, when James Bryce made his report for the Taunton Commission, it was evident that nearly thirty years of teaching the young had taken their toll. Bryce commented 'this is virtually the public elementary school of Newport. Its master has an income of about £62 from the endowment, and has at present some 33 pupils under his charge. All are free, and the attendances consequently very irregular, and the efficiency of the school inferior to what one would expect from the capacity and reputation of its master.' He suggested making it a preparatory school under the supervision of the Grammar School Master. A public meeting in Newport in 1865 established a committee to investigate the Free English School and the Grammar School, with which many were dissatisfied. The Rector, the Reverend David Mountfield, personally went to London to discuss the problem with the Charity Commissioners. It was agreed that the English School by this time 'was a miserable affair, with some twenty boys – no discipline – and the master worthy but old and incompetent'. The Master was willing to retire but could not afford to unless the whole income could be guaranteed to him. Mr Mountfield stressed that a Boys' National School was urgently needed; in fact, the Privy Council Inspector of the Girls' and Infant Schools had threatened to withdraw their grant if nothing was done for the boys. But the Commissioners would take no action until they had an integrated scheme for the whole area.[14]

That same year the Marsh Trust gave a site on Avenue Road for a National (Church of England) School for boys and girls. The Haberdashers were asked for their backing, with the suggestion that it be called Adams' Preparatory School but they replied they had no mandate for that.[15] The school was built in 1872 without their help, so the Free English School was no longer essential to local education.

Finally in 1878 the Charity Commissioners published their scheme to close the school and sell the site. Governors were to administer the funds, allocating £50 a year to Mr John Lees, the present Master, and the rest to provide Exhibitions of between £5 and £10 a year tenable at Adams' Grammar School or some place of technical education. These were in the first place for boys who had been educated for three years at a public elementary school in Newport School District and then for any Newport boy, as a reward for merit. The Rector and churchwardens pointed out that it would be more in line with William Adams' original benefaction to use the money to help poorer boys stay at school and learn a trade, rather than encouraging them to move on to the Grammar School. They deplored the current notion 'that the occupation of a clerk is more genteel than that of an artisan', which this scheme would rein-force. However, the Commissioners would not move, so the English School endowments from now on supported the Grammar School.

As for John Lees, his friends subscribed to an annuity for him so that, with his pension, he was able to live in comfort for the short time left to him. He died aged 73, in September 1879 and was buried at Chetwynd. He had counted several eminent men among his old pupils and friends, and 'was remarkable for his mild and peaceful disposition'.

Tom Collins
Headmaster 1871–1903

When Tom Collins[16] took over in January 1871 he brought a breath of fresh air to the school. A tall, imposing, charismatic sportsman and Cambridge Blue, aged 30, he was a complete contrast to his predecessor. He was not in Holy Orders, being a barrister although he never practised at the Bar. At Christ's College, Cambridge, he spent so much time on sport – cricket, fives, racquets, billiards and shooting – that he had to work very hard in his last six months to get through his finals. In 1863 he gained a second-class degree in Classics and was always firmly convinced of the value of Greek in training the mind. His first job was as assistant Classical master at King Edward's School, Birmingham, but it seems he was appointed mainly to improve the school's cricket.[17] He enjoyed the social and sporting life of Birmingham, playing whist and bridge as well as golf and fishing, but when he got engaged 'desirous of settling as soon as possible' he applied for the Headship at Newport. Incidentally, there were 27 candidates for the post, more than ever before. He later wrote, 'The School when I took over was in a most unsatisfactory condition. The boys had been caned by my predecessor morning and afternoon. The result was that most of them would lie through a brick wall if they thought there was any chance of getting off scot free.' Collins was very much against corporal punishment and based his discipline on trust between master and boy. As a large confident man he must have inspired respect, but this was reinforced by the personal interest he took in his pupils at work and play. He used humour and encouragement but not sarcasm. He advised teachers never to punish a boy for stupidity but to redouble their efforts to get him to understand. He thought writing lines as a punishment a waste of time (and could lead to a black market in used lines!). Genuine detention, in which one master supervised several boys doing appropriate work, was the best method of punishment. He lived up to his theories; two Old Boys, writing separately in the *Novaportan* in 1931 and 1934, remembered only three canings in four and five years at school.

Significantly, Collins thought that boys in the school cricket and football teams should be excused detention, as it was important for the spirit of the school that teams should do well in matches. He was very keen that boys should take part in manly games such as cricket and football as these would develop their sense of leadership and co-operation as well as exercising their bodies. This was very much part of the ethos of public schools at the time, who adopted the motto *mens sana in corpore sano* (a healthy mind in a healthy body). He thought a good sportsman made a good scholar, but sport should not be the be-all and end-all of life. He introduced athletics, cricket and football to the school, renting a cricket field from the town almost immediately he arrived. His enthusiasm eventually got through to boys and parents. On Speech Day in 1878 he reported, 'The most unsatisfactory thing I have to report is the utter want of interest in manly games manifested by the majority of the school … This is a state of things that I would ask parents of boys to endeavour to alter. If, instead of healthy, manly English games, their sons are allowed to prowl about the streets, they will certainly do themselves no good, and very probably a great amount of harm.'[18] However, he was able the following year to commend the large number of boys who played on the athletics field every night, even though their teams had not necessarily won many matches.

He introduced a 'College Cap' (commonly known as a mortar board) to foster a sense of identity. He made all boys, except the very poor, buy their own books, so they treated them with respect. He set a high standard for entry to the school, examining boys in reading, writing and the four rules of arithmetic; in 1872 he rejected seven out of 22 applicants. A new fourth master, James Griffiths, was appointed early in 1871 to specialise in chemistry and drawing, though the study of chemistry did not get going for a while because of lack of space and funds to buy chemicals.

A significant step forward was taken when Newport Grammar School became a centre for the Cambridge Local Examination (roughly the equivalent of GCSE). Collins had obtained the agreement of schools nearby such as Stafford, Market Drayton, Brewood and Wellington, to send their candidates to Newport. The Cambridge Board required a guarantee of 25 candidates at £1 each a year to establish a centre. The Governors agreed to guarantee that amount, but they were rarely called upon to provide it as enough boys were entered. Of the first 10 Newport boys, eight passed, two with honours, and more successes followed. In 1883 J.E. Quibell out of 3,900 candidates nationwide came first in Latin, second in Greek and 19th in mathematics. The Governors made a grant of £15 to enable him to stay at school a further year as his father could not afford it. The support was well rewarded – Quibell became a noted archaeologist and for many years was Keeper of the Egyptian Museum in Cairo.[19]

It did not take long for Collins' enthusiasm to penetrate throughout the school. It gained in status when he became a member of the Headmasters' Association. In 1871 a new outside examiner, who was also examiner for Rugby and the City of London School, gave it a very good report. He praised Classics as excellent, mathematics of a very high standard (though two papers not so good) and natural history very gratifying – as a new subject it had caught the boys' fancy. In English they had been studying Shakespeare's *Julius Caesar* and Bacon's *Essays*, and were very keen. He observed that the school 'has fewer weak points than most schools and is destined to make still further progress'.[20]

Collins was determined to improve conditions in the school and in 1874 the Governors agreed to pay the first caretaker. A man and his wife were paid £30 a year: he to mow the grass, keep the playground and privies clean and ring the school bell, she to sweep and wash the school and light fires. The two pupils appointed at £1 a year since the time of William Adams to clean the school and ring the bell were no longer needed. Collins paid the caretaker extra so that he was partly his own servant. John Taylor was with him for 26 years, assisting in his shooting expeditions as well as sometimes shielding boys from the consequences of their misdemeanours. If a window had been broken and Collins enquired the cause, Taylor would often say, 'There was a very strong wind last

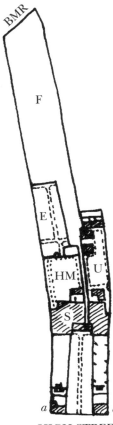

The school site redrawn from the Ordnance Survey of 1881. HM headmaster's garden, E probably an extension to his garden, U usher's garden, S school building (as on 1902 OS map), a almshouses, F field, BMR Beaumaris Road

night, sir'. Collins persuaded the Governors to provide new desks; the old ones were probably 100 to 150 years old! He also had a hot bath installed for the boarders.[21] The main problem, lack of teaching space, could best be solved by an entirely new building, but in the meantime Collins extended into the Usher's house. Mr Hutt, the Second Master, was given £40 a year for giving up a room in his house to be a classroom. This was the small room on the first floor next to the library and a way through was made by the builder J. F. Cobb. Collins' next plan was to use the Usher's house for boarders and grant the Second Master extra money to find his own lodgings. The Governors offered Hutt £90 for this, in addition to his £110 salary, but he wanted an extra £110. After threats of dismissal Mr Hutt resigned in June 1875 and the new master, A.M. Drennan, was the first not to live in the original Usher's house. In 1881 Drennan had six boarders of his own. A second classroom was taken from the house at the same time (presumably the room downstairs next to the portico).[22] All this happened before the 1878 scheme was in place.

The improved prestige of the school by 1875 can be seen by the large number of applicants for masterships that year – 23 for the Second, 56 for the Fourth and 57 for the Foreign Master. The only one who did not leave that year was the faithful Richard Crowther, who retired in 1882. Numbers of pupils also rose spectacularly, to 137 in 1878.

The new spirit was reflected in the *Novaportan*, the school magazine which was first issued in November 1883, price 4d. We have copies up to July 1887, one for April 1890, one for July 1893 and then no more until it was revived under Mr Shuker in 1907. For the first time a schoolboy voice is heard. The first editorial earnestly exhorts 'each of our schoolfellows to do his best for *the honour of the School*. ... this however cannot be upheld and maintained by a mere knowledge of Latin, Greek, French, German, Mathematics nor indeed by any other species of learning but rather by honourable, truthful, gentlemanly conduct both in and out of school; conduct such as becomes all those who wish to maintain the honour of England, and, what is better still, to please in all things the "Great Headmaster in the Heavens".' This first editor, Lonsdale Ragg, gained a Careswell Exhibition to Christ Church, Oxford and had a distinguished career as an author and cleric. Humour had its place in the *Novaportan*: there was a witty 'History of England' and a tongue-in-cheek 'Dictionary of the Latin Language'. There was a list of Don'ts, a 'Manual of Mistakes & Improprieties more or less prevalent among schoolboys', such as 'Don't omit to cheek your elders, nothing is admired so much in a youngster as cheek, Don't prepare your lessons (this old fashioned and ridiculous custom has long since died out).' Later a companion list of 'Always' appeared, including 'Always chuck stones into mud puddles to splash small boys, then chuckle at your own bravery'. Among general knowledge quizzes, serious historical and natural science articles, accounts of travels and poems, we find music mentioned. The boys gave concerts after the Athletic Sports and on Speech Day, with guest singers, male and female. One year, musical talent being low, they acted two comedies, to great acclaim.

By far the most space in the *Novaportan* was given to sports. There were paperchases, extending even to 16 miles in an afternoon, lawn tennis tournaments as well as athletics, cricket and football. The cricket field was in Audley Avenue (later called the Shuker Field) and the Head and other masters played in the teams. Apart from Stafford Grammar School, all the other teams they played against were adult clubs. In 1883 they played the Caxtonians (a Newport side), Lilleshall, Stafford, Hinstock, Mr A.T.Ward's Eleven and Chetwynd. They later played Madeley, Newport Town and Ketley Bank. A similar variety of opponents were met in football, such as Newport Bicycle Club, Wellington, Malinslee, Aston, Stafford Town as well as Market Drayton Grammar School and the Old Hall. The school football ground was at first on the Longford Road. In 1871 the boys played rugby, but soon changed to football which was in its infancy. There was no agreed size or shape of pitch, teams played according to the rules of the home side. In November 1884 the first XI went to Wellington to play Wellington College. 'Our opponents, as usual, played four masters, and being more at home on their own field, defeated us by five goals to one. Our fellows were unable to make either "head or tail" out of the field, which was triangular in shape; one of the corner posts being situated about eight yards from the goal.' The cricket and football activities were paid for entirely by contributions from the boys. One editorial complained bitterly that not all boys were paying their contribution.

Tom Collins played an active part in town life. He was a member of Newport Literary and Social Institute from its beginning in 1883 and an honorary member of the Oddfellows and the Free Foresters (Friendly Societies that provided insurance against sickness, unemployment and death). He was a keen Freemason, joining Audley Lodge, Newport, on its foundation in 1881 and becoming Master in 1886. From this time many masters at the Grammar School were Freemasons. He was a Justice of the Peace and, as Headmaster, *ex officio* Vice Chairman of the Marsh Trustees, who administered the income from the former common land in Newport Marsh (Audley Road area) for the good of the town. Soon after his retirement in 1903 Collins was elected a town councillor with great support from the ordinary working man, but he was impatient with other councillors whom he considered got elected to serve their own interests and retired from this in 1910. He was made a Manager of the Grammar School in 1904 and served for many years. As Chairman and Manager of Newport Gas Company and an Income Tax Inspector he would have received an income, which was just as well as the Grammar School funds were so low when he retired that all the Governors could afford was a single gift of £134 15s. rather than a pension.

On his retirement as Headmaster the Old Boys held a dinner in his honour at the *Royal Victoria Hotel* and presented him with an illuminated address. This meeting led to the formation of the Old Novaportans' Club. Although towards the end of his time the school was declining in numbers, it is evident that he was indeed a great Headmaster, who inspired abiding affection in those who knew him in his prime. Increasingly deaf and blind, he remained a benign presence living across the road from the school, revered by townspeople and schoolboys alike. In 1933, a year before he died, as the oldest living cricket Blue (whose over-arm bowling in 1863 had caused a change in cricketing law), he was made a Member of the M.C.C.

Town and School at the end of the century
Many townspeople disliked the 1878 scheme. They resented the loss of what they saw as their right to free education. The new Rector of Chetwynd, Dr Cosmo Gordon, complained that it excluded boys at Chetwynd National School from gaining free foundation scholarships as the school itself had moved 12 years previously to a position near Chetwynd church. The Charity Commissioners replied that if boys lived in Chetwynd End they would still qualify for reduced fees.

A public meeting at the Corn Exchange attended by many eminent townspeople in September 1884 typified the discontent.[23] The meeting considered the Managers' plan to build a completely new school as unnecessary, saying it would be better to repair and improve the existing one. The money saved could go towards the girls' school. It was also asserted that 230 boys could easily be taught in the existing building, rather than the proposed 150. The meeting demanded the restoration of the 80 free places. Another large meeting resolved that there was no need for a girls' school and that the boys' school should be dealt with first!

Such sentiments surfacing from time to time did not deter the new Managers from trying to do the best for the school. They were, after all, made up largely of local people, such as the Rector of Newport and solicitors E. Hodges (Clerk to the Managers) and C.R.Liddle. They would have preferred to build a new school, surrounded by playing fields, rather

Graffiti on the window-sill in Big School.

than patching up the old. Sir Thomas Boughey offered them free of charge
a site on the Wellington Road but the problem was money. The Charity
Commissioners refused to allow them to take from capital the large sum
a new school would cost, but the Managers had no means of paying back
a loan. They turned to the alternative and in 1886 offered 25 guineas for
the best plans to alter the existing buildings at a cost not exceeding
£4,000, to include a house for the second master. All this while, because
of the agricultural depression, the Haberdashers were allowing tenants on
the Knighton estates to pay less rent. The school income was cut by £240
in 1885 (despite local opinion that this was not necessary), so any action
was put on hold. It was cut by another £250 in 1887, at which the
Managers stated they could afford no further scholarships. Even the
Novaportan reflected the frustration that nothing was being done. In 1883
a long poem entitled *Before and After* protested that the new scheme had
not lived up to its promise:

> The Scheme it came. Five years have run
> Their long and weary course:
> The citizens begin to feel
> The bitings of remorse.
>
> No statelier pile has reared its head,
> An honour to the town;
> The School itself will ne'er be touched
> Until it tumble down.

Over the next few years, there were many more public meetings and
consultations with the Charity Commissioners but nothing was done and in
1896, because of the delay, Sir Thomas Boughey withdrew his offer of a site.

At long last in June 1899 the Managers took action. With the agreement of the Haberdashers' Company they asked the Charity Commission for permission to spend £2,000 on improving the existing building, in accordance with the plans of Messrs Scrivener of Hanley. This amount proved too small and £3,500 was authorised by the Charity Commission, but of that £2,500 had to be repaid to the Charity out of income within twenty years. The changes were pitifully small after the high hopes of the previous twenty years. They were reported in the *Newport Advertiser* on 31 August 1901. An entrance hall had been added to the Headmaster's house and other improvements made. The sitting room in the former Second Master's house was now a dining room for country boys who could not go home for dinner. A movable glass partition had been erected in the Schoolroom (plate 25). The old library had been turned into a classroom and the library itself moved to a partitioned-off section. The second floor rooms had been converted into physical and chemistry laboratories. The whole place was to be heated with hot water 'on the most approved modern principle'. The garden at the rear had been asphalted to be used as a drill ground, and a building provided for storage of boys' bicycles. Much of these alterations are recognisable in old photographs that still exist. The work was carried out by Mr Whittingham of St Mary Street, Newport.

So at the very end of Tom Collins' time as Head something was actually done to improve the school buildings. The following year the 1902 Education Act opened up new possibilities but these did not affect the school until the time of Mr Shuker, the next Headmaster.

31 *Hurlstone, for many years a boarding house kept by Mr and Mrs Gill. In 1934 it became the rectory. It is now a private house.*

32 *Aston Hall, a school boarding house from 1947 to 1968. Pinewoods housing estate, Church Aston, now occupies the site.*

33 *The 1929 New Building with open walkways.*

34 *The library after the Tercentenary refurbishment.*

35 *The Tercentenary 1956. Mr Kenneth Leach, Chairman of Governors and President of the Old Novaportans, opens the Old Boys' gates, watched by Horace Knott, caretaker, Tom Pemberton, who made the gates, Alderman Sir Frederick Wells, Master of the Haberdashers' Company, Robert Glover the Headmaster and Commander H. Prevett, Clerk to the Company.*

36 *Boys admiring their contribution to the Tercentenary, the newly positioned coats of arms on the pillars of the front gates.*

37 *The unbeaten rugby team of 1951.*
Mr R.H. Anderson, Eric Clarke, Keith Howells, W. Prescott, Ewan Henderson, Jim Home, R. Burgess
Harry Lloyd, Don Hillcoat, John Durnall, Dan Chalmers (Captain), Peter Boyle, Michael Bromage, Brian Simmill
John Reece, M. Stephens, Reg Warrington, Nigel Bromage

38 *The unbeaten cricket team of 1951.*
Eric Clarke, Jack Boyle, W. Prescott, Keith Howells, Reg Warrington, Bev Griffiths
John Reece, Jim Home, Michael Bromage, Colin Wright, Nigel Bromage

39 *The Masters, 1958-1959*

J.L. Humphrys, M.D. Watts, J.D. Chambers, R.Q. Cavenagh, C.A. Paris, J.L. Burgess, K. Reynolds, L.E. Seymour-Whiteley.

G.A. Mottershaw, A.S.W. Baker, A.W. Harding, R.H. Anderson (Acting Second Master), R.F. Glover (Headmaster), A.W.C. Johnson, N. Elliott, J.W.L. Birbeck, F.P. Fowler.

Absent: L.W. Taylor (Second Master)

40   *The school staff in 1988*

Back row: C.G.Powell, I.H.Lock, B.M. Lucas, P.R.North, R.G.M.Jones, G.Leach.

Second row: B.S.Thompstone, N.C.Gibbs, J.N.Roberts, K.Orrell, B.K.Banks, T.H.Bate, P.Hunt, K.J.Delaney

Third row: Mrs H.Gosling (HM secretary), Mrs J. Macphee(catering), G.P.Quinton, J.H.Deakin, M.E.Morris, F.L.Gibbon, A.W.Harding (bursar), Mrs M. Lloyd (school secretary), Mrs M. Overton (lab technician)

Front row: Mrs C.M.Charrington, Mrs C.V.Bloor, J.D.Chambers, D.E.Westgate, D.J.Taylor, G.A.Mottershaw, Mrs S. Seymour Whiteley (librarian), Mr L.E.Seymour Whiteley, Mrs B.Wood

Not present: C.A.Jobson, A.M.Newton, Mrs C.Jopling

41 *The Governors at the time the school became grant maintained, September 1990*

Front row from left: Mrs Sylvia Pearce (parent), Revd Roy Hibbert, Captain M. Barrow (Clerk), Mr David Taylor (Headmaster), Mr Harry Wood (Chairman), Mr David Sime (Master), Dr Alan Snead (Vice Chairman), Mr Barry Gillibrand (parent), Dr Barbara Marsh
Back row: Mr Ian Thomson, Mr Charles Hannon (parent), Mr Geoffrey Fox, Mr William Hickman (parent), Mr John Maxwell (bursar), Mr Brian Shawcross, Mr David Smythe, Mr Alan Roberts, Mr Tom Bate (staff), Mr Derek Corlett (parent), Mr Brian Thompstone (staff), Mr Brian Williams (clerk to governors), Mr Geoff Eatough.
Not present: The Hon. L.B.Hacking

42 *Tom Collins 1871-1903.*   **43** *J. W. M. Shuker 1903-26.*   **44** *W. S. Brooks 1926-46.*

Six Headmasters

45 *A. D. C. Peterson 1946-52.*   **46** *R. F. Glover 1953-9.*   **47** *J. D. Roberts 1959-73.*

48 *David Taylor, Headmaster 1974-93.*

49 *David Westgate, Deputy Headmaster 1977-1996.*

50 *The present Headmaster, Jim Richardson, with his deputies Mark Warren-Smith (left) and David Iddon (right).*

51 *Mrs Hazel Gosling, Headmaster's secretary 1975-91.*

52 *Bryan Lloyd, caretaker 1978-1998 with his enormous bunch of keys. Only he knew which was which!*

53 *Walter Harding when boarding bursar in the 1980s.*

54 *Presentation to Joyce Locke of the school support staff on her retirement after 38 years at the school, 1990.*

55 *Kenneth Leach (Chairman of Governors 1956-76) on the left, being presented with school memorabilia by his successor Peter Watson Jones.*

56 *Dr Alan Snead (Chairman of Governors) and Mr Ian Thompson (Foundation Governor) checking details of the new technology centre, 1993.*

57 *Looking down into Big School during major repairs in 1975/6.*

58 *A steel girder being swung into position to support Big School ceiling and the floor above.*

59 *The main classroom block in the late 1980s after major reconstruction of the corridors.*

60 *The old Manual Room in the 1980s, before its conversion to a drama area.*

61 *The new technology area in the Taylor Centre in the mid-1990s.*

62   *Fishing at Longford.*

63   *Dormitory at Longford in the mid-1980s.*

64 *Choir and orchestra in the parish church with director of music Richard Churches, 1989.*

65 *The famous astronomer Patrick Moore with three first-year boys at Greenwich Observatory in 1986. They were invited to appear with him for the press photographs.*

66   *The school prefects in 1994-5 including two of the first intake of girls: Liz Banks, school vice-captain, and Laurie Phillips.*

Nine

1903 TO 1926
THE SCHOOL EXPANDS

J. W. McLellan Shuker
Headmaster 1903-26

Under the headship of J. W. Shuker the school became a recognisably modern institution. Numbers rose rapidly. The 57 boys taught by three assistant masters in 1903 became 138 boys taught by five assistant masters in 1906 and 156 taught by seven masters in 1908. The upward curve continued. By 1919 there were 225 pupils of whom 60 were boarders, and on Shuker's retirement in 1926 the total was 257. Remarkable successes in scholarship and sport brought self-confidence and pride in the school's achievements. These were made possible by two main factors: the strong leadership of J. W. Shuker and the financial aid that came to the school as a result of the 1902 Education Act.

Shuker's background made the developments in sport understandable, but not his enthusiastic promotion of maths and science. He had read Classics at Cambridge where he distinguished himself in athletics: he won the University half-mile in 2 minutes 2¾ seconds and ran in the mile for Cambridge against Oxford. He also played rugby and cricket. He came to Newport from Framlingham College, Suffolk, having been Head of Classics and then Second Master there.

At Newport he recognised that educational needs were changing. Many boys from the state elementary schools were now able to enter the Grammar School. All pupils needed a grounding in maths and science to fit them for the modern world. At last what the people of Newport had been asking for since the mid-19th century, and what had been recommended in the 1860s by James Bryce and the Taunton Commission became a reality. Newport Grammar School rose to pre-eminence in the county. Numbers who gained university entrance and County Council scholarships far outstripped those from other grammar schools.

We owe our knowledge of what went on in the school at this time primarily to the school magazine, the *Novaportan*, which was revived in 1907 and continued to the outbreak of the Second World War in 1939. It was edited by staff in Shuker's time and by pupils after that. The enthusiasm it portrayed for the school's progress must have been not only a reflection of that progress but a stimulus to it. Time and again it waxed lyrical about the 'public school spirit'. It is in the main an account of events at the school; there are very few other articles such as there had been in its previous incarnation. Sadly, no minutes of Managers' Meetings survive from the time they took over in 1878. The minutes of various Haberdasher Committees give us some information about the buildings and finances of the school, but after 1878 they were no longer responsible for the educational side. Main events were reported in the *Newport and Market Drayton Advertiser.*

Academic progress

The academic success of the school can be charted from the results of the Cambridge Local Examinations reported in the *Novaportan*. We noted in Chapter Eight that Newport pupils had gained outstanding results from the first establishment in 1872 of the school as a centre for these examinations. What we are able to see from 1903 onwards is the whole range of results. There were three grades of examination: preliminary for pupils under 14, junior for pupils under 16 and senior for pupils under nineteen. In 1903 five boys were entered for the junior grade. All passed. After that boys were entered for all three grades, most well below the specified age. From 1911 to 1919, when the system was altered, the senior and junior exams alone were taken. These exams superseded the established yearly exam by an outside examiner which had been going on since 1861.

In 1906 all 68 boys in the main school were entered, aged from 11 to 15. 58 passed, nearly one half of the school. In 1907 all 92 boys in those forms took the exam of whom 84 passed. We get a flavour of the excitement of those times from the *Novaportan* of April 1908: 'February 10th was a red letter day in the history of the School. On that day the results of the Cambridge Local Examinations arrived. For some weeks we had all been living in an atmosphere charged with suppressed excitement. When the school had assembled to hear the lists read out, the excitement seemed to be let loose, and as name after name was read out, the cheers rang louder and louder. The loudest cheer of all greeted the name of Lloyd; when the Headmaster called for an extra cheer for him – our youngest success – there went up such a shout as has probably not been heard in the School for many years. On the following day a whole holiday was granted, for which we thank the 84 boys in whose honour it was given.'

We have no consistent record of what subjects were taken, but in 1907 we know all boys took religious knowledge, English language and literature, history, geography, French, arithmetic, mathematics and drawing. Almost all also took Latin and chemistry. It was a sign of the times that Latin was no longer compulsory. A substantial number of boys gained honours and distinctions and exemption from London Matriculation (which saved them having to take a separate exam if they went on to London University). Frequently they took the lead among all entrants nationwide.

From 1910 through to 1915 the school was the first in England in the number of distinctions in English and history, and in 1910 it was joint first in chemistry. Three times Adams' pupils won the Silver Medal of the Royal Geographical Society. In 1917, the last year the Cambridge Syndicate published individual positions, Newport Grammar School, out of 5,222 candidates, gained first in history, second in geography, third in chemistry, fifth in physics and many more outstanding results. In total, from 1903 to 1917 the school gained 836 Cambridge Local certificates, of which there were 109 first class and 62 second class honours and 437 distinctions. First position in the whole list was achieved 16 times; an amazing achievement for a school of its size.

In 1918 the system was changed. The earliest examination now was the School Certificate of the Northern Universities Joint Board. Boys sat this in July at the age of 15 or 16. (This was changed to the General Certificate of Education, Ordinary Level (GCE, O Level) in the 1950s and General Certificate of Secondary Education (GCSE) in the 1980s.) It seems that at first, when the school was big enough to have two parallel forms, A and B, the VB boys were not entered for School Certificate. From 1931 they were, but the subjects they took were not identical; for instance, they did general science instead of separate sciences. For the first time in 1919 boys could also sit the Higher School Certificate at the age of 17 or 18. This became Advanced Level GCE in 1951. The school was now recognised by the Board of Education as one of only three in the county to provide an advanced course in mathematics and science (for which an extra teacher was provided), so the sixth form was basically a Science Sixth. The December 1921 editorial in the *Novaportan* proudly recorded that, in the list of academic distinctions gained by Shropshire schools, Newport had 31 names, while no other school had more than eight, and the 31 Old Novaportans currently at university equalled the total for all other schools in the county.

It was not until 1928 that the new Headmaster, W.S. Brooks, arranged for a separate Arts Sixth Form to take Higher School Certificate in history, French and English. Latin was soon added. This is not to say that there were no boys going on to university in arts subjects before this. A determined boy could pursue his chosen subject despite the curriculum, with help from a dedicated teacher. J.W.Corbishley gained an Open Scholarship to read history at Keble College, Oxford in 1915. At the Old Novaportan Dinner in 1920 he recalled the last two years of his school life. What little he knew about history, he said, was largely due to the guidance of Mr Dyke. It should be noted that Mr Dyke was not a history graduate; his subject was English, in which by all accounts he was inspirational. He also read up zoology and botany when the school set up a biology laboratory in 1919. He got many boys through their First M.B. examination, which saved them a whole year at medical school.

Entry to university could be surprisingly informal. Reg Lees, born 1910, recalls how Mr Brooks came into the Sixth Form room with a letter from Durham University which had had some good students from Whitchurch, and was enquiring whether any other Shropshire boys might be interested in going. Reg volunteered and went to read mathematics.

We must remember that not all boys were at school for the full five years; many stayed only two or three. Shuker frequently reminded parents at Speech Day of the benefits of completing the whole course. Paying pupils could come at the age of eight into Form I or II. There was for a while a preparatory department below these forms. In Form III they were joined by the scholarship pupils from the state elementary schools. Thus Form III was the first form in the main school. It was later known as the First Form, and nowadays as Year 7. Eighty boys from the privileged area of Newport and Chetwynd End still paid less than the others. When Ray Elkes' parents asked the Headmaster whether he could come at the age of eight he was accepted from January 1922, but they had to pay the full amount until the autumn, when there would be a vacancy among the eighty. He recalls that the 80 could come from as far away as Edgmond or Lilleshall in his day.

Sport and other activities
It was not just in academic work that the school forged ahead under Shuker. It continued its fine performance on the sports field and there were several new activities.

Shuker organised the boys into Houses: Boarders, Town, Country A-L and Country M-Z. Later these were known by the names of the housemasters. Inter-house competitions in football, cricket and athletics, with 'colours' and caps for each team fostered community spirit. Old Boys and well-wishers gave House trophies, so they competed for the Sir Oliver Lodge Cup for Athletics, the Silvester Horne Shield for Football, the Sir T. F. Boughey Shield for Cricket and the A. J. Davies Shield for Shooting. Scratch sixes – six-a-side football matches – had large numbers of entries; the Headmaster gave medals to the winners. A large proportion of the *Novaportan* was given to detailed accounts of football and cricket matches and the performance of each team member. Over the years the school had some highly successful teams. Fixtures included the same schools for decades: Edgmond College, Ellesmere College, Stafford, Wolverhampton, Whitchurch, Brewood, Stone and Wem Grammar Schools; the Priory School, Shrewsbury and many others. And of course there was the annual cricket match against the Old Novaportans – 'Past v Present'.

The cricket field was on Audley Road, just beyond and behind Audley Villa and in the early days a professional cricket coach was employed. Football was played on the other side of the road, where Burton Borough School now stands. The pavilion on the cricket field, erected in 1923 by public subscription, was used for both sports. Hot showers were added in 1931. The cricket field was rented from the Marsh Trustees until Mr Shuker bought it and presented it to the school in 1924. Still known as the Shuker Field, it was leased to Newport Urban District Council when the school moved its playing fields to Wellington Road in 1958. Rather mysteriously, the Headmaster's report at Speech Day 1913 refers to facilities for swimming, 'though without a swimming bath these must perforce be inadequate'. We should like to know what these facilities were! All we know for certain is that boys used to swim in the canal and the Moss Pool near

Forton. In 1909 some early-rising boy-scout boarders swam behind a barge on the Strine out of sight of their clothes. When they got back the clothes were gone! There was talk of a swimming pool in the early 1900s; the Old Novaportans planned to fund one in 1910 and again in 1919 as a war memorial. In the event, the school had to wait until 1958 when the family of Kenneth Leach, Chairman of Governors, had one built.

Sports Day was the highlight of the athletic year. Boys had always competed on an individual basis for the honour of being Victor Ludorum and a cup was given for this by the Old Novaportans. From 1907, with the presentation of Sir Oliver Lodge's House Cup, the honour of the House was also at stake. Points were given for the first six in many events, so everyone could contribute and many keen boys were seen practising well beforehand. In 1927 an Inter-House Cross Country Run (or steeplechase) was added. Shropshire Inter-School Sports are first mentioned in 1915, when they were held on Newport School field. Six schools took part: Bridgnorth, Coalbrookdale, Oswestry, Wellington, Wem and Newport. The six events were: 100 yards, mile and quarter mile races, long jump, high jump and a relay race. Bridgnorth won four events, Newport won two. When the first post-war Inter-School Sports took place in 1924 nine secondary schools competed and Newport won both Senior and Junior championships. Newport won the senior shield again in 1926 and 1927. Individuals played a large part in these successes. E. H. Foinette was an outstanding all-round athlete and J. Lineton an excellent runner at this time.

No sport was timetabled during the day. It was after school ended at 3.30p.m. that boys could go up to the playing fields to play amongst themselves or practise for the school teams. This was the highlight of the day for many of them!

There were activities other than sport during Shuker's time. The Literary and Debating Society was founded in 1909, restricted to forms V and VI. The subjects of debate reflected contemporary concerns, some still relevant today. They approved of capital punishment (1909), Home Rule for Ireland (1911) and nationalisation of English railways (1912). In 1910 they agreed by a narrow margin that England was in danger of invasion from Germany, but they disapproved of extension of the franchise to women (1913), of subjecting aliens to more severe restrictions and supervision (1911), and in 1929 and 1932 voted strongly against blood sports, hunting, and vivisection. Many boys honed their debating techniques on these occasions. Two protagonists in the early 1930s were Kenneth Mynett, who became a judge and QC, and Kenneth Leach who became Chairman of Serck Audco and also of the Grammar School Governors. The Society also bought newspapers and periodicals from its subscriptions which the boys eagerly awaited every morning. It then branched out to form a lending library. In 1913, 100 books were in circulation, some bought, some donated. As funds became available more books were added and a library was started for the junior boys. These were of great benefit, as the official library consisted of reference books

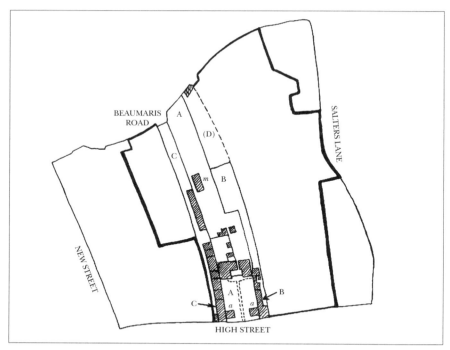

School site 1656-1926. a: almshouses, A: the original school site, B: 117 High Street bought from Tom Collins in 1919, C: Old Crow Inn outbuildings and land bought in 1926, (D): land and cottages behind 117 High Street bought in 1938, m: 1926 manual room. Heavy outline shows boundary of present school site.

which only the senior boys could use. Boys who were at school during the Second World War remember this library as their only source of books. Chess and draughts were encouraged and competitions held regularly.

A Boy Scout group for the younger boys was started only a year after Baden-Powell founded the movement in 1908, and a Miniature Rifle Club was formed the same year.

In July 1915, when no fewer than 165 Old Boys were serving in the forces, at least three had been killed and several wounded, the Headmaster set up a School Cadet Corps (plate 24). This was the 8th Company of the Secondary Schools Cadet Battalion, attached to the 4th Battalion of the King's Shropshire Light Infantry. Immediately it numbered over 80 boys, practically everyone who was eligible to join. There were two Platoons (Senior and Junior) which were subdivided into Sections according to Houses. Activities included drill, signalling with flags, route marches and field days. To start them off, Lieut. W. D. Budgen (the Rector's son) put them through their paces on the drill ground and in the lecture room. Later, as a Major in the RAF, he received the OBE. There was great enthusiasm and a band was soon formed. The officers were teachers, the NCOs were senior pupils. In 1918 the Corps gained the coveted Lucas Tooth award for the best corps in a Shropshire school, after twice coming second. In July 1920 the War Office presented the school with a captured German howitzer gun. This was hauled from the station by a team of boys and came to rest on the grass in front of the school. It was still there during the Second World War and many ONs we interviewed remembered it well. The Corps was disbanded in 1920.

The school was able to move to more peaceful activities with the formation of the school Dramatic Society. This put on the subplot of *Twelfth Night* in 1920, followed by *The Merchant of Venice* in 1922 and the complete *Twelfth Night* in 1923.

Finance and Buildings to 1939 – A Curious School

The amazing expansion at the beginning of the century would not have been possible without financial help from the government. The William Adams' Charity administered by the Haberdashers for the school (now separate from the William Adams' Eleemosynary Charities that dealt with all his other payments), was woefully inadequate. The 1902 Education Act changed matters completely. It set up Local Educational Authorities in all 120 County and County Borough Councils. These were responsible for all secondary and elementary education, including voluntary schools. They could build new schools, for girls as well as boys where necessary, and take over private schools. Voluntary schools whose four-year course had been approved would receive aid from the rates. The endowment body (in Newport's case the William Adams' Charity) was to remain responsible for capital expenditure on buildings, structural repairs and alterations and the appointment and dismissal of teachers. Of the 12 Shropshire endowed schools whose fortunes we have followed over the centuries, six became state-aided, one (Oswestry) became independent so the County founded its own Grammar School there, and the others became elementary schools or were closed. The six who continued as grammar schools were: Bridgnorth, Ludlow, Market Drayton, Newport, Wem and Whitchurch. Of the new schools set up by the County Council the one most likely to be in competition with Adams' was Wellington Grammar School, opened in 1912. From 1907 a quarter of grammar school entries at 11 were reserved for free pupils from state elementary schools, chosen after an educational test. All others paid fees. The school was given extra money for these free 'scholarship' pupils.

The County Council took a year or two to sort out what was needed, but fairly soon they began to contribute something towards Adams' Grammar School's running costs. This was very welcome. Time and again the Managers had to ask the Haberdashers for an advance because they could not make ends meet. In 1905 when the net income for the school was about £750 they were due to get only £124 because they had used the rest the previous year. In December 1905 F. N. Hodges, Clerk to the Managers, begged the Haberdashers for £300 to keep the school going that term. He hoped they would be in a better position the following year as they expected the Board of Education to give about £150 for the year's work. The Haberdashers paid up.[1] Again, during 1907 the school Managers were paid £900 on account, so at the end of the financial year they were overdrawn by £74, but in 1908 they underspent so they were in credit by £437. The Managers complained that the rents on the estates were too low and too much was spent on repairs. The Haberdashers disagreed; in 1911 they spent £325 in rebuilding Knighton Grange Farm. All expenditure by now had to be sanctioned by the Board of Education.[2] From 1906 to 1911 Shropshire County Council contributed £50 a year towards the school's running costs. In 1912 they asked for the annual accounts so that they could decide the amount of grant according to need. This resulted in much higher grants: £200 in 1913, £300 in 1915 and £433 in 1918.[3]

The County Council did, however, expect the William Adams' Charity to pay for new buildings. The Haberdashers insisted there was not enough money in the funds to do so and looking at the following figures one can understand their reluctance to take money out of capital. For the rebuilding in 1901 they had sold stock to produce the £3,500 needed. Capital assets were reduced from £10,689 in 1900 to £7,160 in 1905.[4] This was the situation that led to a paltry gift of £138 to Tom Collins instead of a pension. The Haberdashers were also wary of borrowing money, which would have been the only way out. Meanwhile Shropshire paid £7,676 in 1909 to rehouse Bridgnorth Grammar School, £10,401 in 1912 on the new Wellington Grammar School, and in all spent £75,110 on new buildings for nine schools between 1909 and 1914.[5] Adams' Grammar School soldiered on with increasing numbers bringing in more income but putting an impossible strain on accommodation.

The Managers had plans for a new laboratory in 1906, which would cost £350. They suggested the cost should be covered by loans from the Company but the Haberdasher representatives privately recommended against this.[6] The Managers then produced a plan for a new Manual Room, Dining Room and two Classrooms costing £1,200. This was authorised by the Board of Education, to be paid for out of capital and repaid by the Managers over 30 years. The Haberdasher Endowed Schools Committee agreed to this, even when the cost rose to £1,700, but nothing was done.[7] Meanwhile, the Managers were having to rent property to keep the school going. By 1908 they had rented no.134 Church Square, across the road from the school. (This was between Hurlstone and Musgrove House, where Tom Collins later lived. Both no.134 and Musgrove House were demolished when the Post Office was built in 1959.) This provided accommodation for Forms I and II (later IIIA and IIIB) and the caretaker, who ran a tuck shop from there. The Haberdashers were eventually persuaded in 1922 to buy it for £516 and sold it in 1931 (for £400) after the new teaching block opened.

To receive support from the state the school had to be recognised as efficient by the Board of Education. After official inspection this was duly given in 1907. It meant a grant for all boys following the four-year course approved by the Board. In addition to that, a new scheme of organisation had to be agreed on, to take the place of the 1878 scheme. The Haberdashers were not happy with this as it diluted their influence, but financially they knew that there was no alternative. Long-drawn-out negotiations resulted in the scheme of 1909. The main difference was that the Managers now numbered 15 instead of 13. As the Haberdashers still appointed seven, they no longer had a majority. Four were appointed by the County Council; two each were still appointed by the ratepayers of Newport and the Urban District Council. The Magistrates were no longer involved. Of the Haberdasher representatives only one – the Master – was *ex officio*. Two others would be London Haberdashers who as long-standing members could take a permanent interest in the School's affairs, and four, as previously, had to live within 10 miles of Newport Church. The fear of hostile County Council nominees did not materialise. W. H. Lander, an Old Novaportan active in county politics and a great supporter of the school, was their first Manager. Otherwise the scheme was very similar to that of 1878. The age range was from eight to 18 or 19 (instead of 17), but the fees were set within the same limits, and the Privileged Area was the same. The Head's stipend was still £150 a year, with a capitation fee of not less than £2 a year for each boy. A limited number of maintenance allowances of £15 a year were available for scholarship boys from elementary schools. No details of curriculum or numbers of pupils were given.

It is noticeable that there is no mention of a girls' school in this scheme. In fact in 1908 Shropshire County Council had asked the Adams' Charity to erect one for 100 girls but the cost would have been so high that, despite the County Council's being prepared to contribute towards it so that both secondary schools would be vested in the Haberdashers' Company, the Company and the Managers decided against the project. It is somewhat surprising that the Managers agreed that a 'Girls' School was not required at Newport at the present time'[8] rather than saying that they could not afford to provide one. A good opportunity was lost because of course a girls' school was needed. Shropshire County Council turned to an existing private school, Merevale College. Ten years later this became the Newport High School for Girls and moved into new buildings on the Wellington Road in 1925.

Adams' raised its fees in accordance with the Council's requirements but the problem of accommodation would not go away. The School was warned several times that the Board of Education's requirements as to buildings must be complied with. Despite being offered the *Old Crow Inn*, 103 High Street (next to the school on the south side) in 1912, the Haberdashers refused to buy it until 1926, but then did not use it for school accommodation. It was later demolished and its site used for the driveway at the side of the school. Luckily Tom Collins had had the foresight, in 1902, to buy the premises on the other side of the school, 117 High Street. This was

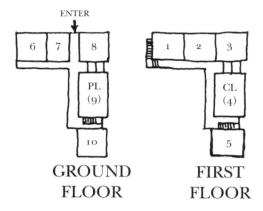

ENTER

| 6 | 7 | 8 |

PL (9)

10

| 1 | 2 | 3 |

CL (4)

5

GROUND FLOOR   FIRST FLOOR

Classroom Block with room numbers in 1929: PL physics laboratory (R9), CL chemistry laboratory (R4). After the new science block was completed in 1960 R9 became the geography room and R4 the art room, the entrance was moved to its present position between R8 and R9, and R7 was enlarged.

occupied by the Boughey family, a firm of saddlers and included many outbuildings at the back, a long orchard and garden. The Haberdasher Governors bought it for £550 in July 1919, the first extension to the school site since its foundation. By December the Headmaster was able to write in the *Novaportan* that the building had been adapted in a most satisfactory manner 'and there is now ample accommodation for the 225 boys attending the school'. This was just as well; Form I had had to use the Parish Room for a few terms.

The new building, known as the Annexe, provided two laboratories for physics (plate 29) and biology, two classrooms for Forms I and II, cloakroom, lavatory, reading room, armoury, bicycle shed and dining hall for the 60 boarders. The only other new accommodation in Shuker's time was the Manual Room, built in 1926. Here woodwork was taught by a local carpenter, and it also served as the Geography Room. It seems the sale of the Woodseaves farm provided a bit more cash for this and the purchase of the *Old Crow Inn.*

It was not until W. S. Brooks took over in 1926 that the Governors made serious efforts to erect new buildings. The Company's architect, Mr N. D. Sheffield, estimated the cost at £9,000. The Charity could only afford £3,000, and privately decided it would have to raise a loan on the Knighton estates, as it could not expect the County Council to make such a large grant. But it did so! £6,000 was voted at first but when the building was opened in July 1929 it had cost £12,500, of which Salop County Council provided £8,500 together with all furnishing and equipment. The new block could accommodate 300 boys in eight classrooms with three laboratories – for chemistry, physics and biology. This is still the main school building. Its corridors were originally open to the air, but were glassed in in the 1960s (plates 30, 33). There was no electricity in the school until 1931.

J. W. Shuker returned to give out the prizes at Speech Day 1929. He recalled an HMI coming into his study and saying, 'Mr Shuker, this is a curious school, you know. If I had to sit down and write a report on the building I should condemn it wholesale. Everything as regards equipment is lacking. But, when I go through it with the boys and masters in, I am conscious that the spirit of work and service is there. When I come to the sports field I am conscious that the spirit of sportsmanship is there in a high degree.' In 1928 the front portico facing the High Street had been glazed in, and the room became the boarders' Dining Room (plate 27). At the same time a building at the side of the Headmaster's garden, the former stables of the *Old Crow*, was converted into a Dining Room for the day boys. It was called the Sykes Room in honour of Lt. Col. H.P. Sykes, Chairman of the Managers. Old buildings at the side of the front lawn were also demolished.

A crisis in boarding occurred in 1933 when the Ecclesiastical Commissioners bought Hurlstone, to be Newport Rectory (plate 31). This had for many years been a boarding house run by Mr and Mrs Gill. The Governors looked into rebuying 134 Church Square or Musgrove House, but did neither. The chemistry lab and geography room above Big School had been converted into dormitories in 1929, but no other provision was made (plate 28).

Mr Brooks kept insisting that more classrooms were needed and that there was a demand for boarding that could not be met. By 1937 the Governors were in active discussion with the LEA; it was even suggested that the Almshouses should be moved elsewhere to provide more room. Plans for a new gymnasium, Assembly Hall, Music Room, Art Room and classrooms were drawn up, finance was agreed (SCC meeting most of the cost), and the lowest tender was accepted in July 1939, but all had to cease on the outbreak of war.[9] The Governors had managed one useful acquisition in 1938: they had bought three cottages in Beaumaris Road whose land backed onto that of 117 High Street. These were later demolished.

The First World War

At the outbreak of war in August 1914 Old Novaportans were quick to enlist. In December 1914 the *Novaportan* published the names of 122 who were serving their country, of whom only eight were in the regular forces. In April 1915, 141 were serving and by December, two hundred. Of these, 162 out of a possible 240 were boys who had been at the school between 1905 and 1914. Conscription in January 1916, of all males aged 18-41, seems to have made very little difference: numbers in April 1916 were 217 and in December, 255. These are those the school knew of and there must have been others. By the time the War Memorial was unveiled in Big School in 1921 it was known that 362 ONs had taken part. The sheer numbers of ONs actively involved in the war had an enormous impact on the school and neighbourhood, but news of wounded and dead began to come through. By December 1915 five had been killed and 11 wounded. The dead included Clifford Grail, School Captain in 1908 and Gordon Budgen, School Captain in 1913, both Careswell Exhibitioners. Clifford was killed at Gallipoli; his letter to school from the troopship at Gibraltar on his way there had been printed in the previous *Novaportan*.

The death toll rose slowly: in July 1916 it was 10; in July 1917, 21; by July 1918, 40. The final number was 45 dead. In addition 77 had been

wounded, some more than once. Most fatalities occurred on the Western
Front (eight in the battle of the Somme), but ONs were also lost at sea, in
the Middle East and at home (fatalities occurred in England during RAF
training). Most of those who died were aged between 21 and 25, the majority in the infantry, and 11 in the King's Shropshire Light Infantry. Nineteen
were officers and six NCOs.

Many Old Boys came back from all parts of the Empire to serve in all
three armed forces. The war seemed to draw them closer to their old school;
many came back to visit, many sent letters and photographs that were
published in the *Novaportan*. J. W. Shuker kept the Roll of Honour of those
who served. He wrote, 'one and all have shown that they have gained
something much more valuable than either book knowledge or skill in
games, viz., a sense of duty and patriotism and a spirit of self-sacrifice in
their country's cause.' The horror of the so-called 'Great War' is made very
clear as the Roll of Honour lengthens in successive issues of the *Novaportan*.
Reports on the exploits of school heroes on the sports field are too often
followed a year or so later by news of their deaths on the battlefield. John
and Bernard Bocking, sons of the Rector of Gnosall, aged 22 and 20, were
killed within four months of each other in 1918. Maurice Cadman, a brilliant and popular member of the school, having gained distinction in his
medical exams at St Thomas' Hospital, London, became a surgeon proba-
tioner in 1918, only two years after leaving school and lost his life in an
accident at sea. There was pride however in the 46 ONs who received war
honours. Major General Ventris was made a Companion of the Order of the
Bath. Among the others were two DSOs, two OBEs, 11 MCs one DFC, five
Croix de Guerre, two DCMs and four MMs. Many gained foreign decorations or were mentioned in dispatches. Two older Old Boys, Lt.-Col.
J.Oldfield RAMC, and Lt.-Col. T.E.Lowe, who joined up with his two sons,
were awarded Territorial Decorations.

The school did what it could to help the war effort. We have already
mentioned the formation of the Cadet Corps. From October 1914 Belgian
refugees were housed at 117 High Street (the Boughey family having moved
to St Mary Street) and three boys attended the school. A school War Relief
Fund was set up, with contributions from staff and pupils. It contributed to
such causes as pipes and tobacco for Soldiers and Sailors, the Red Cross and
Serbian Relief Funds, and Belgian Relief Funds in both Newport and
Gnosall. It also supported a Christmas treat for wives and children of Newport soldiers. No prizes were awarded during the war, certificates and
money being given instead and many boys donated their money to the War
Relief Fund (plate 20). In 1917 the Managers produced a scheme to encourage boys to invest in War Savings Certificates. Boys promised to buy a
certain amount and the Managers bought them, for the boys to pay for in
weekly instalments.

But the strain of war and shortages of many types began to show. There
was a shortage of food – in 1917 the school paddock was dug up to grow

vegetables. The railway service was drastically cut and there was a shortage of paper. The editorial of the *Novaportan* in April 1917 was sad and depressed:

> It seems more than ever difficult, in looking back upon the School life of this term, to see, through the obscuring mists of war time tension and anxiety, even the remnants of the happy irresponsible life, the wholehearted work and play of pre-war days. Calling up papers, medical examinations, and Tribunal Appeals are disturbing factors; and the taste for school sports and academic successes is inevitably dulled by the wormwood draughts which all, in varying measure, have to drink today. At the time of writing, the science of the School is at a standstill, because the War Office has withdrawn all exemptions of schoolmasters classed in the higher medical categories, and – unfortunately for us – Mr Robinson is of their number ... . We do not complain, but an Editorial which is honestly to convey the spirit of the School to readers of today or the future could not ignore such disquieting elements.

Appeals to a Tribunal had become necessary because of a recent decree that men join up at 18, instead of 18 years 7 months if taking examinations. Appeals for postponement were not automatically allowed. This may have been the lowest point. The school had a bad outbreak of measles in April 1918 and in November it was shut for three weeks because of the influenza epidemic. Luckily there were no fatalities.

It was with a heartfelt sense of relief that the boys joined in the Peace Day Celebrations in July 1919. They expended much ingenuity in constructing ships and aeroplanes for the parade. The prize-winning tableau was the Big Four of the Versailles Conference – Lloyd George (England), Clemenceau (France), Wilson (USA) and Orlando (Italy) – represented by some of the smallest boys in the school, heavily disguised.

Old Novaportans

The Old Novaportans Club (the ONC) was formed in 1905 and supported by an enthusiastic hard core of a few dozen Old Boys. It existed mainly for an annual get-together: a dinner which coincided with Speech Day and a cricket match against the school. The Club's events and news of Old Novaportans (ONs) were fully reported in the *Novaportan*. The Club as well as individual ONs presented trophies and prizes to the school. Early attempts to endow a scholarship fund came to nothing, but a Memorial Fund was set up after the First World War to help the sons of ONs and those at university. This took some time to reach its target of £1,000. It set up a memorial tablet in Big School to those who died in the War. In 1930 the ONC acquired its own blazer and badge.

Josiah Oldfield (1863-1953) was the moving spirit in founding the ONC. Son of a blind organist, he became a teacher when he left school at 17, in order to save enough money to go to Oxford. While at university he earned his keep as a council roadman, breaking stones from 5.30 to 7.30 a.m. A man of tireless energy, he took a degree in theology, studied law and was called to the Bar, and then qualified as a doctor at St Bartholomew's Hospital, London. In 1910 he founded the Society for the Abolition of Capital Punishment and wrote many books on penal reform. He was made Doctor of Civil Law by Oxford University. His other great love was vegetarianism. In pamphlets and lectures he was indefatigable in pointing out the benefits of a 'fruitarian' diet (one consisting solely of fruit). As well as being senior physician to several hospitals, he founded a fruitarian hospital and a self-supporting colony nearby for men too old for the labour market. As a young man he had shared rooms with Mahatma Gandhi. He was concerned about the effect of colonial rule on subject peoples and visited India and Jamaica to study this, practising at the Bar in Jamaica as well as England. Sir Oliver Lodge (1851-1940) was the most eminent Old Novaportan; his schoolboy reminiscences have already been related. He left Adams' at the age of 12 and two years later entered his father's business. At the age of 15 he was inspired by a course of science lectures given for working men by Professor John Tyndall of the Royal Institution and resolved to qualify for a London University degree. He was almost 23 before he was able to give up working for his father and study full time. After graduating Lodge made extraordinarily rapid progress, doing teaching and research at University College until the age of 30 in 1881, when he was appointed the first Professor of Physics at Liverpool University. There he did his main scientific work before going to be the first Principal of Birmingham University in 1900 at the invitation of Joseph Chamberlain. He was knighted in 1902.

Lodge's scientific investigations were extensive. By the late 1880s he had become famous following a brilliant lecture on the dispersal of fog by electrostatic precipitation. From this we can trace the development of dust precipitators to reduce fume emissions, developed commercially by two of his sons, as well as the more recent application of electrostatic precipitation in photocopiers and ink-jet printers. Two other sons developed Lodge's work in another field, to produce spark plugs for internal combustion engines. He was one of the first to realise the implication of Hertz's discovery of radio waves in 1888 and demonstrated the detection and transmission of radio waves and their use to convey messages in 1894, two years before Marconi. If he had pressed forward this work instead of being satisfied with a laboratory demonstration we should be speaking of Lodge, not Marconi as the pioneer of radio broadcasting. In a way, this illustrated his approach to science: he started off many things but carried through relatively few to a conclusion. Lodge's other major contribution to science was in 1893 when he devised an ingenious experiment to detect the so-called ether. This had been postulated as an all-pervading medium for transmission of light waves. The result suggested that the ether did not exist and Einstein's Special Theory of Relativity of 1905 showed that the concept of the ether was unnecessary.

However it was Lodge's ideas on the paranormal and psychic phenomena, developed in his early days at Liverpool, which brought him to the notice of the general public. In his book *Raymond* (1916) he claimed to have held conversations with a son who had been killed the previous year. Within three months it was in its seventh edition, eagerly sought by a population trying to come to terms with the carnage of the war. Lodge was a prolific writer on psychic research and, although his many books on the subject were written well after his research days were over, they have tended to obscure his considerable scientific achievements. However, there is no doubt that for many years Sir Oliver Lodge was both the face and voice of British science, not only respected for the quality and breadth of his research work but known for his skills as a brilliant populariser. He represented science to the general public in the way Albert Einstein would do in a later era.

A number of other ONs rose to eminence in their professions at this time: Charles Sylvester Horne (1865-1914) was the youngest son of Charles Horne of the *Newport and Market Drayton Advertiser*. A Pastor of the leading Congregational Church, Whitefield's Tabernacle, London, his eloquent sermons attracted large congregations. A man of great charm and wit, he became Radical MP for Ipswich, the first old boy to be an MP since the 17th century. After his early death the ONs put up a plaque in his memory in Big School. His son, Kenneth Horne, was a very popular broadcaster and comedian in the 1940s and '50s. Francis Ventris, son of the Rector of Church Aston, was one of the few ONs to make a career in the Regular Army. By 1908 he had achieved the rank of Major General, and was made a Companion of the Order of the Bath for his work in the War. Harry Wilson made his career in the Navy. He was Fleet Paymaster by 1911 and made Rear Admiral in 1929. J.E. Quibell we have already met. A leading archaeologist who was a pupil and colleague of Sir Flinders Petrie, and also worked with Howard Carter, he was Keeper of the Egyptian Museum in Cairo from 1913 to 1925. He played host to a number of ONs and indeed many other servicemen who came to Egypt during the War.

Many ONs held responsible positions in the Anglican Church including Gerald Lander who became Bishop of Victoria, Hong Kong, in 1907, while a list of medical men who achieved eminence in all branches of the profession would be very long.

One member of staff deserves a special mention: Frederick Finnis (1852-1928) was Master of the Junior boys from 1878 to 1919 and a worthy successor to Richard Crowther who held that post from 1837 to 1882. He was a kindly, patient teacher, straightforward and generous and a keen sportsman, who organised the School Sports for 48 years. He kept the school playing fields in good condition, even if it meant cutting them personally with a small pony and mowing machine! He was Secretary and Treasurer of the Town Cricket Club from 1904 and was closely associated with the ONC from its beginning. In 1919 he had to retire from teaching because of age, but he continued as Clerk to the Managers (from 1911) and was the Headmaster's Secretary until 1923. Ray Elkes (1922-1931) remembers him coming round the classrooms to collect the subscriptions for the School Games' Club of which he was also Secretary. He was loved and respected by all. The ONC raised money to buy him an annuity and the Haberdashers gave him a pension. On his death the ONC put up a memorial tablet to him above the entrance door in Big School.

Another long-serving employee of the school was 'Soap' Talbott, the school caretaker for 26 years until his death in 1924. A charming poem in the *Novaportan* of July 1925 reveals the deep affection in which he was held by boys and staff alike. His place was filled by Fred, his son, who also acted as the Headmaster's chauffeur. His grandchildren still remember how he and his wife used to make cocoa for the boarders at the Tuck Shop down the alley beside 134 Church Square. Fred, a retired waterways ranger, did not stay long, but his son, A. O. Talbott, after education at Adams' went into the office of the solicitors Liddle and Heane, became their Chief Clerk and was Secretary to the School Governors from 1947 to 1958. He regularly visited Tom Collins to read his letters to him when he was practically blind. In all, a remarkable example of family service to the school.[10]

Life from a Schoolboy's Viewpoint

As well as interviews with several Old Boys who were at school in the 1920s and 1930s, we are fortunate in having some memoires written by earlier pupils. They remember Tom Collins with affection, his infrequent beatings being seen as just, but John 'Willy' Shuker, though widely respected, also instilled fear. He was known as 'The Terror'.

Claude Perry (1908-1912) had a very happy and successful year with Mr Finnis 'but being taught Latin by Mr Shuker was quite a different matter. To begin with because Scholarship boys had their tuition and books free he expected very high results in their class work, and when he issued each scholarship boy with his term cheque (to be given to his parents) he would sneeringly remind the boy of the conditions under which he was able to remain at the Grammar School, with a threat of expulsion if he didn't do better … If there was one trap which Shuker hated a boy to be caught with, it was to translate the Passive voice as if it were Active.' For this there was only one punishment. 'He would shout, "Pearce, fetch my cane". Pearce was a boarder who knew exactly where the Head kept his cane in his study, and was soon handing it over to the raging Headmaster, who would say, "We shall now have a practical demonstration of Active and Passive. Active voice – the Master canes the boy – the Master being the Subject Case exercising the verb canes. The boy is the sufferer and in the Objective Case. Bend over". … Shuker then threw his gown over his shoulder and administered six of the best.' This procedure was repeated to show the boy in the Passive Case. 'The result of this method of teaching caused all the boys to hate the Headmaster and Latin. It also influenced the other schoolmasters with the result that I think I can truthfully say it was not a happy school. The better than average boy may have found his schooldays pleasant to recall but I would say the majority didn't.' Claude left school at 15 to become a telegraphist in the Navy and was mentioned in despatches in the War. He rose to be Lieutenant-Commander in the Second World War.

Sydney Poppitt (1911-1915) also remembered Shuker's formidable temper and his stentorian voice. 'He so scared me when he bellowed in a Latin class that my mind froze up – no doubt giving the impression that I was some sort of a half wit.' Shuker always taught in the library from where his voice could easily be heard in the High Street. The boys knew they had to be extra careful when his gout was troubling him. Ray Elkes (1922-1931) gives a graphic imitation of his Scottish voice – 'Get out of my sight boy!'. He would then banish the offender to the 'donkey pen' behind him – the recess before the door to the small room beyond. (In those days there was only one door, not two as at present.)

An astonishing instance of corporal punishment is given by Sydney Poppitt. As punishment for a misdemeanour during prep (throwing a pear core across the room) a boy aged about 15 had to put his hands over the shoulders of the school porter as if for a piggy back. '…That gentleman leaned forward so that the miscreant's feet left the ground, thereby exposing a substantial area of the wrongdoer's buttocks to the tender mercies of a savagely wielded cane.' On that occasion the boy accepted his punishment with equanimity, actually banging the library door as he went out, at which Shuker, amazingly, did not react. The whole story shows what a completely different world this was from that of the 21st century.

Mr Dyke contributed this, from a staff point of view, to Shuker's obituary in the *Novaportan*: 'Shuker did expect much but never the impossible. A man of few words but sound judgement, no one under him ever doubted the wisdom or justice of his decisions. He kept his own counsels, so that his rare confidences were valued, and in a remarkable degree he had the gift of making his staff feel they mattered greatly in the School's successes. A firm believer in hard work, he did not spare himself, his staff or his boys, but his infectious gratification at the School's achievements was in itself a reward for labour.'

Some memorable members of staff during this period were 'Tad' Dyke, 'Tubby' Gill, 'Jimmy' Kilgour and A.C.Robinson. Tad Dyke instilled a love of literature and drama in many a boy, despite keeping conkers in the sleeve of his gown with which to hit offenders on the head. Tubby Gill would sometimes come up behind a boy and hit him playfully on the bottom. Jimmy Kilgour, a Scot, was seen as idle by most boys. He would get out his newspaper and tell them to get on with their mathematics. He had a way of holding a boy on one side of his face and hitting him on the other so that there was no escape. However, boys good at mathematics found him an encouraging and sympathetic teacher. Once when in charge of a football team at Stafford he called in at the *Bird in Hand* and left the boys to find their own way to the playing fields. They did not see him again that day! 'Robbo' Robinson taught chemistry assiduously, with frequent tests, and was respected as a good teacher. Others included 'Pat' Taylor, junior maths and sport, John Sheldon, physics, and 'Fanny' Mullett, a Danish lady who taught juniors (1918-1932) as did H. P. Johnston who had to retire in 1927 because he was losing his sight. Music teachers came and went, the most outstanding, for his inspirational piano playing, was Mr Veitch. A song composed by him is in the school archive.

Looking back, old boys do not remember class distinctions among the boys. Many from poor backgrounds gained an excellent start in life. Reg Lees (1921-28) lived in a public house in Donnington where he had no privacy for homework, no gas, no electricity and only candlelight to read by. After reading mathematics at Durham, he took up teaching and was Lecturer at Shrewsbury Technical College when he retired. The mother of Maurice Stacey, who became Professor of Chemistry and Dean of the Faculty of Science at Birmingham University, had to take in washing to keep the family going. The most striking example of ability winning through despite adverse circumstances was the Speake family. Four brothers were at the school between 1919 and 1936. Their father was a postman whose round took in the villages of Great Chatwell, Blymhill, Brineton and Orslow, a daily walk of 16 miles. Their mother, who had been in service, took in lodgers to supplement his poor wage. She was determined that her boys would have the opportunities denied to people of her generation and all four gained scholarships to the school. Bill (W.P.) was an outstanding pupil and was Brooks' first School Captain. On Mr Shuker's advice he tried for Cambridge and in 1927 entered St Catharine's College as an Exhibitioner. He spent the war in the Secret Service and was subsequently Secretary to the British delegation to the post-war Red Cross Conference on the conventions of warfare, Principal in the Home Office, and Director of Industrial Relations to the East Midlands Coal Board. He was awarded the O.B.E. Guy (J.G.) read history at Cardiff, gaining his M.A. in 1939. After army service he made his career in residential special schools becoming Headmaster of Petton Hall School, Shropshire. David (G.D.) gained an open scholarship to St Catharine's College, Cambridge, worked on radar in the RAF and became Director of Research at Marconi. He also was awarded the O.B.E. Malcolm (F.M.) was not as academic as the others, but made a good career in the Westminster Bank.

Life at School between the Wars

School started with Assembly at 9 a.m. Farmers' sons would come on horse-back or by pony and trap. Several public houses, such as the *Plume of Feathers*, the *Royal Victoria* and the *Barley Mow* looked after these during the day. One ON remembers jumping off his pony just in time for school, leaving it to find its own way to the back of the *Vic*. Farm labourers' sons would cycle, from such places as Tibberton, Edgmond, Great Chatwell and Lilleshall. A large contingent came by train from the Donnington area, even from Wellington. Some of them got up to high jinks on the train but they all marched in crocodile file to school, arriving just in time. After school they made their own way back, but would have to hurry to catch the 3.50 p.m. train. A few came from the Stafford direction by train.

Under Brooks all assembled in house order on the ground at the back before marching in to Assembly. Registration was in the first lesson. Reg Lees remembers 10 rooms for 10 teachers – no free time for them! French orals were held on the landing just above the entrance to Big School or under the trees outside if the weather was fine. Only sixth formers used the library for private study. It was not used as a library, though a few old reference books were stored in it; the lending library and second-hand book shop were in the small adjoining room. At break and lunch time under Shuker 60 to 80 boys would play football in the narrow space at the back of the school beside the Headmaster's garden. The goals were the school entrance and the gate that led to the gardens at the back (where the 1929 building is). Brooks stopped this and introduced compulsory drill at break, taken by the prefects. This was very unpopular.

At lunch time day boys ate their sandwiches in a room at the back of 134 Church Square, next to the caretaker's house and the tuck shop. After 1928 they had the Sykes Room to eat in. Some went into town, to Elkes' café, as did some staff, but Brooks restricted that liberty to older boys, other day boys had to get an exeat to go into town – buying a book at Bennion and Hornes was a good excuse. Local boys went home, boarders had a hot meal in the semi-basement room at the back of the main building (part of which was the kitchen). After the portico was filled in they ate there. All remember Elkes' cakes and buns that were brought for sale at break, and the teas after matches at Elkes' café (where the Midland Bank now stands).

At the end of school at 3.30p.m. most boys rushed off to the sports fields. Boarders had to be quick to get changed in a smelly room upstairs at no. 134 to be in time for tea at 5.30p.m. It was much easier when the pavilion was built, even though there was no hot water at first.

All town boys had to return for prep with the boarders from 6.00 to 7.30p.m. Claude Perry remembers that he and his brothers always found cold porridge when they got home, because his mother put it on the table at the correct time, but they would stay behind to play football!

Dormitories for the boarders were Spartan. At one time each boy had a chamber pot, but this was soon discontinued. Everyone agreed that Mr Gill's boarders got better food than the Headmaster's, and that Mrs Gill was much more approachable than Mrs Shuker or Mrs Brooks. All boys were inspected before breakfast to see they were washed and tidy and after breakfast they went on a half-hour walk, to Cheney Hill or Chetwynd. The oak-panelled room downstairs in the Headmaster's house was used for boys to recuperate after illness, under Matron's watchful eye; so many boys brought back mumps or German measles after half-term that for a time half-term holidays were cancelled. Baths were on Friday and Saturday nights. There was no school on Saturday. They all went for a long walk in the morning and played football in the afternoon. Boys could go into town to spend their pocket money – they were given 6d. a week. After deducting 1d. for two church services and 1½d. for a letter home, there was only 3½d. left, but you could get a lot of sweets for ½d. On Sundays senior boys went to church twice, juniors once; they marched there and sat at the front while the girls of Merevale College sat at the back! Dress for church was Eton collars, pin-stripe trousers, 'bum freezer' jackets for the smaller boys and longer jackets for the older ones. Young Sydney Preston, who came from Liverpool in 1939, found to his dismay that he was the only boy whose mother had managed to get him the correct short jacket that year! Brooks introduced bowler hats instead of boaters.

A great attraction for boarders and day boys alike was Pat Collins' May Fair. There were lions outside the school, merry-go-rounds, helter-skelters and all sorts of things to be won on the side stalls throughout the town. Stuart Thompstone (1923-28) longed to win a green parrot and crept out at the back entrance (always forbidden to boys), but the caretaker was waiting among the potatoes and caught him in the act. Stuart received five strokes from the Head next day.

Ten

1926 TO 1952
THE SCHOOL UNDER BROOKS AND PETERSON

W.S. Brooks
Headmaster 1926-1946

Mr Brooks set a high standard of discipline and behaviour. Almost immediately after he came the school was recognised as a public school and he expected the boys to behave accordingly. He fostered interest in the arts, not only by creating an Arts VIth but by introducing art and music into the curriculum and encouraging a variety of new activities. He came from Epsom College where he had been housemaster and Modern Languages Master since 1918. He was thus the first Headmaster of Adams' not to have a Classics degree.

Pre-war memories of 'Sam' are mixed: he came with a reputation for caning and there are many memories of this. The injustice of some of his punishments still rankles after 50 or 60 years. Woe betide any boy who was put outside a classroom and found by the Head on one of his many sorties round the school. The younger staff were scared of him, as well as the parents and boys. Despite this he has also been described as a perfect gentleman who set a high standard of conduct. Firm discipline meant no bullying. He could ride roughshod over scholarship boys whose parents had little influence and almost invariably put these boys in the B stream, from which there was no transfer, which could prevent an able boy from continuing to university. However he was very helpful to many whose families fell on hard times when a father died and the widow had to exist on a pension of £1 a week. Such was the case with Charles Quant (1929-36) and Maurice Bourne (1931-38). Charles went on to a successful career in journalism and public service in North Wales and Maurice was helped by Brooks after the War to change to Agricultural Advisory work. Ted Brock (1924-36) owed his career in teaching to Brooks. Ted had worked for two years at Harper Adams as a laboratory assistant, having achieved little at school other than in sport. Mr Brooks called at his house to persuade him to come back to school to run in an athletics match against Priory School. Ted agreed (but did not win!), decided to stay on and eventually qualified for Cheltenham Training College. He later returned to Newport to teach at the Junior School, became Deputy Head at the newly formed Burton Borough School, and in his retirement taught with his wife at Castle House School.

Brooks placed great emphasis on the house system. Houses were now named after their housemasters and each had its distinctive colour, sewn on the school cap. They were: Adams (boarders), orange; Robinson, green;

Dyke, light blue; Taylor, dark blue; and Harman, mauve (added in 1934). Maroon school blazers with blue and gold braid were introduced and eventually made compulsory. Competitions between the houses were no longer only sporting; each in turn produced a play or concert. Military-style drill, introduced during break, was done in house order and there was an inter-house drill competition.

Rugby football was now introduced instead of football. Brooks denied he had done this because rugby was a 'public school' game, but this was widely believed to be the reason. It caused difficulties at first as few other schools played rugby, but Brooks was vindicated as more and more schools took up the game. By 1937 the enthusiasm and good feeling between players and coaches led to a largely successful season. Peter Dawbarn (1929-1938), a very good all-round sportsman, remembers that Mr Humphries taught the 1st XV a Maori-like haka to strengthen their resolve when in difficulties. It went like this:

> Belle Bello Belli Bellus
> What the hell's the matter with us
> Ickey Tikey Crikey Crikey
> Damn Damn Damn

This they chanted under the goal posts at half-time in a match against Denstone. It did wonders for their play, but the Headmaster of Denstone complained of their language to Brooks, so he forbade them to use it again!

Athletics got an additional boost with the return of A. W. C. Johnson to be junior science master in 1929. A pupil at the school from 1912 to 1921, he gained many athletic successes while at University College, Cardiff; he was Victor Ludorum three years running at Cardiff and first in the Inter-Varsity Cross Country Race in 1924. It is not surprising that he was an enthusiastic athletics coach on his return and it was probably due to him that an Athletics Club was formed. He organised the first cross-country match against Harper Adams in 1931 and sent many boys to inter-school meetings. He was always known as 'Joby' Johnson.

Mr and Mrs Brooks were personally very keen on the arts and were friendly with several well-known artists. Among these was Gertrude Hermes (1901-1983), wood engraver and sculptor. When Tom Collins died Brooks commissioned her to sculpt a lectern in his memory. This was presented to the school in 1936 by Josiah Oldfield on behalf of the Old Novaportans. It was exhibited in 1938 at an Exhibition of Contemporary Arts and Crafts at Burlington House, London, but it fell into disuse and lay unrecognised in a store until it was found and used by David Taylor (it was too tall for most people!). Its importance was only realised when the Royal Academy asked to borrow it in 1981 for an Eightieth Birthday Exhibition of her work. It could have been through her that Brooks got Agnes Miller Parker to be art teacher at the school from 1933-1936. She

and her husband had both worked with Gertrude Hermes and her husband at the Gregynog Press near Newtown in Wales. Agnes was one of the
most admired wood-engravers of the 20th century, renowned for her book
illustrations (see pp.107, 130, 152, 206).

In 1933, a new club restricted to 12 senior boys, was formed to study
plays outside the school curriculum. At Brooks' suggestion it was called the
Turk's Head Club. This name continued to be used for school plays and for
a printing press started under Peterson until well into the 1980s. He presumably chose the name as the *Turk's Head* was the meeting place of 'The Club'
set up by Dr Samuel Johnson and his friends in London for literary and
intellectual discussions.

In 1935 Mr C.W.S. Dixon, School Manager, local antiquarian and manager of Barclays' Bank, presented the Dixon Cup to commemorate 25 years
of association with the school. This was a house challenge cup for achievement in art, literature and music but during the war it was awarded for
school work. The Debating Society was revived as well as an élite Wrangler
Society for informal discussion on topical events. The first discussion was
led by Koenigsberger on 'Hitler and his Ideals'. Many other clubs came and
went, e.g. Cycling Club, Philatelic Society, Scientific Society and Chess
Club.

Up to the end of 1932 the only music taught in the school was one lesson
a week for forms I, IIA and IIB (by the French mistress) but with the
appointment of the first music master musical activities increased. A school
orchestra and choir gave concerts and professional musicians gave recitals
to the boys. A Music Club met to hear gramophone records of classical
music.

There was a scare in November 1936 when fire broke out on the ground
floor and spread up the stairs to Big School. A boarder in the dormitory
above raised the alarm and staff and boys worked hard to contain it until
the fire brigade arrived. Lessons had to be in the Parish Room and the
Council Offices for six months. Burn marks from the blaze can still be seen
on some of the woodwork inside Big School to the left of the entrance.

The 1929 Smoking Case

An incident in which W.S. Brooks caned a boy for smoking in the street
made legal history. On 6 December 1928 Frank Wright, aged nearly 16
and due to leave school at the end of the term, was seen by a prefect
smoking with another boy in the street after school. The next morning
after Assembly the Head dismissed the lower school and called the two
boys out to the front. He said they had been reported for smoking in the
street. When they admitted it he said he was going to cane them for
breaking a school rule. Wright refused outright and tried to escape up the
library steps, but his way was barred by prefects. The Head ordered two
members of staff, Mr Harman and Mr Lowe, to bring him back for his
punishment. He struggled so much that his coat was torn in the process.

They held him over a desk, kicking violently, while the Head caned him three times. He accepted his fourth stroke without restraint, but then threw himself 'bellowing' on the floor. Meanwhile the Head caned Williams, the younger boy, and turned back to administer one more stroke to Wright. Both boys then apologised to the school for letting down the school by their behaviour. Wright went straight home, told his father and showed him his injuries. Ernest Wright was the owner of a garage and the town Picture House in Stafford Street. He was Chairman of Newport Urban District Council and a Magistrate. He immediately went to see Brooks to complain of the brutal treatment of his son. He said he allowed his son to smoke, and on this occasion he and his friend had been on an errand after school to collect some cases of films from the station. The operator of the Picture House had given each boy a cigarette when they brought him the cases. As it was well out of school hours he considered the boys were no longer under the school's jurisdiction. He contended his son knew nothing of a school rule forbidding smoking and if he had known about such a rule he would not have allowed him to smoke. Brooks, for his part, maintained he must punish a boy for behaving in a way unsuitable for a grammar school. He said there was no written rule forbidding smoking but he was constantly telling boys they must act in a decent manner. Ernest Wright later said Brooks was scared of him and apologised for caning the boy, but Brooks denied this. The upshot was that in February 1929 Wright brought a charge of assault against the three masters in the Magistrates Court. Evidence was brought that the boy knew smoking was not allowed. The magistrates decided the Headmaster had acted within his rights in punishing a boy for action outside school premises and the punishment was reasonable. They dismissed the case. Wright then took the case to the Court of the King's Bench presided over by the Lord Chief Justice. He claimed the schoolmasters had no authority to make and enforce a rule about acts done beyond the precincts of the school and in public, and that they therefore had no defence to a charge of assault. But the judges argued that a parent sending a boy to school authorised the schoolmaster to administer reasonable punishment for breach of a school rule. The punishment administered was reasonable and the case was dismissed.

The case reached the national newspapers. The town (and country) was divided: some declared Brooks was far too free with the cane, some that he must uphold the standard of behaviour in the school. Presents of cigarettes were posted to the Wright family. It must be remembered that smoking was accepted throughout society then and its health implications not fully understood. The School Managers stood firmly beside their Headmaster.

This judgement of the High Court is recorded in educational law books, but it must be said that if it were tried again today Mr Wright would win his case. Corporal punishment of a pupil by a teacher is now illegal under the Education Act of 1986 but the authority of a school to punish its pupils outside school is still a grey area.

Refugees from Nazi Germany

With the rise of Nazi rule in Germany after 1933 many refugees fled to England. Surprisingly, several found their way to Adams'. The Koenigsbergers deserve special mention. Being Lutherans they were not aware of their Jewish ancestry until Nazi propaganda turned others against them and they were gradually forced to realise there was no future for them in Germany. Helmut (H.G.) entered Adams' in 1934 aged 15. His brother knew Dr Quibell in Cairo and his mother met Dr Pooler in Derbyshire, both of whom recommended their old school. He played a full part in the life of the school, as scrum half in the 1st XV, in the astronomical society and the orchestra. He won an Exhibition to Caius College, Cambridge to study history, served in the Royal Navy during the war and became Professor of Modern History at Nottingham and then at University College, London. He was a well-known authority on Philip II of Spain. His cousin, Peter (H. P.), followed two years later. His English was very poor when he arrived, but he was awarded a Law Society Scholarship in 1939, so he must have made rapid progress. His parents moved their business from Saxony to Ireland early in 1939. Peter was interned on returning from there soon after war broke out and was moved to Australia, from where he joined the Forces. After the war he continued his law career in England. He hated the food at Adams', but 'the teachers were a revelation after the stodgily distant martinets in Germany'. Konrad his brother joined him in January 1939. At school in Germany he had indignantly exclaimed, 'I am not a Jew' when told by his Nazi Headmaster he should be particularly careful, as a Jew, to obey school rules. This was held to be 'trying to hide his Jewishness' and he was expelled. At Adams' he was demoted from his prefect's duties, not because of his Jewishness, but because one Sunday he decided to go to the Congregational church with his friend John Ward, instead of to the compulsory Anglican service (which he found boring). The Headmaster had not been consulted, so even when his parents wrote to ask for him to change his religious attendance the request came too late! As a refugee when the war started he got a passage to the U.S. where he could join relatives, although his first ship was torpedoed. He became a Christian missionary and an academic in Thailand.

World War II

Old Novaportans

No school magazines were published during the Second World War so we have no account of who served, nor any descriptions of wartime experiences such as we have for the First World War. Conscription was introduced immediately the war began so there was no heroic volunteering as there had been in 1914. The only names we know for certain are those who gave their lives for their country, recorded on the memorial plaque set up in Big School in 1948 by the Old Novaportan Club. Cerdic Warrillow (1948-55) has transcribed the Commonwealth War Graves Commission burial records of 27 of these; they were serving in all areas of the war worldwide. Perhaps surprisingly only four of them came from Newport itself. Many more ONs must have served in all these theatres of war. Some, such as Peter Dawbarn, were thrown into combat with a minimum of training. He was trained as a bomber pilot but fighters were needed so at the age of 19 he was posted to France in May 1940 with a squadron of Hurricanes. On their first engagement they lost their Flight Commander and Sergeant Pilot. Soon afterwards, returning from a mission over France, his engine failed and he crash-landed in a field and hit a tree. His face swelled up so that he could not see. He got out of the burning plane, heard a horse galloping round and feared he would be trampled on. Luckily an Air Raid Warden rescued him, not knowing whether he was German or British. He spent the next six months in hospital, returned to duty and survived the war.

Two very different wartime experiences, those of Geoffrey Purslow and Maurice Jones, must act as representatives for all those anonymous ONs who experienced danger in defence of their country's freedom.

As a boarder from 1926 to 1935 Geoffrey Purslow played a full part in school life. He was in the first cricket and rugby teams, took part in school plays and was active in the Debating Society. He became Captain of his House and Head Prefect. A High School girl at the time describes him as 'very charming and a complete gentleman'. After completing his medical studies at Birmingham he joined the Merchant Navy and became surgeon on the *Laconia*.

On 12 September 1942 the *Laconia* was sailing along the west coast of Africa bound for Freetown (Sierra Leone) with a load of several thousand Italian prisoners when it was torpedoed by a German U-boat. What happened then has been recounted with amazing recall and in harrowing detail by Doris Hawkins, a nursing sister on the ship.[1] Some of the survivors were rescued by the U-boat but had to be returned to the sea when it was attacked by an Allied plane. Doris Hawkins managed to get on board one of only two lifeboats available with 67 others, including the young ship's surgeon, Dr Geoffrey Purslow.

The 30-foot wooden boat had 68 people packed inside it with five oars and no rudder. The U-boat Commander, before submerging, had told them that the nearest land was 600 miles away. The boat leaked so that water had to be pumped out continuously, there was no room to move, it was pitilessly hot during the day and dreadfully cold at night. Many had virtually no clothing. They had 15 gallons of drinking water and Dr Purslow took charge of that and of their meagre food supply. They took turns at rowing, but each day they became weaker until it had to be discontinued. As their journey continued their numbers decreased: each day someone died. 'One wondered how long one could remain sane.' On 27 September the survivors saw a three-funnelled ship about four miles away, but it did not see them. The disappointment and dejection was profound but they realised that they were nearing a shipping lane so that another boat might soon appear.

The saltiness of the sea water produced sores, septic fingers and toes. Doris Hawkins describes how she and Dr Purslow opened up sores with a pen-knife to let them discharge. Eventually Dr Purslow himself developed severe blood poisoning, and became too weak to continue his task of distributing rations.

Doris Hawkins writes 'One morning, about nineteen weary days after the ship was torpedoed, I heard voices, and after a while realised that one was his. Although I could not hear exactly what was being said I gathered that, realising he was a potential source of infection to the rest of us, Dr Purslow had come to a great decision.' In a voice stronger than she had heard from him for many days he said '"As I cannot be of any further help, and if I am now a source of danger to you all, it is better that I should go."' Whereupon he heaved himself up to the side of the boat, said goodbye and took a final step backward. The sea closed over him. Doris recalled that as he departed she recovered her voice to say '"Greater love hath no man than this, that a man lay down his life for his friends."'

Twenty-seven days after being torpedoed, their small craft beached on the coast of Liberia. There were 16 survivors out of the original sixty-eight.

Maurice Jones left Adams' in 1939 at the age of 16 and, as soon as he was old enough, he joined the King's Shropshire Light Infantry (KSLI). He saw service in North Africa and Italy but on 4 October 1944 he was captured by the retreating Germans in northern Italy and taken to Stalag VIIIB at Lambinowice (German name Lamsdorf) near the town of Opole in southern Poland. Conditions in the camp were unpleasant but improved significantly by the Red Cross which was allowed to send food parcels and other items such as record players and records. Without Red Cross food parcels, many of his comrades would have died. New Year 1945 opened with blue skies, deep snow and a bitterly cold wind, with a temperature of minus 35°C. The war was going badly for the Germans and the Russian army was advancing rapidly through Poland. On 22 January the prisoners were each allocated a blanket, a Red Cross food parcel and a loaf of bread to be shared between two, and marched out of the camp in columns of two thousand.[2] As they marched west, German troops passed by heading eastwards, forcing them off the road into the deep snow. They marched continuously for ten days to reach Stalag VIIIA, some 150 miles away at Gorlitz, just inside the German border. After the first five days their food rations had been eaten; for the next five days they had nothing. They were allowed only a short halt of about five hours each night, huddled together in some farm or derelict building, but were often too exhausted to sleep. Many could not keep up the rapid pace demanded of them over the frozen, rutted snow and risked being shot by the guards. Some of the men decided that the column must walk at the speed of the slowest, to avoid stragglers, so on the sixth morning five of them, including Maurice, in the first rank of the column, proceeded at a much more sedate pace than previously. Despite the fury of the guards at the front of the column, this slower rate of progress was eventually accepted, much to the relief of those at the rear.

After several days at Gorlitz, the march was resumed. A thaw made marching easier, but soon a severe drop in temperature brought ice and bitterly cold winds. After one particularly cold night Maurice found his boots frozen solid so that he had the utmost difficulty in forcing his swollen feet back into them. He kept his boots on overnight after that. Food was scarce though rarely absent, their scanty rations consisting of thin watery soup, some bread and a small cube of margarine. When they passed by Dresden, recently almost completely destroyed by Allied bombing, the guard was doubled and the prisoners were told to march in silence at a quicker pace to protect them against possible reprisals by embittered civilians. However, by the time they reached Weimar their condition was so poor that the local population provided them with extra bread, hot soup and coffee. 'Deutschland kaput' was now on the lips of many civilians. In a small village a woman managed furtively to pass a newspaper to one of the men from which they gathered that the war could not last much longer. This gave them hope that they might survive.

As they continued their westward march the column became smaller as malnutrition and exhaustion took their toll, with men dying where they stopped overnight and by the roadside during the day. The fight against death is a mental as well as a physical one and Maurice was determined to survive, believing that if he could reach a British hospital he would live.

They eventually reached Duderstadt, a small town some 16 miles east of Gottingen, where they were accommodated in a brick factory with little shelter and even less food. During the next seven days men continued to die each night, their bodies being removed before the others stirred next morning. On 9 April the Americans were so near that their German captors abandoned them. They were now alone, they had had no food for 24 hours and for most of them life and spirit were running out; they just wanted to go to sleep and not wake up. But at midday there was a commotion outside, one of their number struggled to the window and shouted, 'There's a Sherman tank coming down the road'. They chose an American prisoner to go and greet it, for his uniform would be recognised. The survivors were conveyed to Kassel to an American tented hospital; for several hours Maurice was ignored because the American nurses thought the eagles on the sleeves of his RAF tunic were German ones! On returning to England, Maurice spent over six months recuperating in the Royal Salop Infirmary, Shrewsbury. His hair was so long that in those 'short back and sides' days he was mistaken for a woman!

Maurice had endured and survived what has since been labelled 'The Death March'. Thousands set out but only hundreds survived. The figures, understandably, are imprecise but the *Daily Telegraph* report of 13 April 1945 says: 'From Gorlitz 3 columns of 2000 men each set out marching

westwards. Today there are only 449 including 104 British at Duderstadt.'
Old Novaportan, Maurice Jones, was one of them.

World War II in School

The war made an impact on the life of the school with the evacuation to
Newport of Holly Lodge School, Smethwick on 1 September 1939, two days
before war was declared. 294 boys came by train with their Headmaster and
twenty staff, along with seven wives and 10 mothers. They used the school
in the afternoons and early evenings while Adams' used it in the mornings,
including Saturdays. Adams' pupils spent the afternoons in a variety of
activities involving music, science, literature and, of course, games. The
Parish Room and the British Schoolroom on the Wellington Road as well
as Musgrove House and the ballroom of the Town Hall were pressed into
service. This did not last long: boys began drifting back to Smethwick and
Holly Lodge officially returned in March 1940. The expected aerial bom-
bardment of the Black Country had not materialised and most families
preferred to be together at home. At the same time 148 boys and girls from
Corbett Street Junior and Infant School, Smethwick had also been sent to
Newport, which caused disruption at Newport Junior School. All these
pupils had to be billeted on Newport families so there was a general sense
of relief when, except for a very few, the visitors went home.

Clothes rationing made it impossible to enforce the school uniform of
grey suit for schooldays and black jacket and pinstriped trousers for Sundays
but every effort was made to ensure that all boys had a school tie and cap.
Andrew Casewell's grandmother made him a cap as Whitmore's had sold
out. Every boy had to carry his gas mask with him at all times. The school
windows were taped across to prevent splintering if a bomb fell near and
blackout curtains ensured no light showed outside. No outside bell was rung
– that would have been the sign that the invasion had begun – so changes
of lessons were announced by hand bell. Newport itself was not in real
danger from the air, but enemy planes could be heard overhead on their
way to Liverpool. Two air-raid shelters were built and there were air-raid
practices and fire practices. Martin Likeman remembers water battles on
summer Saturday evenings after fire practice was over. 'The boarder prefects headed two teams, one on each lawn armed with stirrup pumps and
supplied by chains of buckets of water. Everyone wore rugger kit with
pumps [trainers] and got thoroughly soaked. The general technique seemed
to be to squirt the opposition pump man and so disrupt the enemy fire
power as much as possible.'

The school took part in special weeks, such as Wings for Victory Week
and Warship Week, held to encourage people to buy National Savings
Certificates to help the war effort. Boys enjoyed missing lessons to do agricultural work, for which they were paid! Lorries would pick them up from school
to pick potatoes, hoe cabbages or single beet, sometimes in school time,
sometimes at weekends. In the holidays many boys helped on local farms.

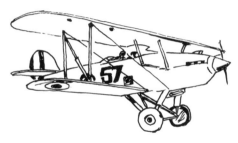

A Hawker Hart biplane.

In 1941 an Air Training Corps squadron was set up at the school, open to all boys in the town. This was run after school hours by L. W. Taylor and J. Sheldon. Class instruction was given in astro-navigation, Morse code and aircraft recognition (using cards) and there was a certain amount of drill. Highlights at weekends were flights from RAF aerodromes at Wheaton Aston and Tern Hill. There were lectures by visiting speakers and the RAF recruiting officer. At this time a biplane, possibly a Hawker Hart, was parked in the playground at the back of the air-raid shelter. There is no record of where it came from. ONs remember clambering into the cockpit imagining themselves as Battle of Britain pilots. It became a joke to tip it forward onto its nose; one member of the School Rugby Team convinced a visiting school that it had crash-landed there and the school had had a lucky escape. It seems it was gradually denuded of its canvas body by passing boys. We do not know when it finally ceased to exist. The World War I howitzer was still on the front lawn in 1941; it was probably taken away for scrap shortly afterwards. Boys who did not join the ATC had to 'Dig for Victory', producing vegetables at the back of the school just as their predecessors had done during World War I. Mr Brooks' personal contribution to the war effort was to command the Newport Company of the Home Guard. After the war, the ONC had tennis courts made as a War Memorial.

The main effect of the war was that younger staff left to join the forces and women and older men took their place. 'Tubby' Gill, who had retired in 1935, returned to teach geography and woodwork. Others continued after they would otherwise have retired and several died in harness. Of the female staff the one who was remembered with most affection was Miss Abrams (known as Old Fogey), who took over the Prep department early in the war. She supervised the junior boarders in the Annexe from her flat at the front of the building. She would invite boys to listen on her wireless to 'Dick Barton, Special Agent', an extremely popular cliff-hanging radio serial. Radios were rare in those days, certainly no boarder had one, so this was a real treat. She had her breakfast with the boarders and took them out on long walks at the weekend. She was known to help boys if they were in difficulties with their English or maths, and was also remembered by many for her inspirational teaching of English. She retired as Head of the English Department in 1949. Eric Cliffe, a charismatic music master and piano-player, was succeeded by a series of female teachers when he left to join the Army. When he returned in 1946 he was emaciated from years as a Japanese prisoner-of-war. The boys responded with horror-struck sympathy. He wrote a fascinating account in the *Novaportan* of July 1946 of how he and fellow musicians were allowed to organise makeshift orchestras in successive prison camps, creating instruments out of whatever was available.

One result of staff shortage was that Brooks allowed two girls from the High School to attend chemistry and physics lessons at Adams' as there were none at the High School. One girl stayed only one day, which left Margaret Davies alone. She studied in the class for two years, on condition that she never spoke to the boys and left immediately the lesson ended. There was no biology teacher at either school able to teach botany and zoology separately, so the pre-medic boys and Margaret cycled to Harper Adams for this. Margaret's father was a lecturer there, so it was probably he who persuaded Brooks to allow such an innovation. She later married Ken Coulson, whom she first met at the school and claims to be the first female ON!

Life as a boarder during the war continued much as before. Two dormitories in the Annexe housing six and 14 boys were supervised from the staff flat overlooking the High Street. The three dormitories under the direct control of the Headmaster were on the top floor of the old building above Big School. Dormitory A, the largest, was central, having windows giving onto the back of the school and overlooking the balcony at the front. Dormitory B, accessible direct from the Headmaster's house, was at one end, and Dormitory C, the smallest, at the front of the old Usher's house. Brooks' excursions to see that boys had settled down were preceded by the smell of his cigar smoke, so there was a little time to rush back into bed. Each boy had a drawer in a chest of drawers, but there were no chairs to sit on. Boys made their own beds and swept the floor. The maids prepared the food. In effect, the prefects ran the boarding houses and could enforce correct behaviour with a slap or two on the behind with a slipper.

ON's main memories are of poor food and the cold! Sydney Preston and Raymond Holland remember the last 'Boar's Head Feast' in Big School in December 1939. This was followed by a master telling ghost stories by candlelight from the library steps. It seems the boar's head was made of brawn on this occasion. Ken Coulson remembers its revival in 1945 when it was made of Spam (tinned meat) beneath a cardboard head! We have no other record of this tradition. Food was in short supply but there seems to have been unlimited amounts of brown bread (called National Bread) available. Boys collected their own cheese and jam ration from Midgley's in Lower Bar and it was up to them to make it last until the next ration was due. Some jam was kept so long it grew interesting multi-coloured mould! Frank Newton preferred Women's Institute damson jam to bought strawberry as it tasted stronger and you could suck the stones. Porridge was traditionally lumpy. At bedtime cocoa and bread and dripping were supplied. Those on duty had to be up at 6 a.m. to peel the potatoes for midday dinner. (The day boys, who had their cooked dinner at a different sitting from the boarders, had to peel their potatoes the day before, under the stairs up to Big School.) Italian prisoners-of-war were drafted into the kitchen in

1942/43 to help with the washing up, later doing some of the cooking. Mrs 'Bunty' Brooks could be seen up the High Street with an Italian prisoner-of-war in tow carrying her shopping. Towards the end of the war some boys found the Headmaster's cellar was well stocked with tinned food. They would creep down the main stairs at night, past the maids' rooms, and take a tin or two. No retribution followed. There was no tuck shop during the war. Boys could get burnt buns at Elkes' shop – they suspected that these were sometimes overcooked deliberately! Day boys who shared their packed lunch sandwiches with hungry boarders were very popular, but the fillings, such as lettuce or beetroot, would not be considered very enticing now. Day boys ate their sandwiches in Big School or sometimes in their form rooms. The Sykes Room by now acted as a common room for boarders, where they kept their sports gear. It had a coke stove in it on which they could roast chestnuts and make toast.

Fresh air was the order of the day, even to the extent of having snow blowing in on one's bed in the dormitory! The Annexe was particularly cold: boys would leave bottles filled with water overnight to see whose had cracked in the morning because the water had turned to ice. In hot weather Ian Byrd recalls they were allowed to take their beds out onto the balcony from A Dormitory and sleep in the open air. Shortage of fuel, even after the war had ended, was such that there was no hot water except at weekends, and no heating. Baths were taken twice a week, in the regulation four inches of water, and later only once a week. Sheets were changed once a month.

There were no activities outside school hours except for practice on the sports field. Staff who were supposedly in charge of rugby put in very few appearances, but 'Joby' Johnson regularly came to encourage athletics. One season Brooks cancelled all cricket fixtures after a particularly bad defeat by Stafford Grammar School. There was no member of staff to coach the boys. Boarders' activities were physical: long walks or even a fight for Lilleshall Hill, organised by a prefect. In the summer there could be swimming at Stafford baths and enterprising boys and girls still swam in Moss Pool near Forton. There were few books to read for relaxation.

Life was enlivened by the occasional high jinks: Sydney Preston remembers dancing naked on the balcony one night, in full view of any passer-by, and then trying desperately to get in again as the other boys held the window shut against him. An initiation test in the big Annexe Dormitory was to swing right across the room on the bars that held the roof up. One boy was caught in the middle when Miss Abrams was heard approaching. He panicked and dropped onto a bed – luckily without injury. Boys in the Annexe would let down a shoe on a rope and swing it so that it knocked on the back door of the almshouse; they hoisted it smartly upwards when the old lady came to the door! Alan Holland as the youngest in A Dormitory had so many 'apple pie' beds made for him he gave up bothering about them and learned to sleep curled up. Frank Newton remembers how boys from A Dormitory got under the clock turret by picking the lock and poured water down the bell rope to drench the boy ringing the bell in Big School. This must have been after the war ended. He describes the last Sunday of term as 'Bawling Sunday'. Attendance at church was, of course, compulsory. The boys would sing the last hymn very loudly but stay silent on the penultimate line. This was very disconcerting for the choir, and indeed the congregation!

Boarders all remember severe winters when they were alone in the school, as there was no heating and day boys remained at home. The worst crisis was in the spring of 1947. Although the war was over rationing continued and there was no fuel for heating. Sliding on the frozen canal, shovelling snow and snowball fights all increased the feeling of comradeship. David Basford remembers his amazement on returning after Christmas that year to find the new Headmaster and Mrs Peterson joining with the prefects and boys in sliding right across the front of the school, some dropping over the edge into the yard behind the Annexe. This had been sacrosanct territory up to then.

A.D.C. Peterson O.B.E.
Headmaster 1946-1952

W.S. Brooks retired in 1946 to become ordained and was for many years a chaplain in the south of France. He died in 1963. A. D. C. Peterson was a completely different character. After reading Classics at Oxford he had spent two years in industry before teaching at Shrewsbury School. During the war he served in the Far East, becoming Deputy Director of Psychological Warfare on the staff of Earl Mountbatten. When he arrived he was 38 and his new wife Corinna was 23. Traditionalists expected a martinet but what they got was an intellectual, an idealist who believed in the innate goodness of mankind. He fostered self-discipline through example, not the use of the cane. This was a shock to everyone; some boys revelled in the freedom and responsibility now offered them, but some became disorderly. Peterson found he had to use the cane occasionally, but he did so reluctantly and never in public. He took an active part in school life and he and his wife would have boarders round to Sunday tea. The atmosphere in boarding became more relaxed. The Petersons had three children over the years and some older boys almost became part of their extended family. One of them, Nigel Bromage, gave his tribute at Peterson's memorial service in 1988: 'It is no exaggeration to say that in six years Alex transformed the school. His vision, drive and vigour acted as a spur to all but especially the boys ... For those of us who were privileged to live through this striking transition, it was heady stuff. I have no doubt that the values he taught us and the respect for others he imbued in us influenced all of us who were lucky enough to have our lives run briefly alongside his.'

Although Peterson threw himself with enthusiasm into school life, the wider world had its attractions. He was recognised as an authority on the Far East, writing and broadcasting about it. In 1952 he was asked by

General Sir Gerald Templer, High Commissioner for Malaya, to come out for three months to advise on the Communist threat there. On his return he accepted a two-year post as Director General of Information Services in the Federation of Malaya, and resigned from Adams' at half-term that year. He subsequently became Headmaster of Dover College, Head of the Department of Education at Oxford University, and a great supporter of the broad-based International Baccalaureat as the final school exam instead of A level.

Mrs Peterson kindly allowed us to see her late husband's private memoires of his time at Adams'. He recollected a school that had been allowed to run down during the war years so that academic and sporting achievements were poor. There was no school secretary, not even a list of boys – the first day he sent the head prefect round to each classroom to compile one. The school was heated by an inefficient antiquated boiler, and Brooks had allowed the supply of coke to run low, possibly because he did not want unsightly piles of it in the yard for his last Speech Day. From January to March 1947 Shropshire was snowbound in the worst winter of the century. The coke soon ran out and there was no means of heating the school. Day boys stayed at home, boarders shivered, but the school doctor said they had never been healthier.

Brooks had kept the County at arm's length, sometimes even ignoring the new catchment areas, but Peterson knew Martin Wilson, the County Director of Education, as an old friend. They willingly co-operated together in the County Development Plan which was put forward as a result of the 1944 Education Act. Peterson saw the Haberdasher Governors, though well disposed, as too far away to make much contribution to the school's development, but found the active Chairman of Governors, T. C. Ward, a great ally. His aim was for Adams' to take its place as a bridge between the predominantly boarding public schools and the day schools under the local authority. He soon employed a secretary, Evelyn Lucas, who shared his office at the front of what had been the Usher's house. She recalls that he always asked her to leave the room if he had to give 'the whack'. She would go across to Matron's room and when she saw a boy walking past holding his posterior she knew it was safe to go back! Her desk was near the window which she kept open on warm days. Sixth-formers would creep up to the window and beg for cigarettes!

Peterson encouraged boys to broaden their outlook; art and music flourished. The last period on a Wednesday was devoted to cultural activities. Room 10 was converted into a Current Affairs Room, managed by the fifth forms; French Impressionist paintings, borrowed through a County scheme, were hung on the walls. As a result many boys developed a lifelong interest in art. The Sixth Form Common Room was moved to the Sykes Room so that the library could be used for teaching and private study. Numbers of lessons increased to allow all the Lower Sixth to take a course in economics and geography, and the Upper Sixth to take political science. All boys were soon able to have a cooked midday meal brought in containers from a central kitchen in the new canteen built by the LEA by the Beaumaris Road entrance. Thus the boarding houses were responsible only for breakfast and evening meal. Music flourished under the talented leadership of Mr Cliffe. A Newport Music Club, open to townspeople, provided several professional concerts a year.

The Turk's Head Club became very active with full productions as well as play readings. They broke new ground when in March 1948 *Laburnum Grove* by J. B. Priestley was produced with ladies in the cast, including Miss Lucas, the school secretary. The Headmaster himself took the role of the Angel in *Tobias and the Angel* in 1949, when girls from the High School were also involved. The Dixon Cup, the Debating Society and the Chess Club all came to life again, with many new societies as well, such as the Gardening Club. The Turk's Head Press printed programmes, fixture cards and menus on an antiquated press brought back from Secret Service use in the war.

Boys attended biology classes at the High School where they had a specialist teacher, so there was no need to go to Harper Adams any more, but co-operation extended also to joint ballroom dancing lessons there after school – a common feature in many sixth forms of that era.

The school also revived academically. Two boys gained Open Scholarships in Modern Languages at Queen's College, Oxford, having been tutored in Italian by the Headmaster and in English by his wife. The transition from School Certificate and Higher School Certificate to Ordinary and Advanced Level General Certificate of Education (GCE) in 1951 was made smoothly.

A full inspection by H. M. Inspectors in October 1947 gave a generally favourable report. There were 284 pupils, of whom 71 were boarders, compared with 232 with 58 boarders at the last inspection in 1930. There were 14 full-time staff and one visiting mistress for art. There were two forms in each year, the boys being streamed after the first year. The A stream took separate physics and chemistry for School Certificate, the B stream taking general science (as we saw in the 1920s). Art was taught to the first two years and one third year only; there was no specialist art room. 32 boys were in the sixth form, of whom more took science than arts subjects. The inspectors reported that the school's greatest need was a gymnasium and a hard-surfaced playground outside for physical education. Big School had been declared unsafe for exercise. House P. E. was currently being taken by boys under a master's supervision, for which the boys 'do not change into gymnastic kit or shoes, but with jackets removed, spread out over the paths beyond the school and perform a few movements in a listless manner'. This was likely to produce distaste for exercise. Games was time-tabled only once a fortnight. Plenty of boys stayed to play after school but this was voluntary and not all could do so. The other pressing need was for improvement in the library, which contained about one thousand books. Non-fiction was open only to the Upper School but many subjects taken at sixth-form level

were hardly represented at all. It was noted that the first medical inspection had taken place in 1946.

The school could do nothing about the lack of a gymnasium, but new staff were able to bring fresh impetus to many subjects. One of these was A. W. Harding, geography, who had known Peterson in the army, having been involved in Intelligence work in the Far East. He became a popular institution, retiring from teaching in 1981. He organised the first school foreign visit: he took 49 boys to Switzerland in 1949. In July 1951 the Headmaster and five members of staff took about half the school (154 boys) by rail to the Festival of Britain in London. Going on the Underground was in itself an exciting experience.

The first Physical Training master, Mr Ashurst, was appointed in 1948; he also taught history. He took classes in the Parish Room as there was no gym at school. J. L. Guise, former Middlesex and Oxford cricketer, soon made an improvement in the school's cricket performances. He had a practice concrete wicket laid down. The return of R. H. Anderson from his service in the RAF made a vast difference to school rugby as well as French. He was an effective player himself and a great supporter of the newly formed Newport Rugby Club, many of whose players were ONs. A. W. C. Johnson continued to nurture athletics, which was the one sport that had continued well throughout the war. All this led to the *annus mirabilis* of 1950/51 when the athletics team won all their fixtures, the cricket team won or drew every match for two seasons, and the rugby team had an unbroken series of 18 victories. They scored 463 points to their opponents' 50! Six AGS boys played rugby for Staffordshire (there was no Shropshire team then), and M. Bromage and J. W. Reece played for the Midlands against the Home Counties. They were both selected for the Final English Schools' trial at Cheltenham, Reece being selected as an England XV reserve. One of these keen rugby players, Ewen Henderson, became famous in later years in a completely different field, as a ceramic artist and sculptor. Sadly, he died of cancer in 2001. An anecdote by Ken Broad graphically illustrates the link between Adams' and Newport Rugby Club. The whole school practised Stanford's *Te Deum* for Founder's Day 1945 until they were note perfect. A few years later 'when Newport Rugby Club was being outsung in a bar after a game at Lichfield the captain said "OK lads. Let's hit 'em with the Te Deum". The effect was devastating – two brave souls even attempted the

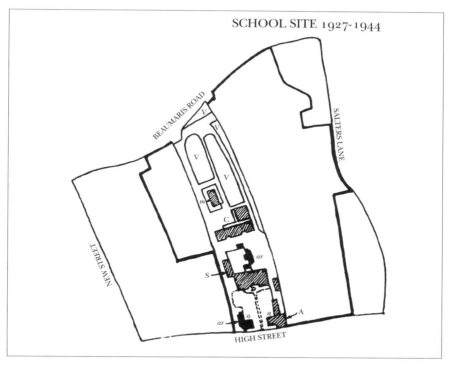

School site 1927-1944. a: almshouses, ar: air-raid shelters, m: manual room, A: Annexe, C: 1929 new classroom block, D: 1928 glassed in portico, S: Sykes room, V: vegetable beds. Heavy outline shows boundary of present school site.

alto parts, the original preserve of 'Pongo' Cooper and Raymond Holland! If only the Bishop had been passing the *Three Tuns* at the time.'

The 1944 Education Act

The intention of R. A. Butler's Education Act, passed in 1944, was to provide a better education for all children, taking account of their various abilities. Instead of elementary schools continuing to provide education for most children to age 14, with some pupils leaving at 11 to go to grammar schools, primary schools now taught children from five to 10 or 11. At that point an examination, soon known as the Eleven Plus (11+), decided what sort of secondary education was suitable for each child. The wishes of the parents and opinion of the teachers were also to be taken into consideration. The most academic gained places at grammar schools, the others at new 'Secondary Modern' schools, where more practical subjects were included, not necessarily tied to a School Certificate course. Technical schools were intended to cater for those with abilities and interests between the other two groups, but few were established. Education was to be free at all stages and the statutory school-leaving age raised to 15. This had to be postponed because of the large amount of school building required, and the additional numbers of trained teachers needed. All three types of school were intended to be of equal status but in practice the already-established grammar schools were perceived as superior and 'passing the 11+' was seen as an important goal by many parents. But selection for some implied failure and rejection for others, an interpretation never intended by the framers of the Act and never used by those whose business it was to administer it. Since 1907 LEAs had paid for up to 25 per cent of pupils at grammar schools through the scholarship system, and more had free places if there chanced to be money left by earlier benefactors, such as William Adams. The opportunity for a grammar school education would now depend on the power of a child's brain, not the power of the parents' purse. There were already sufficient grammar schools, but new buildings usually had to be provided for the secondary modern schools as there were rarely existing buildings available for conversion.

The endowed schools now became known as Voluntary Schools. There were two types: Aided and Controlled. Adams' became a Voluntary Aided School. This meant that the Foundation Governors, the Haberdashers, appointed the majority of local Governors, an advantage they had lost in 1909. The term Managers, used since 1878, was now dropped. The LEA was responsible for educational equipment and internal repairs while the Foundation Governors had to provide for external repairs, alterations, and improvements with a 50 per cent government grant available through the LEA. This percentage was gradually increased until it reached 85 per cent in the 1970s. Teachers were appointed by the Governors but were paid by the LEA. Voluntary Controlled Schools had a majority of LEA representatives on the governing body and the LEA was responsible for all maintenance costs and appointment of teachers. The former endowed schools at Bridgnorth and Wem became Voluntary Controlled, Ludlow and Whitchurch were Voluntary Aided. Schools directly run by the LEA (e.g. Wellington) were called County Schools. The LEAs were to be responsible for the 11+ selection procedure and the allocation of pupils. They were encouraged by the Act to provide boarding for pupils for whom it was considered necessary, either by running their own boarding schools or securing places at Independent ones.

It took some time for the Act to be implemented. Adams' became a Voluntary Aided School in 1949, but the final decision as to the composition of the Board of Governors was not published until 1954. Ten Governors were to be chosen by the Haberdashers. They were: the Master of the Company and nine others, of whom four were to be resident within 10 miles of Newport, one nominated by Birmingham University and two by the Old Novaportans. Five Representative Governors were to be appointed by the LEA, of whom one was to be nominated by Newport UDC and one by Wellington RDC.

As far as Adams' was concerned the greatest effects of the Act were that it lost the power to decide which pupils should enter the school, and the area from which day boys could be accepted was drastically curtailed. The historical catchment area had now gone. One small difference was that the school had to conform to a set number of working days per year, so the holidays given in honour of special achievements were discontinued. The Preparatory Department was phased out so it became an entirely 11 to 18 school.

In order to remain viable with a reduced catchment area the LEA suggested it should become a co-educational school, or increase its number of boarders. The Chairman of Governors from 1942 to 1955 was T.C.Ward. He was a formidable character: a local farmer, Chairman of Governors of Harper Adams' Agricultural College, Vice Chairman of Shropshire County Council and, from 1946, Chairman of the Council of Agriculture of England. He refused point blank to consider co-education. He and Peterson agreed with the County that the school should increase its number to 350 by taking 50 per cent as boarders. This was part of the County Development Plan to decrease the number of small grammar schools and promote larger schools which could offer greater scope to pupils. The aim was also to concentrate boarding in a few schools, and, in Adams' case, obtain equal numbers of boarders and day boys so neither group felt inferior.

Expansion of Boarding
T. C. Ward took matters into his own hands in July 1947 by buying Aston Hall, Church Aston, together with Dog Bank Cottage, for £7,000. The Haberdasher Governors agreed to buy it from him and make suitable alterations to turn it into a Boarding House (plate 32). This was opened as Ward House in September of that year.

T. C. Ward and Peterson were alert to other boarding possibilities. Beaumaris House, the most elegant 18th-century house in Newport, further down the road from Adams', was for sale in 1948. When private negotiations with the owner, Mrs Morris Eyton, failed, Ward bought it at auction on behalf of the Foundation Charity for £5,250. It had been the Rectory from 1874 to 1933 and in the 1860s had been a ladies' boarding school. There was talk between the Foundation Charity and the Governors of buying Roddam House, 127 High Street, but Shropshire County Council wanted it as a clinic for two to four years, so they decided to wait until they could get vacant possession – which did not happen until 1954. Meanwhile Ward had taken the initiative and personally bought the Old Post Office in 1949. This was 119 High Street, next to the Annexe, facing it across the yard at the back, and therefore ideal for the school. The Haberdashers bought it from Ward's executors in 1957 and converted the top floor to staff flats, but it was not until the Post Office moved across the road in 1960 (on the site of Musgrove House and 134 Church Square), that it could be incorporated into the school. That left Picken House, 121 High Street, with its long plot stretching back to Beaumaris Road, which formed a barrier between the main school premises and Beaumaris and Roddam Houses. To reach the swimming pool and the tennis court one had to go out onto the High Street. C. R. Picken, a well-known pharmacist and seed salesman was an ON and a Manager of the school from 1936 to shortly before his death in 1948. He left £2,000 to provide a scholarship for boys studying pharmacy. His widow continued to live at Picken House despite pleas from the Haberdashers that she should sell to them, so it was not until 1963, after her death, that the Haberdasher Governors were able to buy it and open up the land at the back of the school. One property, with no land attached, remained unobtainable, 123 High Street. Successive owners have refused to sell, so it is still separate from the school.

All these purchases by the Foundation Governors were eligible for a 50 per cent grant through Shropshire County Council, but only on the price the District Valuer put on them. This was often much lower than the asking price, which caused many problems. The legacy of T. C. Ward's initiative was a unified set of buildings on the High Street but, as they were all listed as buildings of special architectural interest under the Town and Country Planning Act of 1971, repairs had to be done to a high standard specified by the Department of the Environment which has involved the Charity in a great deal of expense.

Life as a Boarder at Aston Hall
Aston Hall opened in September 1947, with 16 boarders, some new, some transferred from Adams' House on the main school site. The numbers quickly grew to a maximum of 36 and the boys formed a new school house – Ward House. John Sheldon the housemaster and his wife Catherine were kindly but firm. Those who transferred from the main school thought they were fortunate because there was so much more space and freedom. There was a walled garden, a small rear paddock, room for two tennis courts at the front (though the grass was rather bumpy) and a space used for cricket or rugby. There were trees to climb, a rookery at one end, a model room in the cellar and a room for a model train in the stable loft. The site occupied the whole of what is now Pinewoods, the main entrance being on the Wellington Road. Dog Bank Cottage was used as married staff accommodation. David Basford remembers excellent food. As farmers' sons he and another boy helped look after the two pigs, which were fed on kitchen waste. When they were slaughtered the boys helped Mrs Doody, the cook, salt the bacon and make pork pies. The boys would all march to Church Aston church on a Sunday and return to a traditional Sunday lunch. Some joined Church Aston scouts. Mr Sheldon encouraged boys to play a musical instrument (he did not like jazz or popular music) and Ward House usually won school music competitions.

Boys used their bicycles to get to school and go into the country at weekends. Alan Holland would take his tame rook with him everywhere, sitting on his handlebars. Sheldon would vet the film at the Picture House in town before allowing the boys to go. Cerdic Warrillow remembers how most boys would go instead to the *King's Arms* for a drink, and learn the plot of the film from their friends on the way home. It must be remembered that there were open fields from the back of the Grammar School to Aston, past the back of the High School. On the last night of term there would be skirmishes across these fields and sometimes dormitory feasts. The most audacious ploy was when boys from Adams' pulled up the posts from the rugby field (by then next to the High School) and left them across Aston Hall doorway.

After the Sheldons, Mr and Mrs Palmer took over in 1953 and then 'Andy'Anderson and his wife, Barbara, were in charge from 1954 to 1968, when they all moved to Longford Hall. From 1956 Aston Hall housed juniors only.

T.C.Ward maintained a special interest in Aston Hall. When in 1955 the other Governors wanted to cut down the number of gardeners there from two to one, because of the expense, he left the meeting and never returned. A new Chairman was elected, Mr Kenneth M. Leach, ON, Chairman and Managing Director of the Audley Engineering Company, who served from 1956 to 1976. At the same time Mr Peter Watson Jones, local farmer and also an ON, became Vice Chairman. T. C. Ward died a few months after resigning.

Eleven

1953 TO 1973
THE SCHOOL UNDER GLOVER AND ROBERTS

R. F. Glover
Headmaster 1953-1959

Robert Glover was 36 when he took over as Headmaster of Adams', having been Head of Classics at King's School, Canterbury before coming to Newport. In many ways his era was one of golden years, a time of expansion, optimism and grasped opportunity. Vigorous and a strict disciplinarian from a public school background, he was welcomed by some as an antidote to what they had perceived as the relaxed regime under Peterson. He certainly used the cane as an instrument of education as well as punishment. He was ably supported by his wife, Jean, also an Oxford graduate, who shouldered the responsibility for boarding and catering while bringing up three young children. (As soon as she arrived she had to sack the cook for pilfering the food supplies and was left alone to cook for 80 boarders.) Although Glover was only at Adams' for a little over six years, a great deal was achieved in that time. His success was such that when the Haberdashers were looking for a new Head to give firm direction to Monmouth School they invited him to take over there. After he retired in 1976 he continued to be influential in education as Secretary to the Headmasters' Conference and Deputy Secretary of the Secondary Heads' Association. He died in 2001.

Within a week of arrival Glover had struck two blows in his campaign to tidy up Adams' Grammar School: he announced that school uniform must be worn, and he caned a boy. There is an oft-quoted story among ONs that he rushed up to B Dormitory above Big School where there was a lot of noise at 2a.m. on the night before a Haberdasher visit and caned the lot of them before retiring to bed and sleep. He recalled that they were proposing to do something to make the school look silly the next morning and that his action effectively stopped this. Exeats were tightened up and he introduced a new punishment: the writing out of Bill's Will instead of lines. Bill's Will was the informal name for the list of William Adams' benefactions (not William Adams' actual will), inscribed on wooden boards and displayed on the east wall of Big School where it remains today. In an attempt to smarten up the boys' public appearance Glover decreed that a tassel should be worn on a prefect's cap but the prefects felt embarrassed to wear it.

Glover was determined to increase the number of boys going to university, particularly Oxford and Cambridge, and inspired many a boy to raise his sights higher than he had thought possible. He never appointed a master who had not got a degree from Oxford or Cambridge. Instead of using the Joint Northern Examining Board he entered the school at O and A level for the Cambridge Board examinations, which he considered more exacting and prestigious. For some time O level Latin had seemed an impossible target for most boys but Glover, a stimulating teacher, soon showed it was attainable by all. He even taught Greek to a few pupils whose parents requested it. One or two boys obtained Open Scholarships at Oxbridge Colleges, as indeed the brightest Adams' pupils had over the years.

Newport continued to lead the County in numbers of O and A levels and in numbers of County Scholarships obtained. In 1957, when 22 per cent of grammar school leavers in Shropshire had A levels, the figure for Adams' was 35 per cent. A high point was reached in 1955/56 when the school gained two Open Awards, two State Scholarships and 12 County Scholarships. The numbers of ONs at university doubled between 1953 and 1959 (from 20 to 40) as did the numbers in the sixth form (from 30 to 60). Glover himself was convinced of the advantages of a Classical education, but the strong scientific bias of the school continued. At Speech Day, 1958, he reported that 70 per cent of ONs at university were reading science (including medicine): a very considerable contribution to the nation's need for scientists and technologists. 1958 was the first time he referred to the threat to grammar schools from the supporters of comprehensive education, asking parents and townspeople to speak out in their defence. Answering the criticism that grammar schools were too small to provide a wide enough range of subjects, he pointed out that 19 subjects were available at O level, with no individual taking more than nine, and 15 different subjects were currently being taken by ONs at university. He persuaded the Haberdashers to introduce a Closed Exhibition to Corpus Christi College, Oxford, available only to an Adams' pupil nominated by the Headmaster. The first, of £50 a year for three years, was awarded in 1960 to A.G. Dykes to read physics.[1] Closed Exhibitions were being abandoned rather than started at this time and the Exhibition was ended in 1984.

Glover's time is remembered as one of expansion. More boarding accommodation was acquired and the new gymnasium built some twenty years after it had first been promised. Behind this burst of activity was the fact that the Company at last decided to sell the Knighton estates and convert their capital into investments. This freed cash for building projects and increased the Charity's annual income. The purchase of Roddam House for boarding, a new kitchen for the Headmaster's house and the new gym were all funded from the sale to Cadbury's of their holding at Knighton. The new Science Block, changing rooms and lavatory accommodation, and a new Masters' Common Room begun in 1958 were paid for out of the sale of the rest of the estate to Sackville Estates in 1957.[2]

The aim, as under Peterson, was still a 50/50 balance between boarders and dayboys (though this was never achieved). Roddam House remained a County Council clinic until 1954, but the school had rented the upper floors for boarding while the clinic was in operation, so it was imperative to buy it when the opportunity arose.[3] Use of the Old Post Office, although bought in 1957, had to wait until 1960.

Mrs Glover earned the gratitude of later users of the Headmaster's house by insisting on having a kitchen built. When she arrived the only kitchen was that for the boarders in the semi-basement at the back of the boarders' dining room (Room D). This was inconvenient especially in the holidays, but also in day-to-day provision of meals for three children. It seems that when boarders were admitted to School House a number of years previously (we do not know when), the Headmaster's kitchen was dispensed with. We think it must have been the front room which is now the School office. At first she had to be content with a gas stove in the small top room, now the archive room (it had absolutely no ventilation!), but then a narrow kitchen was added on the side where the *Old Crow Inn* had stood. It could be very cold – one winter the Taylors went into the larder to find a bottle of squash had shattered and left the frozen contents still standing upright.

The school playing fields in Audley Avenue were needed for the new Secondary Modern School (later Burton Borough School) so new ones had to be found. It had taken 13 years for the 1944 Education Act to be fully implemented in Newport! John Swinn, the first Headmaster in 1957, recalled Glover's blunt assertion when they first met: 'Your school is built on my Rugby ground.' Luckily the Governors were able to buy five and a half acres of land on the Wellington Road (where the Boughey Road estate is now) from Dr Sowerbutts for £650. This was not eligible for a grant so had to be financed by the Haberdashers themselves.[4] Three years later the Governors erected a pavilion and changing rooms, using the £2,000 bequest left to the school by T. C. Ward. The Shuker Field remained in Haberdasher hands and was let out to the Urban District Council. The annuity from the field was paid to Mrs Shuker until her death in 1964. A swimming pool was officially opened in July 1958, the gift of the family of Kenneth Leach, Chairman of Governors, in memory of his father, R. W. Leach. Thus at last what had been talked of at the beginning of the century came into being and the boys welcomed it with enthusiasm. Swimming sports were held at the opening and every year after that.

The School's tercentenary was celebrated in great style in 1956, from 23 to 26 July. *The Pirates of Penzance* was presented in Big School and an exhibition of the life, activities and history of the school was opened by an eminent ON, Professor Maurice Stacey, Professor of Chemistry at Birmingham University. Kenneth Leach, Chairman of Governors and President-elect of the ONC, presented a pair of wrought-iron gates on behalf of the Old Novaportans. Local craftsman, Tom Pemberton, had made them at Puleston Forge. They gave access to the new driveway which had been

constructed by the County
Council at the side of the
school on the site of the *Old
Crow Inn.* So successful had
the ON appeal for the gates
been that a further £200 was
given to the library. The pupils gave two shields for the
front gateposts, one of
William Adams' coat of arms
and the other of the Haberdashers'. Unfortunately, the
former was stolen a few
years later, so the other is
now above the door of the
Headmaster's office. The
Master of the Haberdashers
laid the Foundation Stone of
the gymnasium which was
first used for Speech Day the
following year. The LEA

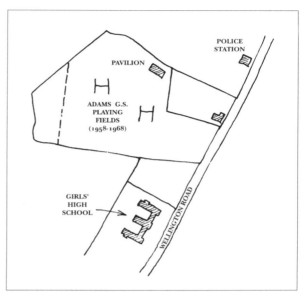

Wellington Road playing fields.

made their contribution by refurbishing the library, redecorating it and
supplying new bookcases, tables, chairs and reading lamps (plate 34). Dick
Talbot, the local carpenter who taught woodwork at the school, did most of
the woodwork such as the panelling and the tables. (He with six pupils later
made the movable Communion rails in the parish church). The Haberdashers gave £300, £1 for every year of the school's existence, which was spent
on library books.

The school said goodbye to three long-serving members of staff at this
period. L. W. Taylor (Pat), whom ill-health forced to retire in mid-1959, had
been at Adams' since 1916 and was admired and respected by boys and staff
alike. He had been appointed to teach maths but was also a great asset on the
sports field and ran the ATC during the Second World War. His help in
staging school plays was invaluable and he even took over woodwork teaching when Gill retired. He was made Second Master in 1947 when A. C.
Robinson left and was a great support to both Peterson and Glover, holding
the fort in the absence of Peterson, and for two terms before Glover arrived.
When he made John Smith Head Prefect of Clive House he told him, 'Smith,
you are to be captain of all the boys in this House, not just of those who win
prizes'. After Taylor died in 1960 the ONC presented in his memory a clock
for the pavilion on the Wellington Road playing fields. Sadly, it does not
seem to have made the transfer to the new Longford pavilion in 1968.

L. P. Ibbotson, idiosyncratic but effective teacher of French since 1920
and John Sheldon, physics master since 1922 (the first specialist physics
master the school had) and first housemaster of Aston Hall, both retired in

1958. The school's success in science owed a lot to Sheldon's meticulous teaching. Their replacements were John L. Humphrys (French and German) and Keith Reynolds (physics), both of whom maintained the high standard of learning in their departments.

Extra-Curricular Activities

Many activities flourished at this time; a complete list would be tedious but a few must be mentioned. R. H. Anderson (Andy) combined his love of French and rugby football by organising a link with the Lycée Fontanes, Niort, near La Rochelle. Throughout the 1950s rugby teams from each school visited the other on alternate years. Adams' usually won and their rugby gained quite a reputation over there. After a few visits staying in school accommodation the boys were given hospitality with families, both here and in France. It was an exciting experience for all, even the host parents! After 1961 the visits did not involve rugby any more, but continued as cultural exchanges.

A. S. W. Baker (Sam) was a worthy successor to Eric Cliffe as Director of Music and enthused generations of boys with his own love of the subject. His production of *Messiah* in March 1955 was the first in Newport for over forty years. The school choir of 120 was augmented for the occasion by friends of the school and the leader of the Shrewsbury Orchestral Society led the string orchestra. Among the soloists were Joyce Carter (for long afterwards conductor of Newport Male Voice Choir) and Tom Pemberton (the blacksmith who was also a noted local bass). In subsequent years Sam presided over equally ambitious performances such as Mozart's *Requiem* and Haydn's *Creation*. Perhaps his greatest achievement was Bach's *B Minor Mass* in 1964. For this Miss Angela Dove of Newport High School trained the combined chorus of the two schools, to which were added choirs from Wrekin College and Wellington Girls' High School. The orchestra consisted of amateurs from Shrewsbury and Wellington, reinforced with professional help, which included Sam's son Julian, Principal Horn of the Hallé Orchestra and two trumpet players from the Hallé. The soloists were all professionals. The new school organ, given by the ONC, was moved from Big School to the gym for the occasion. It was a musical triumph, repeated at Wrekin College the next day. This was such a success that the same combination of schools performed Brahms' *Requiem* two years later. Sam Baker also encouraged boys to learn to play musical instruments and the school orchestra gave regular concerts.

David Grundy, who took over as Director of Music in 1971, carried on this fine choral tradition, involving parents and friends in the Adams' Choral Society. In 1974, when David Taylor arrived as Headmaster, Bach's *St Matthew Passion* was in rehearsal. Adams' Choral Society continued under successive Directors of Music until 1980. When Keith Orrell became Director of Music he founded the Beaumaris Singers. He left to take up freelance choral work (he is currently Choirmaster of the Hallé Choir), but continued with the Beaumaris Singers who have received acclaim throughout the region for their high standard of musicianship. Incidentally Keith Orrell's school choir gave great delight to all at the Haberdashers' Schools Music Festivals when they started in 1986.

The flourishing Music Club started by Eric Cliffe had by 1953 almost as many townspeople as pupils of Adams' and the High School in its membership and was no longer organised by the school. Glover encouraged them to change their venue to the High School. A few years later Sam Baker organised a series of subscription concerts open to parents and pupils. These were a great success, offering recitals by professional artists as well as local ones. This continued as The Music Club throughout his time at Adams'. David Grundy continued with this, but when David Taylor became Headmaster they agreed it would be better to run a Town music club, to be self-supporting financially instead of relying on the Boarding Account. Thus was born in 1974 the Newport Music Club, which is still flourishing at the time of writing and is one of the few music clubs in the West Midlands devoted to classical music. After Grundy left, the organisation of the concerts was left to the Committee, many of whom had had boys at the school, in particular to the Headmaster as Chairman and his wife, Ruth, as Secretary. The school continues to give the Club hospitality.

The third master who took the lead in many activities in this period was A. W. Harding. His performances in Gilbert and Sullivan operas became legendary, from the first *Mikado* in 1953 to the *Pirates of Penzance* and *HMS Pinafore*. His Pooh Bah in 1959 earned him a well-deserved nickname. He was always involved in production and continued to produce in the 1960s even though he no longer performed. J. D. Roberts made him the first Careers Master in 1959 and he handed over the headship of the geography department in 1973 so that he could spend more time on careers. The present structure of careers advice is still based on the one he created. In 1957 he revived the Debating Society, now to be called the William Adams Arts and Debating Society. In 1960 for the first time the President was a pupil (Graham Millington) but it has always had a lot of support from the staff. It was open to fifth and sixth formers only. Most topics debated were questions of national importance but frivolous subjects such as balloon debates were also included. Over the years it has been decided that TV is not an unmitigated evil, that blood sports are a slur on the British way of life and ought to be abolished and that trade unions are too powerful. The society was not in favour of corporal punishment in 1961 but was in favour of capital punishment in 1964. It supported Britain's entry into the Common Market in 1963 but no one was in favour of depriving the British Fascists of free speech that year. It approved of factory farming by a narrow majority in 1954 and opposed any merger between Adams' and the Girls' High School in 1968! The Society was a useful forum in which young people could have practice in presenting their ideas in a coherent manner – essential for the adult world.

The Combined Cadet Force

The other school activity in which Walter Harding played a major role, and which still thrives, was the Combined Cadet Force (CCF). A contingent was formed in 1955, its first public test being to parade with the British Legion on Remembrance Sunday. Since then Adams' CCF has been a familiar part of Newport civic ceremonial and its band much in demand. An RAF section was added in 1964 and a Royal Navy section in 2001.

The CCF gives boys (and now girls) a taste of military life that, since the end of National Service, they would otherwise not experience. A visiting Inspecting Officer described the CCF as the biggest youth club in the country, and it certainly enabled the school to provide a wide range of adventurous and sometimes arduous activities and the opportunity to develop initiative and leadership in practical situations. While the CCF has never been compulsory there has been a strong expectation that the boys would join when eligible to do so.

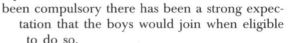

From the first the CCF has had keen support from the boys at Adams', made possible by dedicated leadership from the staff. Proof of this is the favourable mentions it has frequently had in *The Silver Bugle*, the magazine of the Light Infantry, with which it is linked. At first the CCF was restricted to fifth and sixth forms, but later fourth forms were admitted. A lecture room on the end of the Manual Room and a miniature rifle range in a Nissen Hut were soon provided by the Army.

The contingent was organised in house platoons and sections under NCOs. Each recruit had to pass a series of written tests as well as do practical drill. On the annual Inspection Day a formal inspection and march-past taken by a Regular Officer would be followed by classroom inspection and demonstrations of battlecraft, an assault course, abseiling and negotiating a RAF cable slung across the paddock by the swimming pool. Field Days and the Annual Summer Camp gave more chances to put theory into practice. Map reading, orienteering, signalling and basic survival skills all had their place in the programme. Initiative tests would involve, say, two cadets being sent off to reach a point a hundred miles away and return within a certain time, armed only with food, tent and ten shillings. Hitch-hiking came in useful. Camping weekends could involve skirmishes against 'enemies' or simply treks with map and compass over wet Welsh mountains. All this, and the chance to be sopping wet and covered in mud, was embraced with enthusiasm.

RAF skills have included navigation, meteorology and gliding. Over the years many boys have been taught to fly after winning RAF Flying Scholarships. The section very soon won the trophy as the best unit in the North West zone of Great Britain. In 1974 the summer camp was at RAF Lyneham, where the group found themselvs involved in helping with evacuees from the Cyprus crisis. They became experts at making up beds and cooking for large numbers and gained high praise from the Commanding Officer. A highly successful aspect of CCF has been the band, which has played outside the area, for instance at Dragey, near Avranches during the fiftieth anniversary of the D-day landings. All this would not have been possible without members of staff giving up their free time as officers. Lt.-Col. A. W. Harding was followed as Commanding Officer of the CCF by J. L. Humphrys, L. E. Seymour Whiteley and B. S. Thompstone. The RAF section was started by L. E. Seymour Whiteley. Innumerable others have played their part. The contingent has also been fortunate to have assistance from ex-regular soldiers as School Staff Instructors.

J. D. Roberts
Headmaster 1959-1973

Jeffrey Roberts, a reserved bachelor of 32, was a complete contrast to his predecessor. He had been housemaster and Senior Mathematics Master at Kimbolton School, Huntingdonshire. He had read natural sciences at Cambridge and gained First Class Honours in mathematics and psychology at London, so he was the first Headmaster of Adams' not to have an Arts degree. His interest in and encouragement of the pupils fostered a happy atmosphere in the school and he soon let the cane fall into disuse – in fact he later forbade its use by any member of staff. A very effective teacher of mathematics, he took Holy Orders in 1965 and worked closely with the Rector, James Hill. He ended compulsory church attendance and himself took a Sunday service for boarders at school. He resigned in 1973 to become head of a Church of England comprehensive school, St George's School at Gravesend, Kent. New schemes for reorganisation of education in Newport at this time are dealt with in Chapter 12.

The active support of the Chairman of Governors, Kenneth Leach, and the Clerk to the Haberdashers, Commander Prevett, meant that several developments in school buildings were achieved in Roberts' time. Shortage of funds did not seem a problem, compared with the restrictions of the 1970s and 1980s. The new Science Block and Masters' Common Room were completed in 1960, as was the new Tuck Shop, provided by the ONC, which backed onto the Headmaster's garden. Picken House, 121 High Street, was at last bought in 1963, which gave the space to add a new science block to the 1929 New Building. The caretaker moved to a new bungalow near the swimming pool when Beech Grove was demolished, and rooms at the back of Picken House became the Ward housemaster's house. In 1972 a new house was built for the housemaster of Adams' at

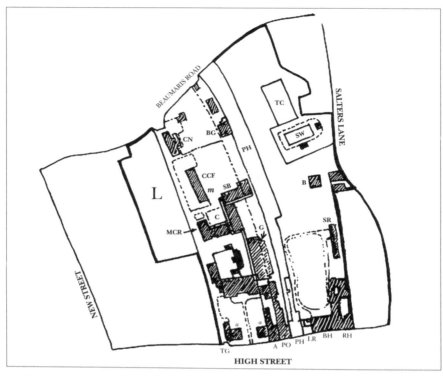

School site 1944-60. a: almshouses, m: manual room 1926, A: Annexe 1919, BG: 1958 Beech Grove (caretaker), B: bungalow (caretaker after Beech Grove demolished 1961), C: 1929 classroom block, CCF: 1956 armoury and store (lecture room added 1964), CN: 1949 LEA canteen (replaced by Dining Hall in 1964), G: 1957 gymnasium, L: land gradually acquired 1961-85 (car parks and grass), MCR: 1960 staff common room, SB: 1960 new science block, SR: 1957 shooting range, SW: 1958 swimming pool, TC: 1953 tennis court, TG: 1956 Tercentenary gates, PO: 1957 Old Post Office, ------ boundary of land acquired when PO and BG bought, PH: 121 High Street (owned by family of C.R. Picken), divided school into two sites until bought in 1963, LR: 123 High Street (at one time Lloyd and Robinson solicitors), not owned by school, BH: 1948 125 High Street, Beaumaris House, RH: 1954 127 High Street, Roddam House.

the back of Beaumaris House in place of the laundry which was moved to Longford.

In 1964 the new dining hall was opened, with its own kitchens. It had been designed to extend as far as the boundary of the land belonging to Picken House before it was acquired by the school; hence the unsightly kitchen door and dustbins next to the main entrance. This enabled day boys and boarders to eat together, which they had been unable to do in the existing canteen as numbers rose. For some time boarders had had to revert to eating in Room D. Kenneth Leach was alert to the opportunity of gaining land at the back of three buildings to the south of the school, as far as Lloyd's Bank, which broadened the school site.

The main change came in 1966 when Longford Hall came on the market. The school had been aware for some time that if it were to reach its target of 175 boarders it had to find accommodation for 50 more. Aston Hall took 40 juniors while Beaumaris, Roddam and Picken houses on the main site housed 85 boarders. A proposal to build a new boarding house on the main school site had been abandoned on grounds of cost, so the opportunity to buy Longford and remove the playing fields there as well as the junior boarders was too good to miss. Roberts was alert to its boarding possibilities because something similar had happened at his previous school, Kimbolton, which had bought Kimbolton castle for boarding use. He had been its first housemaster and his experience there convinced him that boys would appreciate and respect the elegant surroundings of Longford Hall which was one of the outstanding late Georgian houses of Shropshire (plate 15). It was designed by the Italian architect Joseph Bonomi in 1789 for Ralph Leeke, the second son of an old but undistinguished Shropshire family, who had gone out to India at the age of 16 and returned 16 years later as a wealthy man. Kenneth Leach quickly got the support of the Governors and Haberdashers, and the LEA, and it was bought in May 1967 for £40,000[5]. It was paid for by the sale of Aston Hall and the Wellington Road playing fields – both for building development. Aston Hall was sold in November 1967 for £23,000, but the sale of the playing fields dragged on until 1972. The developer whose offer had first been accepted went bankrupt and adverse market conditions and the problem of access meant fewer buyers came forward, but soon Boughey Road was constructed and new houses were built. Despite adjustments necessary to turn Longford Hall into a boarding house the junior boarders were transferred there in September, under the care of Mr and Mrs Anderson, who had spent all the summer holidays getting it ready. It was too expensive to move the pavilion from Wellington Road so a new one was built when the playing fields had been prepared at Longford. The school now had a magnificent house standing in 100 acres of parkland a little over a mile from the school with formal gardens, driveways, lakes, woods and fields, together with the Home Farmhouse and walled garden, with cottages and two lodges, barns, stables, dovecote and other outbuildings. Princess Margaret, Honorary Freeman of the Haberdashers' Company, officially opened Longford Hall in May 1968. Adams' now had some of the finest playing fields in the country – and one of the most elegant boarding houses.

Roberts put forward the idea of the school's acquiring its own cottage for adventure training and fieldwork and so the cottage near Foel in mid-Wales was bought in 1967 (plate 89). Lynn James, Welsh-speaking PE master, was a great asset in the management of the cottage and negotiations with the local farmer. It was used for CCF activities, ornithology, botany, fishing and form outings, but eventually it was found that staff did not want to be tied to one area for their activities and its use declined. It was sold in 1990 and the School Cottage Fund set aside for outdoor activities.

In the 1970s it became evident that a school architect based in Watford (J. L. Caldwell had been appointed in 1950) was not best placed to maintain the buildings in good order. Ken Griffiths, surveyor to the Urban District Council, was local Clerk of Works for new buildings but was not asked to inspect established property. So the Haberdashers agreed to appoint new architects, Wood, Goldstraw and Yorath of Stoke-on-Trent. They carried out a detailed inspection of all buildings just before D. J. Taylor arrived as Head, which led to a continuous programme of repairs throughout the 1970s and '80s.

In 1963 Roberts launched an Appeal Fund to provide equipment for school activities. Parental contributions and a fête got it off to a good start and further fêtes and school dances were organised by staff and wives. The purchase of the Welsh cottage was partly funded by this, as was the first school minibus in 1965. Another landmark came with the formation of a Parents' Association, the Adams' Grammar School Society, in 1972. Parents automatically became members when their sons joined the school. This has always worked closely with the school and has, over the years, raised thousands of pounds for it as well as being a social focus. Successive committees have put a lot of energy and money into projects such as making the school cottage fit for use (including a long driveway to it across the fields), funding for more computers when they were beginning to be used in schools and for another school minibus in 1986. They have organised (and still do so) very successful summer balls, in Big School or at Longford in a marquee.

The 1960s ethos of great social change and student power meant that the autocratic methods of previous Headmasters would have been impossible to maintain, and they did not accord with Roberts' own approach. He ended streaming: both parallel forms were of equal ability, there was no difference in their curriculum so neither felt inferior. Greek came to an end when it was offered as an alternative to chemistry at O level, and Roberts stopped the teaching of Latin when it was no longer required for entry to Oxford and Cambridge. Roberts changed the prefect system, abolishing the selected few and making all members of the sixth form responsible for leadership. He did not go so far as to establish a school council but he consulted the sixth form in a way his predecessors would never have done. He began to appoint two joint School Captains instead of one head boy and one deputy. The boys benefited from extra facilities in careers advice when the school became a member of the Governing Bodies' Association of Public Schools and thus a member of the Public Schools' Appointments Bureau, later called Independent Schools' Careers Organisation (ISCO). Boys were able to attend courses in the holidays during which they explored a variety of career paths.

Sport continued to be the mainstay of schoolboy experiences. Lynn James was an inspirational (and forceful) games and rugby master, ably supported by other masters such as Tom Bate and Rodney Jones who maintained the tradition of coaching teams in their spare time. Roberts

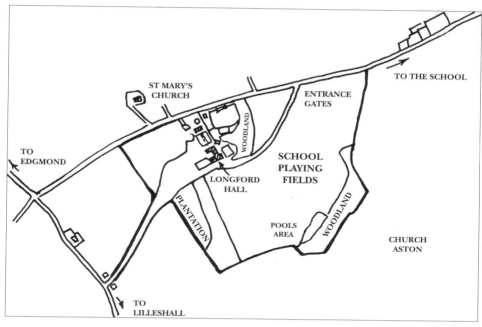

ST MARY'S
CHURCH

ENTRANCE
GATES

TO THE SCHOOL

WOODLAND

TO
EDGMOND

SCHOOL
PLAYING
FIELDS

LONGFORD
HALL

PLANTATION

WOODLAND

POOLS
AREA

CHURCH
ASTON

TO
LILLESHALL

Longford Hall grounds.

ended boxing, which had been introduced under Glover. Other alternatives made their appearance: the Duke of Edinburgh Award Scheme was begun in 1962 and individual boys had the opportunity to participate in Sail Training Association voyages thanks to sponsorship by Kenneth Leach and the Haberdashers. As always activities flourished according to a master's own interests; for instance, R. Q. Cavenagh was a keen fisherman and introduced many boys to its delights. The Film Society made their own film – *Exeunt Omnes* – as well as showing professional films. Visits abroad continued and C. A. Paris, head of English, produced many plays. In 1964 Mrs Margaret Humphrys produced a staff play, *The Importance of being Earnest.*

For the first time numbers of pupils rose above 400 in 1971. In 1966 a record 27 boys went to university. Despite this the majority of boys remained content to leave after O level to become bank clerks, trainee accountants, even teachers, as no A levels were then necessary for this.

Boarding in the 1970s and 1980s
Junior Boarding
Although boys at Longford lived in the house of a country gentleman, they did not live the lives of one. Life there in the 1970s was spartan and institutional as it was in most boarding schools of that era. Nevertheless it is life at Longford that many boarders choose to recall, often with affection.

Numbers did not at any stage reach the architect's planned 100, although 84 was reached in the mid-1970s. However, as the demand for boarding decreased and the expectation of comfort increased, the maximum number was reduced to under sixty.

Stuart Everall, now himself a housemaster in a boarding school, Paul Malone, John Pemberton, and Richard Oliver have contributed to this picture of boarding.

Although the new boarder might be struck by the beauty of Longford, the over-riding impression on first arrival was the size of the Hall and the space in the grounds. It was different from anything he had known. Walking through the big front entrance with its tall double doors was a daunting experience for it marked the start of a new existence separated from his family – especially that 'personal assistant' called Mum. He was stepping into a life of routine, rules and rotas, of living in public where individual affection was replaced by corporate care, where quivering lips had to be replaced by stiff upper ones. Symbolic of the change in the young boy's life was the loss of Christian names, to be replaced by surnames by the staff and nicknames by his friends.

The day began with the rising bell, and breakfast at a place at table fixed for the year. If you were on the serving rota there could be hot buttered toast from cook in the large kitchen and if your place was near the staff table there could be extras. Country gentlemen dressed for dinner and so did boarders – school uniform was worn at every meal!

There was the bath rota (baths twice weekly) and a rush to the wash rooms on other evenings – some basins had no plugs so wise boys took their own. The last one out had to mop the floor. It was a shock to young boys getting ready for bed to be helped by a 19-year-old assistant matron! Beds in the 1960s and '70s were in large dormitories of up to ten in a room (not as large as many schools), with no posters allowed on the walls, though this rule was later relaxed. Each 'dorm' had its own colour of blanket with iron bedsteads and thin mattresses. In the morning beds had to be made with the sheets turned down with 'hospital corners'. Beds were checked by Matron and if they weren't satisfactory the unfortunate boy would return from school at the end of the day to find his bed clothes in a heap so that he had to do it all over again. Stuart still wears his watch on the inside of his wrist, a relic of the days when he had to avoid scratching the watchface on the metal of the bed as he tucked in the sheets.

Although a coach and later a school minibus would take boys down to school in the morning, they often had to walk back at the end of the day. It was only a mile but to a small boy it seemed like ten. Some had bikes and riding in the slipstream of the bus was an excitingly dangerous and forbidden activity. Few who were boarders in those days will forget the sight (and smell!) of the 'boot room' and the long passage with a row of pegs, one for each boy to hang up his coat, cap and blazer, backing on to the games rooms and leading to the notice board and the warm radiator at the foot of the back stairs.

After tea, prep was in two cold rooms in the 'Sundial building' at the bottom of the gardens behind the Hall. Afterwards a simple supper was followed by a bedtime much earlier than at home, but occasionally enlivened (for First and Second Year boarders) by attack from Third Year marauders.

Pocket money was issued on a Saturday morning and soon spent in town (wearing school uniform), often on sweets from the 'Green Shack' near the school. These and other food were kept in a locked tuck box which also held other precious belongings. On many Sundays boys had to join the tiny congregation at Morning Service in Longford Church, with an inspection of their 'Sunday Best' school uniform beforehand.

When Longford Church closed and was converted to a private house, the organ was transferred to the boys' common room and services were held there. During part of the '80s Longford boys played a significant part in the life of Chetwynd Church where services were organised by RE teacher Christopher Jobson with the help of senior boys.

As society changed so did boarding. Previously, fathers were happy and indeed keen for their sons to experience the same tough regime that they had known at school. Rodney Jones who joined the school staff as teacher and boarding house tutor in 1970 recalls a father asking about his inoffensive son, 'Haven't you caned him yet? It did me no harm'. Increasingly, mothers, in discussion with their sons, were making the decisions and they looked for something more akin to home comforts. Boarding was not to be endured but enjoyed. So curtains, carpets and lampshades appeared and boys were allowed in their dormitories for recreation when previously they had been forbidden. The furniture was boy-friendly with bunk beds, duvets brought from home and each dormitory reflecting the personalities of its inhabitants. Posters now adorned the dormitory walls, their themes changing as the onset of puberty awakened awareness that girls existed. Headmaster and housemasters devoted much thought as to how boys' lives could be made more comfortable. Although they initiated the 'culture change', it was achieved by the attitude and care of successive housemasters' wives, matrons, cooks and other boarding staff. Eventually there were young female staff as house tutors as well as male. In returning to their house, boys were returning to their home, so 'play clothes' replaced uniform in out-of-school time and life became altogether more relaxed. Young boys were allowed to grow up gradually and emotions could be expressed. Evidence of the change of culture was the emergence of teddy bears encouraged by Rodney Jones, housemaster in the mid-'80s. They or equivalent 'mascots' first appeared in First Year dormitories but eventually in the Third Year ones as well.

Crazes and fashions in games, sports and hobbies came and went as for young boys anywhere. Skateboards, computers (dating back to the 'Sinclair ZX Spectrum'!) astronomy, 'Dungeons and Dragons', 'Escape from Colditz', the Rubik cube and Tolkien's *Lord of the Rings* will stir memories for some and leave others perplexed. Out in the grounds there was for a time a craze for gardening organised by Lynn James. Fishing became particularly popular when Philip North (tutor and later housemaster) founded the angling club in 1985. How many schools have their own fishing pool and offer tuition in country pursuits!

Senior Boarding

The Third Year boys were the Longford élite with many more privileges – and responsibilities – than the others. They had to make the most of their year because they would then transfer to Senior boarding and be at the bottom of the pile once more. Roddam, Beaumaris and Picken houses were built as gentlemen's town residences in the 18th century but behind the handsome High Street façades lay a rabbit warren of over 30 rooms with arcane names such as 'big front', 'small top', 'middle front' and 'dungeon' – a striking contrast to the space at Longford and its numbered dormitories. There were, however, many attractions with all the school facilities available on the site and exciting but forbidden ones in town. There were William Adams' Society debates on Friday evenings (High School girls were members from the early '80s) with lawful exeats to buy chips and unlawful ones to pubs, or to visit girlfriends.

Returning to the boarding house undetected after such an outing could be a problem. A sudden fire-practice would catch out some while there was always the danger that a 'commando' crawl through the Paddock grass would end up in the beam of a housemaster's torch. By the 1980s refrigerators and cookers were available though anything more exotic than pot noodles was seldom attempted. With gymnasium, swimming pool, snooker room and common room there were many of the benefits of a gentleman's club. Watching TV during the lunch break was a great bonus. Senior boys eventually had individual study-bedrooms or shared with another. Powerful audio equipment and other gadgetry appeared so that trailing leads became a concern of the Fire Officer. Much stricter Fire Regulations eventually put an end to the ultimate luxury of bringing an electric fire from home and leaving it on all day!

Twelve

1970s: Re-organisation

Circular 10/65

The 1960s were times of great social and political change to which education was not immune. The scene was set by a 'child-centred' approach to learning at primary school and by 'student power' with its accompanying riots and 'sit-ins' at university. At secondary-school level it was the admissions procedure for grammar schools that came under attack. The tests used and selection at the age of 11 were seen as unfair, especially as the selection rate could vary from under 10 per cent in one part of the country to over 30 per cent in another. Selection was also seen as not making full use of the nation's brains in an increasingly technological society. So when a Labour government replaced a Conservative one in 1964, educational reform was a high priority.

In July 1965 the new government published its plans for abolishing selection in a White Paper – Circular 10/65. Henceforth primary-school children would transfer to secondary education without reference to their ability. To this end existing schools would be reorganised on so-called 'comprehensive' lines. Purpose-built comprehensive schools would be created where necessary. Circular 10/65 marked a defining moment for grammar schools: the government's intention was to abolish them. From now on they would be the objects of attack and not approval. Where once tradition had been revered, traditional now meant 'outdated'. Elite (good) became élitism (bad).

Local Education Authorities were required to produce suitable schemes for each area under their control. Some agreed with the policy and some did not. With subsequent changes of national government and therefore of policy, in 1970, 1974 and 1979, education became a 'political football'. Nowhere was this more true than in Newport, where planning for reorganisation (and ultimately survival) occupied an enormous amount of time and energy for over 22 years. It was only in 1988 that Adams' could say it was remaining as a grammar school, one of 164 survivors from the 1,285 there had been in 1965.

Negotiations between Shropshire County Council, as the Local Education Authority, and the Governors of the two grammar schools in Newport began amicably enough in late 1965. Adams' with around 400 boys and Newport Girls' High School with around 200 girls were each too small to be comprehensive on their own so amalgamating them seemed a logical first step towards full comprehensive status. This would produce a three-form-entry grammar school of around 600 pupils. The problem was how to amalgamate a long-established Voluntary Aided boys' school having a large number of boarders with a County high school having day girls only. The LEA could impose its plans on its own school but not on Adams'. It had to secure the approval of Adams' Governors who made it clear that they would only consider plans that fulfilled certain conditions. These were that the school was on a single site, remained Voluntary Aided and retained its boarding and sixth form. In addition the Adams' Charity had to be satisfied that it could provide its 20 per cent share of the cost of new buildings and their subsequent maintenance. (This was later reduced to 15 per cent).

Another factor to be considered was the growth of the local school population due to the expansion of Dawley New Town (soon to be re-named Telford), the expansion of Donnington REME Depot and Sankey's Engineering Works at Hadley, as well as the raising of the school-leaving age to sixteen. If the population statistics were correct, the High School could be converted to primary use after the grammar schools had been amalgamated and Burton Borough School could be reorganised as an 11-16 comprehensive school. Negotiations between the LEA and the governors of the three schools continued throughout 1966 ... and 1967 ... and 1968. The delay did not worry the two grammar schools but was frustrating for Burton Borough School, which had much to gain from reorganisation. By July 1968 a plan had been produced in which both grammar schools agreed to merge. The school would be Voluntary Aided on the Adams' site, and would provide for 200 day boys, 200 day girls and 200 boy boarders. By this time Longford Hall had been purchased and Aston Hall sold. The sale of the Wellington Road playing fields was under way. If a good price could be obtained the net profit on the three transactions would enable the Charity to meet its share of the cost. For Burton Borough to develop successfully as a comprehensive school it would need a share of the most able children in the Newport area. The grammar school would therefore have to look outside Newport to make up its number of 400 day pupils. It was calculated that this could be achieved by taking three per cent of the 11+ age group within a 12-mile radius of Newport. Such a small percentage, the LEA believed, would have a negligible effect on the comprehensive schools in that area. When the scheme was published the teachers in those schools thought otherwise, claiming that Adams' would cream off their most able pupils, making true comprehensive education impossible. The scheme was no more popular in Newport. People objected to having to share their grammar schools with outsiders. Instead of 60 Newport children entering grammar school each year there would be fewer than a dozen. The local newspapers reported a 'storm of protest' with banner headlines proclaiming 'Adams' to be a Super School'.[1] The proposals were those of

the LEA but Adams' took the flak. Although its Governors were prepared to press on with the plan despite the vociferous opposition, the
LEA decided it was politically unacceptable and abandoned it.

A year later, in 1972, it produced a new scheme. The central feature was
still the establishment of a 3FE (three-form-entry) co-educational grammar
school on the Adams' site but with equal numbers of day pupils and boarders. A third of the day pupils would come from adjacent (comprehensive)
areas and one third of the boarders would be girls. Because the town population was growing rapidly the selection rate for the grammar school would
fall from the current 25 per cent to around 10 per cent by 1980. This would
allow Burton Borough to grow into an 11-16 comprehensive school with 750
pupils (i.e.5FE). Because of increased population a second 11-16 school for
750 pupils would eventually be established. Sixth-form education for these
two schools would be provided in Telford, not Newport.

The new scheme was attractive to the Adams' Governors for it allowed
the school to enlarge to the three forms of entry which they deemed essential for its long-term survival. The idea of girls' boarding was but a small
extra step. The main drawback was that Adams' would have to rely on
boarders to increase its numbers and boarding schools are chosen by parents, not allocated by LEAs. The main reason for parents seeking boarding
at Adams' was its academic excellence, but if their local comprehensive
school was successful they would not need to consider Adams'. The success
of boarding would depend partly, if not entirely, on parents' dissatisfaction
with other schools. Another problem was that Adams' would need to attract
boarders from outside the county. Education Authorities other than Shropshire would therefore be responsible for the tuition fees (parents cannot be
charged for these). Before the 1980 Education Act was passed LEAs could
refuse to pay for children to be educated outside their area. In the financial
climate of the 1970s many LEAs adopted this course of action. Adams'
Governors had two other fears: if this merger of the grammar schools was
a step on the way towards comprehensivisation would a 'comprehensive'
Adams' have the same attraction as a 'grammar school' Adams'? And would
a co-educational Adams' be as attractive as a single-sex Adams' for prospective boarders?

Despite these misgivings Adams' Governors agreed to the scheme. A
detailed timetable was drawn up which, if followed, would have seen the
new school open its doors in September 1976 with girl boarders being
admitted a year later. The formal Public Notice of the scheme under Section
13 of the 1944 Education Act was issued on 1 June 1973. This was an
important moment for Adams' Grammar School. When a Public Notice is
issued it is the right of groups of ten or more electors to write to the
Secretary of State stating their objections. Instead of voicing protests at
public meetings or writing to the Press, they could now make a formal
contribution to the decision-making process. They had two months in which
to do so. The Secretary of State would make the final decision.

The Secretary of State, Mrs Margaret Thatcher, received twenty or so letters signed by 185 people. This was not a large number considering the number entitled to reply and their case was weakened by a misunderstanding of the role of the Haberdashers' Company in the affairs of the School – a misunderstanding that surfaced every time the future of the school was discussed publicly in the '70s and '80s. They did not realise that the Haberdasher involvement in the school's affairs was restricted to administering the William Adams' Charity. Even the District of the Wrekin wrote, 'the Haberdashers' Foundation has ample funds from which to finance improvements, extensions and new buildings at Adams' Grammar School if it so desires. The obvious solution … is for this extremely wealthy foundation to declare Adams' Grammar School an Independent School.' It is surprising that objectors over the years have not taken the trouble to find out more about the Haberdashers' Company instead of being content to accuse it of being a hidden power behind the Governors, an alien organisation unduly interfering with local democracy and the will of the people. There were no 'Haberdasher millions'; the Charity's activities were limited by modest capital assets of around £100,000. By the 1970s there were many demands on this money because of the dilapidation and decay of the school buildings.

The Governors and the LEA were asked to comment on the objections but by September it was up to the Minister to give her decision.

At this point the Headmaster, Jeffrey Roberts, gave notice that he would leave the school at the end of the year and David Taylor (joint author of this book) was appointed to start on 1 January 1974. He had been Deputy Head of a 3FE Voluntary Aided boys' grammar school at Spalding, Lincolnshire, with experience of boarding when Head of Physics at Sherborne School, Dorset. From this point on his personal involvement is reflected in the narrative. On 18 February 1974 the Minister gave her approval for Adams' to become a co-educational grammar school. The High School would close and all the girls transfer to Adams'. This was an exciting time to be at Adams', to take part in possibly the most important change since the school's foundation over 300 years earlier. The euphoria was short-lived. Within weeks the Prime Minister, Ted Heath, was forced to call a general election and a Labour government led by Harold Wilson now took office. The new Labour MP for the Wrekin, Professor Gerry Fowler, was a great supporter of comprehensive schools and a voluble critic of the Newport proposals. The worst was feared but the worst did not come immediately. The Minister said he had no power to intervene in the decision of his predecessor. The school architects drew up plans for the new building. However, severe cut-backs in public expenditure meant the project had to be deferred. At first this was only for a year, but in June 1975 the LEA stated it could not be included in the building programmes for 1976/77 or 1977/78. Adams' had been in this situation many times before: an ambitious plan proposed and approved – but abandoned for lack of money.

Lack of money was not the only reason for the postponement. It was now found that the birth-rate was declining. (Nationwide more women were taking up careers and postponing childbirth by the use of contraception. It was the contraceptive pill that was destined to play a significant part in education planning.) There was no longer any need to use the High School buildings as a primary school, and only 9FE at secondary level would be needed in the town instead of the 12 originally envisaged. This was only one more than existed already, since Burton Borough had already grown to 5FE. The situation was changed yet again by the Education Act 1976 which stated that secondary education was to be provided only in comprehensive schools. The 1973 scheme was now dead.

Comprehensive Schemes

The 1976 Act might demand reorganisation on comprehensive lines but with the economy in a poor state and high inflation the government was now restricting new building to 'basic needs', which usually meant providing for increased numbers. Although it did not seem so at the time, the reluctance of the government to part with money was a blessing in disguise, for it allowed Adams' Governors to object to LEA proposals on the grounds of cost without having to disclose that the majority did not want comprehensive education. If the government had used the carrot of new buildings instead of the stick of legal action the pressure to go comprehensive would have been difficult to resist.

In May 1976, the Chairman of Governors, Kenneth Leach (ON) stepped down after 20 years of magnificent service and Vice-Chairman Peter Watson Jones (ON) took over. Negotiations with the LEA began again. The Governors of the three Newport schools were offered four possible patterns of reorganisation:

a) Two 11-16 schools, one at Burton Borough and the other based on Adams' and Newport Girls' High School. Sixth formers would go to colleges in North Telford.

b) A two-tier system in which Burton Borough became an 11-14 school and Adams' and NHS together formed a 14-19 school.

c) An 11-16 school at Burton Borough and an 11-19 school at AGS and NHS.

d) Two 11-16 schools at Burton Borough and AGS with a sixth form centre at NHS.

The attitude of Adams' Governors at this time was carefully stated by the Chairman: 'The Governors would not wish to oppose the school's taking its proper place in a comprehensive system of education.' But what did this actually mean? Was its proper place as a comprehensive school – or as an island of selection in a sea of comprehensives?

Of the four proposed alternatives not one found favour with all three schools. There were only two points on which they were all agreed: the sixth form should remain in Newport and there should be two schools and not one large one. Adams' Governors were prepared to consider an 11-16 school at Burton Borough and an 11-19 school at Adams' but the other schools objected, saying that parents would choose the school with the sixth form. They believed that the two schools should be perceived as being of equal status. 'Parity of esteem' became an important guiding principle and so in July 1977 the LEA proposed a new scheme based on it. There would be two 11-18 schools, one at Adams' and the other at Burton Borough. Adams' would have to double in size but little building work would be needed at Burton Borough. Pupil numbers of 670 (4FE) and 830 (5FE) respectively were assumed, giving sixth forms of 70 at Adams' and 80 at Burton Borough. These were too small to be autonomous and co-operation between them would be essential. This scheme hardly accorded with government thinking which was moving to a preference for large sixth forms or separate Sixth Form Colleges.

Many of the Adams' teachers thought there would not be 'parity of esteem' under the LEA plan. The romantic view might be that Adams' was an ancient foundation in attractive buildings on a historic site, but a realist might see them as overcrowded, dilapidated and out-of-date. Burton Borough already had modern purpose-built buildings and facilities. The balance of esteem would not lie with the new school at Adams' if it had inferior or inadequate facilities, and the likelihood was that it would have to use the Girls' High School buildings for an interim period of unknown duration. Parents, especially of boarders, might not press so strongly for Adams' once it ceased to be a grammar school.

Out of this mood of dissatisfaction emerged a movement to consider Adams' becoming independent. In April 1977 a staff committee produced an optimistic report on the prospects for independence and by early autumn it was on Governors' meeting agendas. By the end of September it was public knowledge and the *Shropshire Star* had a front page item, 'A school may go it alone'. Shortly afterwards the Association for Adams' Independence (AAI) was formed, its first public meeting in November 1977 attracting an estimated 300 people. The President of the Association was Kenneth Leach and the Chairman was a parent, Dr Alan Snead, who had just become a School Governor. The Association conducted a survey and concluded that Adams' could survive as a small co-educational school. The Whitehead Report, a professional survey commissioned by the Haberdashers' Company and completed in December, came to the opposite conclusion.

In November the Haberdasher representatives had stated that the Charity could not afford its share of the cost of expanding Adams' from 2FE to 4FE; it could only cope with one extra form of entry. This would mean a split-site school with 3FE at Adams' and 1FE at the High School, which was just what the supporters of AAI had feared. The alternative was for Adams' to become Voluntary Controlled, so that the LEA would be in control and entirely responsible for the building costs. Both the LEA and DES would have preferred this but the Governors rejected it. Despite the pessimism of the Whitehead Report, independence was given further consideration. David Taylor produced a paper on the organisation and running of a small independent school. Lucton School in Herefordshire was visited as an example of the sort of school that Adams' might be. Soon after, Lucton had to close rather suddenly on financial grounds (though it was to reopen a few years later). This was a sober warning about the risks of independence.

There's rather a mixed feeling in our house. Dad's anti-grammar, mum's anti-comprehensive and I'm anti-school!

Newport Advertiser, *27 October 1978.*

The County Council did not know how seriously independence was being considered. A sense of frustration and annoyance was creeping into its thinking. Had Adams' Governors been negotiating all this time when in reality independence had been their aim? If the school were to go independent it should do so immediately, its indecision was holding up the rest of Newport. Adams' was beginning to be seen as the villain of the piece and it was not receiving a good press. The view of some was that Adams' should 'get out of the way' so that Newport education could be planned without historical baggage. But could Adams' 'get out of the way' so easily? If it did so, it would be withdrawing over 400 places out of the Newport area which the LEA would have to replace. The LEA said it would require compensation of £1,500 per place for this withdrawal, giving a total of over £600,000. It sounds a large sum now, but it was an enormous sum then and effectively put independence out of the running.

The Company still had the problem of finding enough money to put the LEA scheme into effect. A public appeal was considered and rejected – who would support a grammar school to go comprehensive? Part of the Longford estate could be sold but why dispose of the 'family silver' for a plan that was not of the school's choosing? The forthcoming general election might also alter the situation entirely, for the Tories were well disposed towards grammar schools.

It was at this point that the LEA formally put their scheme to the government, despite lack of agreement with Adams' Governors. The Minister found the proposals satisfactory and asked the Governors to produce their own plans within two months. Instead of complying, the Governors replied that the Minister's interpretation of the 1976 Act was wrong![2] They argued that they need only submit their own proposals if the LEA proposals were not satisfactory. But the Minister had said that the LEA proposals were satisfactory. The Governors agreed with them – but couldn't afford them. The local press reported the Minister's letter as an ultimatum. The Governors' response was seen as conceding defeat but it was the very reverse![3] The local MP Gerry Fowler wrote that Adams' Governors were ignoring the law of the land, Peter Watson Jones replied to disagree. The impasse gave AAI further hope despite the required compensation and its membership grew to 680 supporters.

By the end of 1978 two possible sources of finance had been found but both were controversial. At the suggestion of James Hill, Rector of Newport, and an Adams' Governor, the Diocesan Education Council had been approached about the possibility of Adams' becoming a Church of England comprehensive school. The Council agreed to consider a £40,000 loan to help it to do so. No immediate decision was made because the LEA also offered to consider using its powers under Section 137 of the Local Government Act 1972 to pay the 15 per cent of the cost of replacing the Girls' High School building, that would otherwise fall on the Charity. That the LEA was willing to do this was a measure of the importance it attached to reorganisation. With inflation running at 10 per cent the cost could soon go beyond its reach as well as that of the Charity.

In November 1978 the Minister, Shirley Williams, told the Governors that her interpretation of the 1976 Act was the correct one. She was 'very concerned ... the Governors have failed to comply ... they are in default of their duties and expects them to take urgent steps ...'. At this point the Governors agreed to accept the LEA scheme provided the new school was Voluntary Aided, on a single site and the LEA met the extra cost as already described. Details were agreed by the end of March 1979. The first non-selective intake would be in September 1981 and the school would use the High School buildings until the new building was ready.

Six months later there was a general election and with a new Conservative government came a new education policy. LEAs were quickly relieved of the obligation to reorganise on comprehensive lines but Shropshire LEA wished to continue, for Newport was the only area in the county without a comprehensive plan. Meanwhile, at the request of a re-invigorated AAI, the Governors investigated the new Assisted Places plan which the Government was introducing to help parents on modest incomes send their children to independent schools. It proved to be a non-runner because to qualify Adams' would first have to become independent and there was no guarantee that a newcomer would be able to join the scheme.

So work on the reorganisation plan went on throughout the summer of 1979 with draft procedures for admissions and staffing being drawn up. These were not easy to achieve because Adams' staff were appointed by the Governors (although paid by the LEA) so they could not be moved to another school other than voluntarily. There was also a difference of opinion over 'who goes where'. Burton Borough and the Girls' High School preferred geographical zoning for the admission of pupils. Adams' wished

67   *William Adams from the portrait in Haberdashers' Hall. Painter and date unknown.*

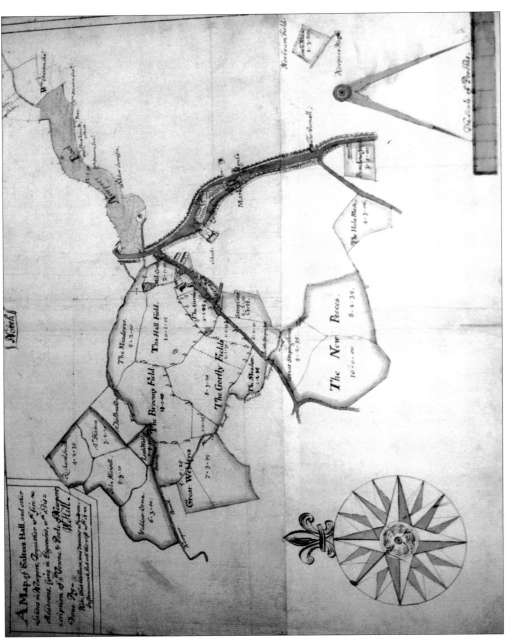

68 *Map of Newport in 1681 by William Hill showing position of school.*

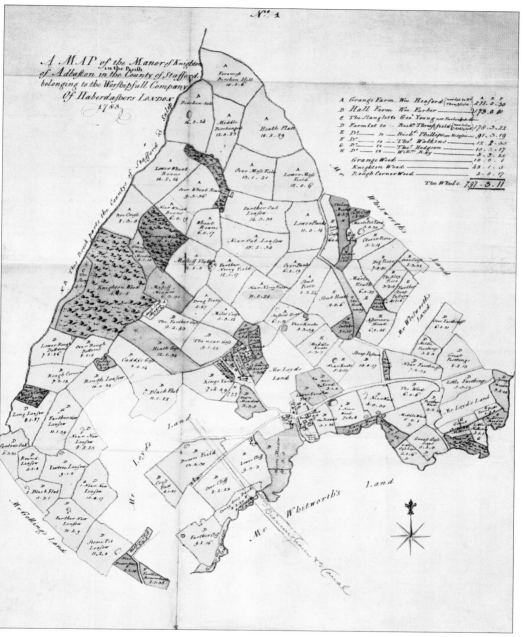

69 *Map of the Knighton estates, 1783.*

70　*The old school building in the late 1990s.*

71　*Sir John Moore's School, Appleby Magna, Leicestershire, built in 1697. It shows a distinct similarity in design to Adams' Grammar School.*

72 *Lantern clock presented to the school by William Adams in 1657. The wooden bracket is of a later date.*

73 *Coat of arms used by the school.*

74 *Coat of arms of the Haberdashers' Company mounted on the wall of the gymnasium – here at ground level after being repainted in the mid-1980s.*

76 *Dole board, originally in the parish church but now in Big School, listing some of the 'pious and charitable deeds' of William Adams. Familiarly known as Bill's Will.*

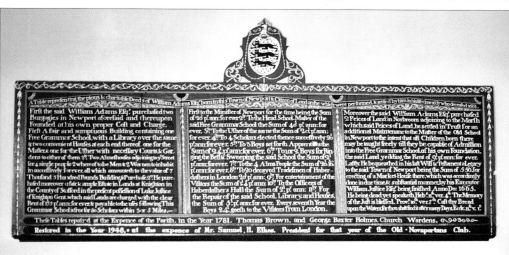

77 *The rear of the old school building showing the bricked-up archway entrance to Big School.*

78 *Knighton Grange on the Knighton estate, a 19th-century rebuilding of an existing farm.*

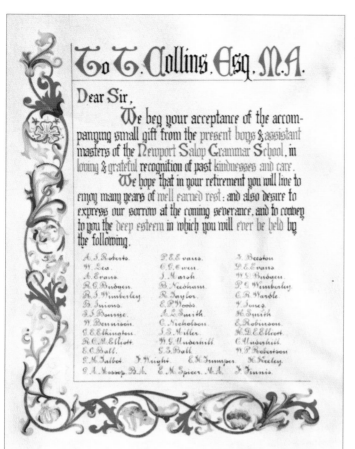

To T. Collins, Esq. M.A.

Dear Sir,

We beg your acceptance of the accompanying small gift from the present boys & assistant masters of the Newport Salop Grammar School, in loving & grateful recognition of past kindnesses and care.

We hope that in your retirement you will live to enjoy many years of well earned rest; and also desire to express our sorrow at the coming severance, and to convey to you the deep esteem in which you will ever be held by the following.

A.J. Roberts.	P.E. Evans.	J. Beeston
H. Lea.	G.G. Owen.	P.E. Evans
A. Evans	J. Marsh	H.L. Budgen
R.G. Budgen	B. Needham	P.J. Wimberley
R.J. Wimberley	R. Taylor.	C.R. Wardle
B. Inions.	E.P. Woods	J. Jones.
J.J. Bourne.	A.L. Smith	H. Smith
H. Bennison	C. Nicholson	E. Robinson
J.E. Ethington.	J.S. Miller	H.D.E. Elliott
R.C.M. Elliott	H.J. Underhill	C. Underhill
E.C. Ball.	G.J. Ball	H.P. Robertson
L.M. Talbot	J. Wright.	E.H. Trumper	H. Keeley.
J.A. Mossop. B.A.	E.M. Spicer. M.A.	J. Innis.

79 *An Illuminated Address presented by boys and masters to Tom Collins on his retirement as Headmaster in 1903. Discovered by the authors in the cellar of the Headmaster's House.*

80 *Two of the Visitors' Chair, provided for their meetings in school dating from the first hal, of the 19th century*

81 *HRH Princess Margaret being shown round a laboratory during her visit to the school in May 1985. Accompanying her are Stephen Fellows (School Captain), Harry Wood (Chairman of Governors), David Taylor (Headmaster), David Pyle and Guy Tindale. Christopher Lowe is in the background.*

82 *Procession of school governors, led by the Beadle and Clerk to the Haberdashers' Company, on their way to the Commemoration Service in the parish church, Speech Day 1989.*

83 Daily Mail *Rugby Cup under-15s team in the semi-final versus Wellington College on the Harlequins' ground, 1988.*

84 *Members of the First VII hoist aloft captain Paul Laffan to celebrate the school's first outright win of the Fraser Bird Rugby Sevens Cup at Longford, 1988.*

85   *The school CCF marching band on Civic Sunday 1989.*

86   *The last year of short trousers! Form I in 1979 with form representative Bryson Wood and form master Christopher Jobson. Two future school captains, Stephen Fellows and Christopher Hillard, are in the photograph.*

87 *Drama class in Big School in the 1980s. (The wide-angle lens makes it look longer than it is!)*

88 *Big School after its conversion to a library in 1992, with Mrs Elizabeth Kosinski, the school's first full-time librarian, at the left.*

89 *The school cottage (1967-1990), Bryn-y-Chwilod, Foel, near Welshpool. Painting by Dudley Chambers.*

90 *The Lynn James cricket nets at Longford, 1989.*

91 *Longford Hall in the summer: a meeting for new boarders and their parents, 1992.*

92 *Longford Hall in January 1982, when a temperature of -26.1°C at Harper Adams' Agricultural College entered the* Guinness Book of Records *as the lowest ever recorded in England.*

93 *Aerial view of Longford Hall in 2000.*

94 *Aerial view of the main school site in 2000. See endpapers for key to the buildings.*

to retain parental choice, a view that was supported by the primary Heads, so the LEA agreed.[4] Adams' would also be allowed to select its own boarders.

If the school had to go comprehensive the Governors felt that the final scheme proposed was as good as any. In some ways the school would be returning to the conditions existing before the 1944 Education Act when Adams' had a wider ability range and brothers could be kept together.

On 21 December 1979 the necessary 'Section 13' notice was published jointly by Shropshire County Council and the Adams' Governors to create two parallel 11-18 comprehensive schools, starting in 1982. The High School would be closed and Adams' enlarged to produce a co-educational school with about 670 pupils, of whom a quarter would be boy boarders. In contrast to 1973 there was no mention of boarding for girls. Burton Borough would have around 830 pupils. The two schools would co-operate to provide sixth form courses.

It might be thought that there would be a lull while the Minister's decision was awaited. This was not the case. In 1979 cracks developed in the gable end of the Headmaster's house. It was found that the oak staircase running up three stories was inadequately supported and in danger of sudden collapse. The Taylor family had to move out quickly and find somewhere else to live. The staircase was dismantled and furniture and other belongings, marooned on three floors, had to be removed by block and tackle! By the time the Section 13 notice was published the cost of repair was estimated to be £30,000; by the end of January 1980 it was £53,000. The entire cost fell on the Adams' Charity which could not afford it so repairs were stopped at a point when the structure was safe. As a result the house lay derelict until 1983 when it was converted into administrative accommodation. With this added burden the Adams' Charity now needed more money. It looked to see what could be raised by the selling of securities and land owned locally. The idea of a Diocesan loan was again pursued but it was too late to change the scheme to accommodate this. The LEA offered to consider an increase in the amount of its financial assistance.

In April the DES said it had received no objections to the scheme, and in late June asked for more information. The signs were promising that the Minister would agree.

His long-awaited reply came on 13 August 1980, but it was not the expected one. The Secretary of State was not satisfied that the proposals 'represented a wise use of resources in the current economic circumstances and is not persuaded that the educational arguments justify such a level of expenditure'.

That a Tory Government could reject a Tory Council proposal came as a genuine shock to all those involved, combined with a feeling of fatigue and frustration. Five years of planning, special meetings, working parties and joint consultations had come to nothing and the whole process would have to be repeated. '11-Plus decision shocks County' said the *Shropshire Star*, while the County Education Committee reactions ranged from 'bitterly disappointed' to 'catastrophic decision'. *The Times* newspaper devoted an article to it noting that the population of Newport was growing, unlike most areas in Britain. The Minister agreed to meet a deputation from the County Council and the three secondary schools. The meeting was polite but unproductive. It was open to the LEA to submit revised proposals if it wished but the Minister reminded the deputation of the current serious financial situation. Rightly or wrongly, this was taken as a hint that a cheaper scheme might be accepted and the whole round of meetings and working parties began again with various other options considered and discarded. The existing plan still seemed the best one especially as it had in a sense been market tested, receiving much support[5] and no opposition. The Adams' Governors agreed to a variation of it as an interim measure, whereby 150 extra places would be provided at Adams', and the Girls' High School building would be kept in use for the First Year and Second Year pupils. To accept a split-site school for an anticipated five years was a considerable gesture of co-operation on the part of the Governors, as was its (albeit reluctant) acceptance by teachers. The scheme could begin in September 1983 starting with a non-selective intake at 11 years of age.

Yet again a Section 13 notice was published (30 October 1981) and the waiting began. With the usual two-month period for objections, the Minister, Sir Keith Joseph, would have all the necessary information to make a decision early in 1982. By July all three governing bodies wrote to the Minister asking for a decision. The suspicion was that he would release it in the summer holidays, a common practice when unpopular decisions had to be made. And this is what happened.[6] In a letter dated 5 August 1982, Sir Keith Joseph rejected the proposals saying that he 'is not normally prepared to approve proposals which would involve a significant change in the character of schools with a sustained and sustainable record of Sixth Form provision'. The Adams' teaching staff took this as a compliment and breathed a huge sigh of relief!

D. J. Taylor 1974-1993
Life from a Headmaster's Viewpoint

I arrived at Adams' in January 1974 during a coal miners' strike and a fuel shortage. The LEA gave schools an extra week's holiday to conserve heating oil and also cut their budgets. One of my first decisions was to cancel the marquee hired for the annual Prizegiving in May, to save money.

The buildings, both school and boarding, were in bad shape. A detailed report on their condition by our new architects arrived at the school at about the same time as I did. It made for gloomy reading, and building problems occupied a lot of my time in the '70s. In particular I got to know my way round the senior boarding houses by frequent visits with the architect, Peter Downing, to inspect various types of rot, decay and leakage, including mould in the showers and fungi growing out of the walls of a sixth-form study. In the summer holidays of 1975 Big School was scheduled for routine redecoration by the LEA. Its ceiling and the floor of the sixth-form common room above it (Rooms A & B) were found to be in a dangerous state. Major renovation work followed, with Big School and the common room out of use for two terms. Steel girders were pushed into the ancient brickwork to provide a new ceiling and floor (plates 57, 58). The appearance of Big School was greatly improved and lighting flush with the ceiling replaced the old pendant lamps. The sixth form had a carpeted area, individual lockers and comfortable cushioned chairs, all paid for by the LEA.

At Longford there was a fall of stone from the portico and in early 1976 high winds blew in the gable ends of the large barn there. Both were listed buildings and had to be repaired to a high standard, costing money the Adams' Charity could ill afford. The drought in the summer of 1976 severely damaged the rhododendrons and azaleas in the Longford gardens. They had been an outstanding feature but were never the same again.

The number of boys in the school continued to increase beyond 400 so in 1973 a demountable (prefabricated) class room was ordered. We saw it arrive during the Headship interviews in October, to be parked next to the toilet block. In 1978 we were able to put another alongside it. These two, Rooms 11 & 12, solved immediate accommodation problems, but they were second-hand and not boy-proof. They deteriorated visibly and until the mid-'90s they formed an unprepossessing 'shanty town' at the centre of the school.

As part of the County's plan to comprehensivise schools, the entry of new boys in September 1974 was restricted to those living in a so-called 'catchment area' based on Newport, Edgmond, Lilleshall and Tibberton. Wellington, Donnington and Staffordshire which had all provided many day boys in the past could no longer do so. They could, however, come as boarders so boarding expanded. Many parents saw it as the price to be paid for grammar school education. Twenty-five 11-year-old boarders came in September 1974 and 30 more in 1975. It was not until 1979 that boarding applications started to decline, no doubt affected by the prospect that Adams' would itself become comprehensive. As these boarding numbers worked their way up the school we ran short of senior boarding space. In September 1974 we had 184 boarders, with 104 seniors. To help accommodate them we converted the Annexe classroom back to the dormitory it had been years before.

A consequence of having a local catchment area was that more boys came to school on bicycles than by school bus. Both sides of the driveway from Beaumaris Road were lined with bicycles – often 'Rolls Royce' models given by parents thankful that their sons had 'passed the 11+' (though pass or fail were words never used by school or LEA).

All boys wore school uniform similar to today except that all first-year boys and second-year boarders had to wear short trousers. This was very unpopular with the boys and there was a loud cheer when I announced the abolition of this discrimination in 1979. In 1974 only the Upper Sixth wore dark blazers but this privilege was soon extended to all sixth formers.

The school day began with Assembly for the whole school in Big School. This was a squash for 400 boys, who had to stand. Occasionally one fainted – usually because he had missed breakfast! The overcrowding could generate a sense of occasion and bonding especially when successes were announced and applause sounded twice as loud as it echoed off the walls. There were moments of seriousness and sadness to be shared as well, when a 'silent' silence descended as if 400 boys had stopped breathing. In particular I remember the deaths of Oliver Atkinson in 1977 and Lynn James in 1986 as such occasions.

In 1974 corporal punishment was not illegal and many schools, especially independent ones, retained it for serious offences. However Jeffrey Roberts had already given up its use and I never used it. So the Headmaster's cane, which has featured prominently in this history, was now a thing of the past. Corporal punishment was formally abolished in Shropshire schools in 1985.

The school had two school captains of equal status, an arrangement I retained throughout my time; usually one was a day-boy and one a boarder. All the Upper Sixth had prefectorial responsibilities but not enough chose to exercise them. Successive school captains urged me to restore the prefect system. In 1979 I did and thereafter around 20 elected prefects exercised a most valuable managerial role, not only performing important daily duties but also taking prospective pupils and their parents round the school. Each form tutor chose a sixth former (a 'Form Representative', not necessarily a prefect), to assist in the pastoral care of his boys.

The '70s was a period when the trend in state education was away from competition, but at Adams' we promoted it strongly. The house system was an ideal vehicle for this and very many activities were put on an inter-house basis. The Dixon Cup, for music and drama, was revived and later a public-speaking competition was introduced. A range of about 20 activities was put into the timetable on Friday afternoon, including the CCF, school orchestra and community service, with squash at Lilleshall Sports Centre available for sixth formers.

In the 1970s schools had control over their curriculum, the only required subject being religious studies, and there was no requirement to achieve a balanced curriculum. At Adams' boys could take three sciences and two modern languages, take English language and elementary mathematics a year early, start additional mathematics in the fifth year and finish with ten or more O levels. O levels were taken after only one year in the fifth form. Unfortunately the achievements of the brightest boys masked the fact that too many left school with few or even no O levels, the pattern being repeated with A levels in the sixth form. In 1974, 60 per cent of the fifth year gained five or more O levels and continued into the sixth form. Many of the leavers took up apprenticeships. At A level 25 per cent went on to university and 30 per cent to polytechnics. Most of the others went straight into a career. Such professions as insurance, accountancy and banking did not require a degree.

To improve the school's academic performance various changes were made. To monitor performance and encourage effort each boy was given a grade in each subject every three weeks or so. Laziness earned a work-card and period-by-period monitoring, with a visit to the Headmaster every Monday morning. I came to know some boys very well! The O level course was lengthened to two years. The O level results improved significantly as did the number of A and B grades. A level results also improved but there were fluctuations superimposed on the upward trend, and they had all the uncertainties of a wine harvest! Vintage years were determined as much by attitude as ability. By the 1980s the A level pass rate was usually 80 per cent or more having risen from 60 per cent. A marked improvement coincided with the introduction of General Studies as an extra A level in 1983. This was taken on a voluntary basis, but soon almost every candidate took it. There was no syllabus, the questions were not easy, but Adams' boys were very successful. Publishing our results each year in the local press became a very effective form of advertising, especially as 'quality of education' became an issue in the school's struggle for survival, related in the next chapter.

Several of the staff had been appointed by Glover or his predecessors and now they were reaching retirement. Mrs Margaret Houlston retired after 21 years as Headmaster's secretary (her part-time assistant, Mrs Hazel Gosling, who replaced her was with me through thick and thin until she retired in 1991). Margaret presented the Houlston Cup to be awarded for outstanding contribution to the school. Ron Anderson retired in 1977 after 43 years; he arrived in the era of the bi-plane and departed with Concorde! Appointed as Second Master by Glover just before he left, he will be remembered especially for his outstanding contribution to school sport and boarding, the epitome of the traditional schoolmaster. A new post of Deputy Head was now created (many schools already had one) and Dr David Westgate, a French specialist from Eastbourne Grammar School, was appointed. He played an indispensable part in the management of the school, successfully seeing in my successor Jim Richardson in 1994 and retiring in 1996. Almost immediately he took an extra job as housemaster at Longford when Oliver Atkinson sadly died of cancer in 1978. Our school caretaker, Horace Knott, a wonderful Black Country character, retired in 1978 after 23 years. In his place came Bryan Lloyd, joining his wife Margaret who was already working in the school office. They lived in the bungalow by the swimming pool until he retired in 1998. A maintenance team of three has replaced Bryan, none of whom lives on site.

In 1978, when the head of the mathematics department, John Edgoose, moved on, I appointed Ken Delaney, by far the youngest candidate, to maintain the school's strong mathematics tradition. He said he could

Novaportan *1982. With acknowledgements to the cartoonist whose signature we cannot decipher.*

improve it and by 1981 there were more grade As than any other grade in O level mathematics and a pass rate of 93 per cent. In April 1979 Ken suggested that the school should buy a micro-computer and I agreed. This was a major step forward – very few schools had a computer or saw the need for one. We went a step further: in co-operation with Newport Rotary Club, of which I was a member, Ken and I organised a two-day 'hands-on' presentation on computers for children in their last year at the seven Newport primary schools. To raise 15 computers we had to borrow from schools all over Shropshire! In the evening we held a public meeting on 'The challenge of the Chip – Employment in the Eighties' with a panel of experts. This was so successful we repeated it in 1981 with the additional assistance of the County Science Adviser, Ray Hills. We organised the purchase of a computer to be shared by the Newport primary schools, Rotary and the LEA sharing the cost. It is worth mentioning that this support from the LEA was occurring at the same time as the negotiations on reorganisation.

In the '70s women rarely applied to teach at Adams'. They might enquire but then withdrew quickly when told it was an all boys' school. In 1979 Frances McMullen (later Butler) did not withdraw and accepted a mathematics post. In 1985 Mrs Borghild Wood was the first woman to head a department when she took over modern languages. In the late '80s Mrs Celia Bloor, a physics teacher, was in charge of the RAF section of the CCF. Today well over a quarter of the staff are women.

Walter Harding retired at the end of 1981 after 34 years at the school. We have already noted many of his contributions to school life since 1947. He never seemed to be off the premises and one wondered how he found time to be a Wrekin District Councillor and twice Mayor of Newport. A catalogue of his contributions does not adequately convey his character, style and exuberance, or his talent for relating to the young, particularly when advising them on careers. To give him an excuse to come to Adams' each day we asked him to act as part-time Bursar, which he did until a full-time Bursar was appointed in 1990 when the school became Grant Maintained.

School was not insulated from the changes in society in the '70s: I recall flared trousers, long hair (staff included!), big ties and shirt collars, with school rules trying to keep up with ear-rings, 'pop' badges, trainers and the use of skateboards. 1977 was the year of the Queen's Jubilee but also of the Sex Pistols and Punk Rock – and the launch of pot noodles, the easy meal for senior boarders!

This period saw a dramatic increase in self-help. Money was short and education cuts became a familiar term. Little new money came our way: curriculum development was for comprehensive education. We embarked on a programme of self-help and fund-raising in which the parents of the young Adams' Grammar School Society played an indispensable role. AGSS acted as a channel of communication to explain to parents what we wanted and why we could not get money elsewhere. School and parents co-operated in fêtes, fairs, draws, sponsored walks, pound-stretchers and discos to raise thousands of pounds. Practical help came in the provision of games-teas by the mums and renovating the school cottage and building a pavilion extension by the dads. The funds were enhanced by annual donations from the Old Novaportans' War Memorial Fund, and various educational charities of the Haberdashers' Company. The munificence of Kenneth Leach was felt again through contributions from the Kenneth Leach Trust. These private school funds enabled us to buy computers, extra equipment and books, a Bechstein grand piano, multi-gym, curtains in Big School, a new minibus ... the list is endless. Materials were provided for the trophy cabinet in Big School, designed and built by craft teacher Jim Clover, and Bill's Will, repainted by parent Peter Imeson. When the school outfitter Tom Whitmore closed in 1979 we formed a school clothing shop run by senior matron and the office secretary, which benefited parents and school funds. Sixth formers redecorated their common rooms (we tolerated some unusual colour schemes!) and boarders did likewise.

Parents contributed to an Activities Fund termly and, from 1982, a Book and Equipment Fund annually. State education might be labelled 'free', but it was parental support and our private funds that allowed us to provide more than the basic model. Statistics at the time indicated that on average the spending per pupil in Independent schools was three times that in the state sector. If you accept that there is a correlation between financial input and academic output, Adams' was a very efficient school!

Thirteen

1982 TO 1987
THE FIGHT FOR SURVIVAL

Confrontation

After Sir Keith Joseph rejected the comprehensive scheme in 1982, the County Council bowed to the inevitable. Although some councillors said the decision was disgraceful, most felt there was little point in submitting another scheme while the existing government was in power. At Adams' we looked forward to a quieter life. But this was not to be.

If the school was to prosper there were some urgent problems to be solved. The derelict Headmaster's house had no staircase and this meant that the sixth-form rooms above Big School had no fire escape and thus had to be closed. The school lacked many of the facilities that other schools took for granted so we put together a list of major requirements. Adams' had only the 1926 Manual Room built when 'Woodwork' was a subject for the 'B' stream. Now it looked more like a large garden shed than a teaching space. The County Adviser, Ken Brown, readily agreed that Adams' had the worst craft facilities in the county.

The Governors met LEA representatives on 6 December 1982 to discuss what happened next. Their ideas were very different. The Governors wished to improve facilities but the LEA was focused on the decline in primary school numbers ('falling rolls'), the 11+ selection procedure and education at 16+. We were told of a predicted fall in the number of 11-year-olds in the Newport area of almost 36 per cent by September 1988. This was amazing information coming so soon after a reorganisation plan which had been based on two 11-18 schools in 1988. The figures now supplied showed that only one school would be needed.

The LEA said it could not spend money on a school which was predicted to shrink in size nor would it accept the responsibility of converting the Headmaster's house into school accommodation. The most it would consider was a 'minor works' project (i.e. costing under £120,000) for Craft Design and Technology (CDT) but not until 1984. It doubted whether the school could maintain viable A level courses as numbers fell. It was clear that it would prefer to provide for sixth formers by expanding New College, Wellington, rather than improving Adams' and the High School. It also criticised our admissions procedure, implying that we were lowering our standards, especially in boarding, so as to maintain pupil numbers. No concrete evidence was produced: we were attacked by innuendo, anecdote and hearsay. In the past Governors and LEA had worked together to submit mutually acceptable schemes to the Minister. But now co-operation was to be replaced by confrontation and conflict.

The project for a small CDT centre came to nothing. The Headmaster's house continued to stand derelict. The Haberdashers' Company was reluctant to commit itself and set up a small strategy group to look at the future of the school. Its mood was clearly supportive but it often reminded me of the sympathy accorded to the terminally ill.

In March 1983 the LEA told us that if Adams' continued to admit 36 boys from the Newport primary schools each year, the selection rate would rise from 25 per cent to nearly 40 per cent, because of falling rolls. The concern was that the quality of intake at Burton Borough would be reduced and that we might have to admit boys who were not of grammar school ability. The proposal was that Adams' should reduce its annual intake from 36 to 30, with a parallel reduction for the Girls' School. This provided the Governors with a dilemma. Their first responsibility was to protect Adams' numbers but they could lay themselves open to accusations that they were indifferent to the problems of other schools. Boarding numbers were already declining in line with a national trend, but also reflecting the reluctance of parents to commit themselves to a school with an uncertain future. Between 1974 and 1982 boarding numbers had fallen from 184 to 119, and school numbers had fallen from 430 to 392 pupils. If the Governors deliberately reduced the day boy intake, numbers would fall dramatically and the school would hover between one- and two-form entry and no longer be able to maintain the 'sustained and sustainable record of sixth form provision' that had impressed Sir Keith Joseph.

In the protracted and often bitter negotiations during the next eighteen months the Governors were alone. The LEA was not proposing a so-called 'significant change of character' so no Minister was called upon to make the final decision. This was the time when the survival of the school was under greatest threat – even more so than during plans for comprehensive reorganisation or the closure proposals of 1985.

Because Adams' was Voluntary Aided the LEA needed the Governors' assent to the proposed change. They decided to oppose it and produce a plan of their own. The key instrument at their disposal was the 1980 Education Act. This effectively abolished catchment areas, giving parents the right to choose the school they wanted irrespective of where it was, provided it had vacancies. The Governors therefore proposed that Adams' should accept no more than 30 boys annually from Newport on condition that, to maintain a total of 60, they should accept 30 others from outside the area, who could be day boys or boarders. The Governors would determine the admission numbers and the LEA would decide which boys were of suitable ability, whether day or boarding, 11+ or older.

The LEA did not at first accept this plan and warned that a refusal to reduce our intake would result in 'other measures being taken'. The press had access to County Council minutes and reported the situation in vigorous detail. 'School gets rap over admissions' was the headline in the *Newport Advertiser*,[1] while the *Shropshire Star* said, 'Move to tame Newport rebels'.[2] The LEA's official report was also robust in its language: 'the governors were obdurate that there should be no reduction ...'. The LEA decided to seek a meeting with Sir Keith Joseph to tell him what an 'appalling mess' had been created by his refusal to allow Shropshire to become completely comprehensive. Tory, Labour, Liberal and Independent Councillors condemned us for shielding the school from the effect of falling rolls. Sir Keith Joseph refused to become involved, saying he might have to rule on the disagreement if it became a formal dispute. The clear message was that the two sides must come to a compromise and so, reluctantly, the LEA accepted the Governors' proposals.

The press informed the general public: 'Governors win victory over pupil intake' and 'compromise wins the day in Adams' fight'.[3] Admissions under the new procedure were to start in September 1985 and we advertised it in the Shropshire and Staffordshire press.

Towards 2000

Looking back we can see that the new admissions agreement was of enormous importance. It marked the start of the school's expansion which continued uninterrupted through the rest of the century and into the new millennium. By 1984 school numbers had sunk to 381 but the next year they rose to 395. Day boys could be admitted from anywhere in the country – provided they could get to school in time! Soon we were accepting 75 and not 60 in a year group. The LEA took over the testing of boarders as well as day boys so they could no longer accuse us of 'back door' entry. They had been very concerned about the number of boarders we admitted at 13+, mostly from Prep Schools, but in the year the LEA took over the testing even more boys qualified for 13+ entry than the year before!

By 1985 the Adams' Charity had been able to repair the Headmaster's house and restore the oak staircase, although the Headmaster and his family would no longer live there and it would henceforth be used for school purposes. The oak-panelled dining room became the Headmaster's Office and the breakfast room was turned into the School Office.

The school now had a reconstituted and enlarged Governing Body, as required by the 1980 Education Act: ten nominated by the Haberdashers' Company, five appointed by Shropshire County Council, and for the first time one elected by parents, two elected by the teaching staff, and the Headmaster. Two of the SCC appointments were particularly significant: Dr Barbara Marsh and Councillor George Raxster. As Chairman of the County Education Committee Dr Marsh had been a formidable negotiator during the comprehensive reorganisation era but now she became a strong supporter of the school. Labour had replaced the Conservatives as the majority party on the County Council in the May 1985 elections. George Raxster was a member of a new Labour-appointed Working Party on Falling Rolls appointed to replace the Conservative one. Two of the Haberdasher governors, Geoffrey Fox and Brian Shawcross, were now Wardens of the Company, giving the Governing Body more 'clout'.

The spring term of 1985 had been one of snow and illnesses with most of the third year boarders laid low with 'flu. One of the few sunny days in the summer term coincided with a visit on 16 May of HRH Princess Margaret in her capacity as an honorary freeman of the Haberdashers' Company. On her last visit in 1968 she had opened Longford Hall as a junior boarding house. To commemorate this visit we converted the two spare bedrooms of the Headmaster's house into a Computer Centre. This was made possible by the use of a generous bequest from Kenneth Leach who had died the previous year. The Princess's visit was a great success and it was clear that she enjoyed meeting boys and staff in preference to the various dignitaries that have to be invited on such occasions.

That year the A level results were good and O levels outstanding. We had a most successful joint Adams'/High School production of Gilbert and Sullivan's *The Sorcerer*, and the joint schools orchestra involving all three Newport secondary schools led by our Director of Music Tom Bayliss had reached a standard comparable with any other school in the county. The house competitions continued with undiminished vigour and the Dixon Cup was won by Aston House – the first win for a day boy house for 13 years. Chetwynd won the Harding Cup and also a new Rugby house trophy, presented by the Smedley family whose three boys had been at the school. The boarders had to be content with winning everything else! The autumn term had started with a splendid First XV victory by 28-4 over Wrekin College. We thought it augured well.

It was therefore with no feeling of apprehension that I attended Shirehall on 5 December 1985 to receive the report of the Working Party on Falling Rolls. I went with Margaret Mantripp, Head of the Girls' High School, and she shared my feelings: both our schools were oversubscribed so we were really attending as spectators. On arrival we were each handed a thick colour-coded document entitled 'Towards 2000'. We turned to the purple pages which were for the Newport area and read:

Proposals
❖ that Adams Grammar (Aided) School and the Newport Girls' High School be closed.
❖ that Burton Borough School become an 11-16 Comprehensive School.
❖ that places at 16+ be offered at the enlarged New College, Wellington.

Newport was not the only area to be affected. Other schools were to be closed and several 11-18 schools would lose their sixth forms. A reduction of almost 20 per cent in pupil numbers was forecast to occur between 1984 and 1995. The Labour-controlled Working Party of seven councillors had been working since June 1985, chaired by Beryl Mason, Chairman of the County Education Committee. 'Towards 2000' was a consultative document and the Governors had January and February in which to reply. If matters went according to the Working Party programme the Secretary of State could make a decision in time for September 1987.

'Towards 2000' had been produced in conditions of complete secrecy with no consultation beforehand. One of the members of the Working Party, George Raxster, as an Adams' Governor was privy to all our Governors' business but had said not a word about the plan. As a yard-stick to determine which schools should be closed the Working Party used the Council's policy formulated in 1984 that an 11-16 school should have at least four forms of entry (assuming 30 in each) with some flexibility to recognise local, especially rural, circumstances. A school of at least 6FE would be needed to produce a sixth form of 150 pupils.

The Governors believed that a grammar school did not require 6FE or even 4FE to generate a viable sixth form. After all, our numbers had risen since 1982 when our sixth form had received the approval of Sir Keith Joseph, and our co-operation with the High School further strengthened it. The Governors' other concern was that the Working Party made no mention of quality of education: it was size that really mattered. The Newport proposals were an overtly political act. For most of the 12 years I had spent at Adams' its grammar school status had been under threat. Now it was under threat of closure. Because this involved everyone, it united everyone – Governors, staff, parents and boys. It was therefore an exciting and exhilarating time to be at Adams'. Those who remembered the Second World War talked of the 'Dunkirk spirit'. We also had an unlikely ally. Terry Gilder, editor of the *Newport Advertiser*, had been critical of the school in the past but now he gave full prominence to anything that the Chairman of Governors or I wished to say publicly. We were quoted at length, often on the front page, enabling us to reach a very wide audience.

As a result of a very well attended meeting of parents on 9 January 1986 an Action Group was formed with Keith Norton as Chairman, Andrea Gillibrand Secretary, David Carver Treasurer, Michael Young Public Relations, staff representative Philip North and a further 15 with designated jobs. Significantly, it included a strong representation of parents living outside Newport who had therefore already made a commitment to Adams' in preference to their own local school. Working closely with myself and the staff this powerful and energetic group played an indispensable role in assisting Governors to produce a strong defence of the school.

A series of consultation meetings was organised by the Working Party including a public meeting at Burton Borough School on 30 January. Over 600 people attended, many of them grammar school supporters. Many had moved to Newport to take advantage of its schools. They challenged the County's population figures and asked why only two months was allowed to respond to what had taken the Working Party six months to prepare. Chairman of Governors, Harry Wood, said that the plans looked more like fact than proposal and he wanted the Working Party to start again with genuine consultation. He pointed out that Sir Keith Joseph had rejected the reorganisation scheme of 1982 because of the quality of sixth-form education, and the County's response was to eliminate it. Two sixth formers, William Parsonage and John Lanham, spoke eloquently in defence of their school, well trained by the William Adams' Debating Society. As the last contributor I said that I feared for the community of Newport. The mass 'bussing out' of sixth formers would turn it into a teenage commuter town. 'I find it disgraceful that we are expected to produce our own plans for survival. Our duty as teachers and parents is to our pupils but it is being diluted because we are having to defend ourselves as well as running our schools. Not only have we done that but we have improved our results. Why can't you get off our backs and let us get on with our real job, which is education.'

The *Newport Advertiser* report on 7 February read, 'Taylor is hero of the hour in Education Officials versus the Rest match' and that 'he captured the mood of most and received enthusiastic applause.' It continued, 'Angry residents gave Shropshire Education chiefs a rough ride ... left them in no doubt of their strong objections ... and sent them back to Shirehall with the message 'think again' ringing in their ears.'

Although there now followed a constant stream of letters to the Press from Adams' parents, boys and other supporters, it was the proposed loss of the sixth form which appeared to generate most concern to the people of the town. Saving the two threatened grammar schools now seemed lower on their list of priorities. It was sad to see such fine schools close, the argument went, but people had to 'grasp the nettle' of falling numbers and accept the inevitable. From the Town Council, local parish councils, from the parent associations of the local primary schools we had sympathy but not support. This was a far cry from the protest meetings at the end of the 19th century. Then Newport Grammar School was Newport's Grammar School and there was a strong sense of ownership. But now in 1986, there were divided loyalties. Other than our present parents we did not know who our local supporters were. Three-quarters of the town might be indifferent to our fate because three-quarters of the town's children did not attend the grammar schools. I was particularly disappointed that the Town Council did not do more to defend the grammar schools. It merely asked the LEA to retain a sixth form in Newport as part of a community school. I wrote an open letter to it, pointing out that Education is part of Newport's business. Closing a school is closing a business and the Town Council shouldn't condone it. Other towns in Shropshire were fighting tooth and nail to preserve their schools. Newport had more reason to fight for its three schools than any other Shropshire town, because their combined examination results were the best in Shropshire. Candidates in Newport obtained an average of 3.8 O level passes each, compared with an average of 2.2 for the county as a whole. I asked the council to take more positive action. My plea fell on deaf ears.

The separate conclusions of the Governors and the Parent Action Group were unanimous: Adams' could remain and flourish as a grammar school. Using information and statistics obtained from Shropshire County Council, they both established in detail that Adams' provided a high quality of education that was cost-effective and that, with the new admissions procedure agreed in 1984, it could maintain its selection rate without damage to Burton Borough School. The parents' report, a spirited and closely argued document written by Professor Tony Hopkins, 'The Case For Adams' Grammar School', was effectively an external audit of the school conferring a seal of approval on its performance. To reach their conclusions parents learned more about the school than they had ever known before.

It was also pointed out by Governors and parents that the Working Party had ignored the contribution of boarding. The Boarding Schools' Association supported us wholeheartedly and wrote direct to the County Education Officer saying that the closure of Adams' would be an 'educational loss for the nation as well as Shropshire'. Since there was united support for Adams' remaining as a grammar school, independence was only briefly considered as an alternative. Ironically, the LEA indicated that it would not be surprised if we wished to go independent.[4] It sounded as though it would ease the Council conscience if it did not have our blood on its hands!

It was not only the articulate professional and business people – the so-called middle class – that supported Adams'. Throughout the school's history a grammar school education has enabled boys from humble backgrounds to go on to university and a successful career. We found the tradition was still alive when a local resident wrote to the *Advertiser* saying that Adams' selected its pupils on social grounds ('if the face fits') rather than academic ones. This drew a vigorous rebuttal from 'Angry Working Class parent' who had children at both grammar schools and described the accusation as 'absolutely ludicrous'. Sixth formers Jonathan Edwards, Ian Hopkins, William Parsonage and Nigel Richardson wrote to the *Newport Advertiser* saying the charge was a libellous insult and that entrants were selected regardless of social background. Nigel and Jonathan suggested to me that the public ought to know more about the day-to-day activities of the school and offered to act as Press Officers. I thought this was an excellent idea and thereafter successive generations of sixth formers performed this invaluable function.

The Editorial by Ian Gilders and Geoffrey Westgate in the 1986 *Novaportan* described very well the mood in the school. 'Although life at the school has more or less carried on as normal ... this report ['Towards 2000'] has been a permanent backcloth to school life over the past year. However, far from bowing down submissively to what some see as bureaucratic whims based on inaccurate facts and dubious predictions, there has been noted, amongst the boys as well as the staff, a certain mood of defiance and determination to prove that Adams' does still ... have a part to play in contemporary education. From our own experiences as Sixth formers we feel that the opportunities offered to senior boys at Adams' would be hard to match at a Sixth Form College. In addition to the academic advantages, the senior boy at Adams' has some chances not available elsewhere for the development of his character, such as holding positions of responsibility in the school, and organising junior boys ... We feel that the Adams' of the present is certainly a more relaxed place than the Adams' of the past ... and bullying has not reared its ugly head for a long time. Although the academic side of school life is important, a friendly community is also vital. We feel that at present, the right balance between the two has been struck at Adams'.' They concluded, 'it is up to everyone of us within the school to take some of the responsibility upon himself to prove that not only is Adams' a good school worth preserving but also that it can be a better school.' When boys can write so well and have such feelings about their school, you know you have something worth defending!

The Working Party did not produce its revised proposals until September 1986. Major changes were made in some areas of the county, but the plan for Newport was unchanged. It would still lose its two grammar schools and therefore the sixth form.

An action group was formed in town to protest at this and in October the Working Party produced a revised scheme in which Burton Borough would have a sixth form. This made the position of the grammar school supporters a more lonely one. What was surrendered was the notion of a small school. Burton Borough would eventually grow to over one thousand when its sixth form was established. But a rise in the birth-rate had now been predicted and it became evident that the mid-1990s could see a demand for another secondary school – just when the two grammar schools were scheduled to close.

The proposals of the Working Party now had three further hurdles to negotiate: the Education Committee, the full County Council and the new Secretary of State, Kenneth Baker. The Education Committee left the proposals intact but it was a different matter when the County Council met on 14 November. In a 9½-hour debate virtually all the Working Party's proposals were rejected by the Labour-controlled Council. Only in Newport, the one area where pupil numbers were not falling, were the proposals unaltered.

However Adams' and its supporters were not downhearted for the final decision would be made by the Secretary of State, whose policy on education included parental choice, good academic performance, and single sex schools. While the LEA was preparing the wording for the Public Notice, Governors and the Parent Action Group were preparing their detailed objections and rallying supporters to do the same. Local MPs John Biffen and Warren Hawksley were stalwart supporters. The formal Public Notice, this time a 'Section 12' one, was published on 26 March 1987, with the usual two months allowed for objections. Judging by the number who sent us copies of their letters there were a large number of objectors.

David Taylor by cartoonist Peter Maddocks.

We were confident that the Minister would reject the closure proposals and expected a decision in June or July. But six months of silence went by and it was not until the very last day of term, Friday 18 December 1987, that I was told in a telephone call from Shirehall that the Minister had rejected the proposals. In coming to his decision the Secretary of State 'took the view that there was insufficient evidence to suggest that the proposals would represent for the majority of pupils, an improvement to the present system'.

Three days later I phoned the *Shropshire Star* and found it had not been told. A few hours later 'No change at Newport' was the banner headline on the front page, followed two days later by 'Christmas Joy for two schools' on the front of the *Newport Advertiser.*

There were of course prophets of doom who said that education in Newport would suffer but their fears have proved groundless and when the year 2000 was reached all three secondary schools were prospering.

Knowing the view of the Minister regarding grammar schools one might ask whether the outcome would have been any different if parents and Governors had done nothing at all. The answer is possibly 'no', but there is no doubt that the reaction of the boys and parents, and the commitment of the staff to 'keeping the show on the road' demonstrated that here was a school worth fighting for. And the Governors did not weaken, declaring from the outset that closure was not on their agenda. The conflict brought all of us closer together and the school emerged stronger and more united than ever before.

Fourteen

1988 AND BEYOND

Grant Maintained Status

Adams' had been defending itself as a grammar school from 1965 to 1987. It could now plan its own route towards 2000. Should it stay the same size or should it grow? Should it remain single sex and should it expand its boarding? We needed more buildings and facilities, as we had done throughout the 22 years. How could we obtain them? These were some of the questions we could now consider. We also had a dream – the school was on two sites in Newport and at Longford. Could we now move the whole school to Longford?

The educational scene had changed during these 22 years. The Labour policy of the mid-'60s was based on equality of opportunity but the Conservative policy of the '80s was more concerned with quality of outcome. A succession of Education Acts in the 1980s, culminating in the Education Reform Act of 1988, provided the instruments of change. The main one was the National Curriculum. A 'core curriculum' of required subjects was introduced with a detailed syllabus in each, and with graded tests at certain key stages along the way. The publication of examination results in a prescribed way would allow parents to compare schools which the Press obligingly ranked in 'league tables'. School Heads acquired the status (and in some cases, the uncertain tenure) of football club managers. Performance was monitored by Records of Achievement for the pupils and Appraisal for the teachers (with performance-related pay on the horizon) and in-service training (INSET). Parents were given much more opportunity to choose a school and then have a say in running it. One Governor was to be elected by the parents and the Governors had to report annually to the parents in written form and at a meeting. Open enrolment ensured that popular schools could expand to the capacity of their buildings and there was a formula to decide what that capacity was. To measure how schools responded to these changes a scheme of inspection (judgmental but not advisory) was set up in the 1990s, known by its acronym OFSTED.

Partly to off-set this increased bureaucratic control from the centre there were local changes, in particular Local Management of Schools (LMS) whereby LEAs delegated a substantial part of their budgets to schools. Even more radical and controversial was the creating of City Technology Colleges, supported in part by industrial sponsorship, and Grant Maintained (or self-governing) schools that would be independent of

LEA control and would receive their entire budget direct from central government.

The new, united Adams' Grammar School imbued with 'post-war' idealism and purged of most of its past reactionary attitudes embraced the changes, sometimes reluctantly and sometimes cynically, but with a determination to show that a grammar school could not only cope with change but also initiate it. Adams' Grammar School was not to be a part of English heritage or a theme park with dinosaurs (though there was a 'dinosaurs corner' in the staff common-room!) The Adams' philosophy was to adopt the best ideas, adapt them to its needs and then if possible improve them. So, for example, we went to some trouble in our curriculum to retain two modern languages and three separate sciences. And in an era when schools were being encouraged to specialise we felt our strength lay in mathematics and science and would do so in technology also if we could but obtain the facilities. Perhaps people will accuse us of arrogance but when educational standards were rediscovered we said 'welcome back!' for we had never lost sight of them.

The main topic to which Governors devoted themselves in 1989 was whether to apply for Grant Maintained status and escape from Shropshire LEA control. It was a big step to take, so big that many schools did not even contemplate it. If Adams' became Grant Maintained the Governors would have direct responsibility for a budget of well over a million pounds. Governors of a Grant Maintained school appointed and paid all the staff and agreed an admissions policy direct with the Secretary of State. They also determined the curriculum within the parameters set by the National Curriculum. They would own all its assets. (The Haberdashers' Company already owned the land and buildings.) The Governing body would also be made up of people appointed to work in the best interests of the school: there would be no Governors appointed by political bodies whose prime allegiance lay elsewhere. There also had to be five elected parent governors. Parents had played a great part in the 'Towards 2000' episode. Here was a chance for them to be involved again.

To become Grant Maintained a set procedure was laid down culminating in a parental vote organised by the Electoral Reform Society. If it were favourable the Secretary of State would make the final decision. The Adams' Governors decided to apply for GM status and the necessary resolutions were passed unanimously by the Governing body in July and August. The Haberdashers' Company welcomed the decision. On 1 September I wrote to all parents telling them of the decision and why I personally supported it. Both the Chairman, Harry Wood, and I were very enthusiastic about this new venture, feeling that Grant Maintained status was purpose-made for Adams'. It is worth recording that at the time the Governors voted, there was no Grant Maintained school in the country, although some would be starting in September 1989.

The professional advice to school Heads was to remain neutral. The official description of Grant Maintained status was 'self-government' but it was soon dubbed 'opting out' which was an unfortunate and misleading term. We told parents that we would not be opting out of our links with the community but would seek to strengthen them. We wished to co-operate with the LEA but not be controlled by it. We assured parents that financially they would not notice any difference, but educationally they would. Adams' would remain firmly in the state sector.

The teaching staff also had to be assured about their conditions of service so the Chairman and I met with area representatives of the main union for the staff (NAS/UWT). The meeting went well and we received a letter soon after expressing the union's satisfaction. There was a period of staff concern after the school had become Grant Maintained because the Governors did not immediately make formal recognition of the unions. However, negotiations resolved the problem and the agreement that was subsequently drawn up became a model that was used by other schools.

Adams' was once again in the public eye and the newspaper headlines. The issue was one for Governors and school parents alone to decide but the County Council organised a public meeting in Newport. We had thought that the County Council would be keen to let Adams' go and that our move would be accepted without dispute. Harry Wood's letter to parents describing the advantages of Grant Maintained status was therefore deliberately couched in moderate language. The County Council also wrote to all the school parents but in a very different tone. It produced a six-page document emphasising the great risks the parents were taking if they voted in favour; there would be 'no way back', 'an uncertain future', if problems arose 'the LEA will not be there'. The document was clearly designed to frighten and not inform. Fortunately we had a parent who was a member of the County Council Education Committee. He wrote to all our parents saying that the presentation and style of the letter had not been agreed by Council members and that many of the points made were inaccurate or misleading.

At the parents' meeting in the school gymnasium just before the ballot was due some of the objections and fears raised by the County Council were implicit in many of the questions asked. Few supporters of Grant Maintained status spoke and by the end I was apprehensive and depressed.

The day after all votes had to be in I was at Shirehall on a management training exercise. A messenger came in, consulted the Chairman and came to where I was sitting. He had a message from my secretary, Hazel Gosling: the result of the ballot was 91.2 per cent in favour. I realised that I was sitting in almost the same place as when I received the 'Towards 2000' proposal to close the school. The wheel had come full circle. 557 parents (almost 78 per cent of the 'electorate') had voted in favour of Grant Maintained status and only 54 against. 'That's more than they get for a general election!' was Harry Wood's verdict. The Press reaction was 'overwhelming' and 'staggering'.[1]

Events now moved quickly for the aim was to become Grant Maintained by the start of the next school year, in September 1990. A great deal of information had to be supplied to the Secretary of State and it was the end of January 1990 before it could be sent and the Governors' proposals published. There was the statutory two-month period for objections. Only one was received, signed by 18 local electors, but the County Council was silent.

Within days of the ballot result Her Majesty's School Inspectorate (HMI) was in touch, to do a quick school inspection. 'Please don't make any special arrangements,' they said. Two HMI arrived the following week and spent a day with us. As we walked round the school I said to one of them, 'This is a very exciting opportunity'. He stopped, looked at me and said drily, 'It's a long time since I've heard a Headmaster use the word "exciting".'

The Secretary of State was now John McGregor (the eighth we had dealt with since 1974!) and he did not take long to decide. On 17 May we were told that he was 'minded to approve the proposals'. In a press statement he said that Adams' had 'an excellent record of achievement, and solid support from parents, governors and staff. I am fully satisfied that it is a worthy candidate to swell the ranks of the Grant Maintained sector.' Adams' would be the 40th Grant Maintained school and we were determined to show that life begins at 40!

We now had to set up a management structure with the appointment of administrative staff – laying the foundations of the school we see today. Making contact with other GM Heads and the DES was easy and informal. The school was visited by bright young people from Schools' Branch 4 (the section at DES that ran the GM system) and the GMS Trust, that had been set up to give schools advice. Everyone was imbued with a sense of pride and purpose in the job they were doing: this was truly a special and exciting time.

Adams' was incorporated as a Grant Maintained school on 1 September 1990. We immediately embarked on a big programme of redecoration and applied for a grant to build a Technology Centre. This was a lengthy procedure and entailed a lot of work by our school architects. Our bid was not successful and we were very disappointed. Was the 'promised land' a mirage after all? We visited the DES and found that the Government had allocated 10 million pounds for capital projects in response to bids from 60 schools totalling 70 million pounds. There was clearly no bottomless 'pot of gold'. DES officials suggested we consider 'remodelling', that is to say, convert existing accommodation to new use. A deputation of sixth formers had been to see me asking for the library to be improved. Here was an opportunity to do something about it. In March 1991 Governors approved a scheme to move the library into Big School (plate 88). The existing library would become an 'electronic library' with a variety of machines to aid individual private study. By September the new scheme was in place thanks to generous support from the Haberdashers' Company and use of a grant from the Government's Technical and Vocational Education Initiative (TVE). Our Grant Maintained funding also allowed us to appoint a full-time librarian and retain the part-time one. No longer could Old Boys visit and say that nothing had changed since their day! The transformation between July and September was amazing. The adjacent sixth form rooms were refurbished

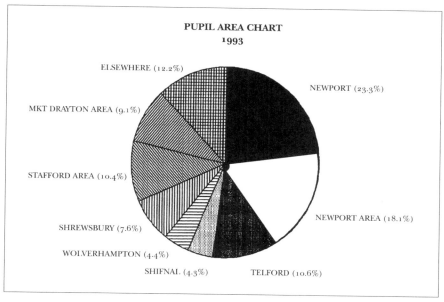

PUPIL AREA CHART
1993

ELSEWHERE (12.2%)

NEWPORT (23.3%)

MKT DRAYTON AREA (9.1%)

STAFFORD AREA (10.4%)

NEWPORT AREA (18.1%)

SHREWSBURY (7.6%)

WOLVERHAMPTON (4.4%)

SHIFNAL (4.3%)   TELFORD (10.6%)

Pupil area chart, 1993.

and the biology laboratory was equipped with the latest designer furniture to emerge as a real showpiece.

Our first year as a Grant Maintained school had produced some notable achievements despite some setbacks. Our first Bursar was replaced by Mike Wilkie, the chartered accountant he had brought in to help him. We had retained many of the LEA's services but found them expensive, so we now looked elsewhere. We also decided to run our own admissions system using nationally recognised and validated tests which candidates took at the school. In this way we ensured that the conditions under which the tests were taken were the same for all candidates and we could now decide which boys would profit from an education at Adams'. The response was such that we had to decide whether to let the school grow or whether to reject boys we believed to be of grammar school ability. We did not wish to measure success by the number we rejected but by what we did for the boys we accepted. And so the school continued to grow.

If the school was to increase in numbers it had to have more buildings. When it became Grant Maintained we had to publish the official capacity of the school as calculated by a DES formula. This was 506 pupils, and by September 1992 we would be very near that figure. So in October 1991 we applied again for capital funding but our bid was again unsuccessful. Then in March, completely out of the blue, we were told that we had been allocated almost half a million pounds under a new scheme 'Technology Schools Initiative'. The scheme was open to all LEA secondary schools as well as Grant Maintained schools and Adams' was one of a hundred chosen to receive funds for developing technology. The thought that we had at last emerged from the wilderness was tempered by the realisation that all might be snatched away from us if there were a change of government after the general election in April. The Labour party was committed to returning Grant Maintained schools to local authority control and abolishing the few remaining grammar schools. However the Conservatives retained power and our plans proceeded. Construction began in January 1993 and the new building was ready for use by the start of the autumn term. At a formal opening ceremony performed by the Master of the Haberdashers' Company in January 1994 it was named 'The Taylor Centre'.

At the Governors' meeting at the beginning of October 1992 I gave written notice of my intention to retire in December 1993, at the age of 60. At the same meeting I proposed that girls should be admitted to the sixth form starting in September 1993. It is worth relating briefly how this came about. Bryan Banks, Head of English and a member of the school management team, had approached me some time earlier, asking what I would do if I received an application from a girl to join the Adams' sixth form. 'I would have to consider it very seriously', was my reply. Co-education in the sixth form was one of the targets in our annual School Development Plan produced in the previous April. Bryan's question would concentrate our minds! Our basic premise was that we should prepare sixth formers for the world of work by providing girls and boys with the experience of working together as well as socialising together. Governors agreed that I could pursue the matter.

There were many people to be consulted as well as bureaucratic hurdles to be surmounted. However what would previously have taken months, if not years, to establish, was accomplished within weeks. By the end of January we had secured the written consent of the DFE (the renamed DES) for Adams' to accept up to 6 per cent of its total school number as girls in the sixth form, without change to its single-sex status. The Governors approved the proposal: the whole process had taken four months. I had been appointed in 1973 to create a co-educational grammar school. Now, 20 years later, a part of that mission would be accomplished. We advertised the fact that we could now admit girls and again Adams' was in the news. The teaching staff had supported the move from the onset but the boys were not so sure. That barometer of school opinion, the William Adams' Society, held a debate on the subject and voted to keep girls out!

Not surprisingly, the first applicant was Elizabeth Banks who was joined by five other pioneers. The number was a little disappointing since we could have taken fifteen. However there was considerable interest and many parents said to me, 'I wish you had done this earlier'. The six girls were very good ambassadors for the new venture and there has been increasingly strong competition from girls for entry ever since. By 2002 there were 52 girls in the sixth form.

School Life in the 1980s and '90s

In 1988 an air of relief and optimism was very apparent among the boys of the school, noted in the editorial of the *Novaportan* and in an amusing speech by school captain Marcus Jones at the annual Prizegiving. 1988 demonstrated the quality of what had been preserved. It was a vintage year for public examination results and more boys than ever went on to higher education. It was the first year of the new GCSE examination which replaced O levels. Boys and staff showed that they could more than cope with an examination far removed from the traditional grammar school approach. We also had one of our most successful years on the sports field. School rugby teams won five of the six County championships (though this was not unusual), and the first XV had a successful tour of Portugal. In March the school won the Haberdasher Schools' Fraser Bird Sevens for the first time, the result in doubt until the first VII beat Elstree 13-0. A month later in the *Daily Mail* National Schools' Rugby Cup the Under 15 team came third equal with Rossall School with a 7-7 draw on the Harlequins' ground in London. Rossall had been favourites to win the Cup having scored 859 points to 78 in 25 games, and unbeaten in the season. Adams' was the only state school to reach the final four and in recognition of this achievement the team was the first recipient of a new County award, the Beswick Trophy.

These achievements and others were remarkable in that in the years 1984-86 there had been nationwide industrial action by the three main teaching unions in pursuit of a pay claim. Almost all the staff were union members and each union took a slightly different stance so I had a lot of negotiating to do. There were days of strike action which affected the teaching programme and an ongoing 'withdrawal of good will' which affected out-of-school activities and parents' meetings. External threats unite but internal threats divide, so this was a difficult time. However local grievances were avoided and relationships quickly returned to normal once a national pay agreement was reached. The achievements of 1988 show that the staff found a way of obeying union instructions without losing their commitment to the boys. I think this was understood by the parents for we had virtually no protests. A motion in the William Adams' Debating Society, 'the teachers' action is justified', was carried.

In September 1986 the whole school had grieved at the sudden death of Lynn James from a heart attack on the rugby field at Longford. In his contribution to rugby and cricket, boarding at Longford, the school cottage (he was the first master in charge) and the tuck shop, he was one of the school's treasures, respected and loved by boys and staff alike. Who could forget his expressive face on the touch-line moving from the stern aspect of exhortation to an angelic smile when things went well or his voice, quiet one moment but capable of travelling the width of a rugby pitch the next? In 1989 new cricket nets were opened as a memorial to him (plate 90). They appeared to act as an inspiration, for the school had one of its best seasons for many years. The Under 12 and Under 16 teams won County Championships and in the latter

Neil Armstrong took six wickets for six runs including a hat trick. In three of the school teams centuries were scored.

In the 1980s a succession of gifted musicians, Tom Bayliss, Keith Orrell and Richard Churches, raised school music to new heights both in quality and numbers involved. After the first Haberdasher Schools' Music Festival at Elstree in 1986 we could with confidence host the second one in 1987. However it was Chris Jobson, Head of Religious Studies, who founded the Newport Joint Schools' Orchestra during the interregnum before Tom Bayliss arrived. The establishment of a CCF marching band in 1989 further enhanced the school's musical reputation and it has been in frequent demand for civic occasions.

Art must not be forgotten: Dudley Chambers' philosophy was that an artist is not a special person but everyone can be a special kind of artist. As a result he was able to draw in boys from a broad academic background. The number who took A level art in combination with A level mathematics and physics was notable. He further expounded his ideas in his annual critiques of the art and craft exhibited in the Harding Cup. Pictures by boys, and some of his own adorned the walls of the school. Particularly memorable were the 35 Van Gogh reproductions painted by groups of boys and displayed in the dining hall in 1990, 100 years after the artist's death.

At the end of the 1980s we achieved a change in the Adams' culture by reorganising the house system. There had been four houses, Adams and Ward (boarding) and Aston and Chetwynd (day). Boarders won most of the house competitions even though they were greatly outnumbered, but as their numbers fell there came a time when they had difficulty in raising rugby teams. In 1982 boys and boarding staff alike vigorously opposed my proposal that the houses should be altered to contain a mixture of day boys and boarders. Instead Adams and Ward were amalgamated to form School House, with house colours of amber and blue. By the end of the '80s with the rapid increase in day boys the imbalance of numbers had returned. In September 1988 a staff pastoral committee recommended the abolition of the old houses and the creation of three new ones with a mixture of day boys and boarders. The names Clive, Darwin and Talbot, used from 1948 to 1970, were revived. With three-form-entry and three houses the form unit and the house unit thus became one, and the forms were named accordingly. Boarders and day boys would now not only work side by side in the classroom but play side by side on the sports field. The change was made successfully – receiving the ultimate accolade of approval in the school captains' double-act at Speech Day in September 1990!

Parent Governor Alan Snead and I found we had similar views regarding the national shortage of engineers. We organised a four-day residential conference, The Challenge of Engineering, based at Adams' and sent invitations to 300 schools. We had no problem in assembling a full programme of lectures, workshops and visits involving top industrialists. It was endorsed by Sir Monty Finniston FRS, who had been guest speaker at Speech Day

1978, and attracted support from the government, County Council and industry. Unfortunately there were not enough applicants and it had to be abandoned. However, it led to our organising a two-day version in 1983 for our own sixth form and that of the High School, which became an annual feature. Participation in the Young Enterprise scheme (in which sixth formers run a mini-company with the help of advisers from industry) began in 1986 and still continues. Such events gave extra depth to the structured programme of careers advice which has been a particular strength of Adams' for many years.

In the second half of the '80s the remainder of the Glover appointees retired. First to go were John and Margaret Humphries, remembered with affection by generations of senior boarders. Next went Keith Reynolds, only the second Head of Physics the school has had, followed by Lynton and Stella Seymour Whiteley and then Graham Mottershaw and Dudley Chambers in 1991. Sadly, there is no space to give adequate biographies, save to say that they had devoted almost their entire careers to the school with energy and enthusiasm.

Long service was not confined to the teaching staff; it has also been a feature of the support staff, many of whom retired at this time after 20 years or more at the school. In particular we remember Joyce Locke who retired from the domestic boarding staff in 1990, having been originally appointed to look after the Petersons' children in the early '50s!

By September 1989 numbers had grown enough for the LEA to allow us an extra member of staff. A technology fund set up the previous year had been so well supported by parents and the Company that we had sufficient equipment to justify appointing Peter Chapman as our first teacher of Information Technology.

Academic Progress

The national publication of examination results allowed us to compare our performance with other schools'. Previous to this we could only compare one year's with that of another. In the 1990s the media devoted an ever-increasing amount of attention to the interpretation and discussion of these results. In 1991 a reporter from the *Sunday Times* telephoned to ask what was our percentage of A and B grades at A level. I told her 33 per cent. It was lower than several previous years so I was surprised when she said, 'Oh, that's good'. In a list published the following Sunday Adams' was 34th and in a list including independent schools Adams' was 96th. In 1992 the government issued performance tables for the first time, as promised under the Parents' Charter. *The Times* printed a list of the top ten Grant Maintained and selective schools. Adams' was seventh in one and sixth in the other, with scores that put us ahead of any comprehensive but below many independent schools. The A level pass rates were impressive: 92.4 per cent (41.9 per cent at A & B grades) in 1992, 94.5 per cent (37.8 per cent A & B) in 1993 and 96.5 per cent (42.4 per cent A & B) in 1994.

GCSE hastened though did not initiate a classroom revolution. In traditional teaching, 'sit up, face the front and stop talking' had been a frequent instruction. The focus was the teacher and silence was the aim. But teaching methods had changed. Blackboards and chalk (and the inevitable chalk-filled air) gave way to white boards and overhead projectors. Locker desks with sloping tops became antique shop collectables and were replaced by large tables to allow for practical work and group activity. Boys no longer sat isolated speaking only to the teacher. They often worked together and therefore talked together. The emphasis moved from teaching to learning. Noise could be a sign of success and not indiscipline. Almost every classroom belonged to a specialist subject so that at a lesson change the corridors were crowded with boys and noise instead of a few strolling teachers. Boys could store their books and belongings in metal lockers in the corridors but usually chose to carry them in large bags that would be left in piles around the school at break and lunch times. These untidy piles, I would tell visiting parents, demonstrated the security the boys felt – they were behaving at school as they did at home!

The culture change spread beyond the classroom. The family type meals in the dining hall of twenty years earlier, with a teacher or prefect serving at each table, gave way to a cafeteria service where there was a wide choice and the customer was king. A new and bigger tuck shop was sited at the dining hall and boys descended on it like a plague of locusts at every conceivable opportunity.

Boys fed their minds as well. In 1992, after one year of operating the new library in Big School, Elizabeth Kosinski reported a six-fold increase in the borrowing of books and at lunchtime the library was packed with boys. It was no longer on the fringe of school activity, it was at the centre and possibly did more to change the ethos of the school than anything else. How pleased William Adams would have been, who attached so much importance to his library!

Fifteen

INTO THE NEW MILLENNIUM

J. M. Richardson
Headmaster 1994-

Jim Richardson took over as Headmaster in January 1994, having been Deputy Head of the Royal Grammar School, Worcester and before that Head of Economics and Politics at Haberdashers' Aske's School, Elstree, where he was in charge of rugby. He was educated at Marple Hall Grammar School, Cheshire, and the London School of Economics; the first Headmaster not to have been educated at Oxford or Cambridge university.

Richardson's first task was to pilot the school through its first OFSTED inspection, little more than a week after his arrival. Adams' was one of the first schools to be inspected so it was a novel experience for both school and inspectors. The report praised the school's 'highly motivated pupils, proud to be part of a school with long-standing traditions'. It said that the school had made great strides since going Grant Maintained and that expenditure per pupil was twice the national average. It identified areas for improvement, saying that the new Headmaster and the Governors had the opportunity to make the school 'equal to, or better than, any other state school in the country'.

The next OFSTED report in 1998 said that 'the quality of teaching was a very clear strength of the school', praising it for its wide range of extra-curricular activities and saying that the boarding at Adams' represented 'very good value for money.'

Richardson inherited a very different situation from his predecessor. In 1994 the school was in charge of its own destiny and there was confidence in its future as a grammar school. The school and the Haberdashers' Company could work together with no education authority to complicate the relationship. Within three years another new teaching block, the Wood Centre, was built next to the Taylor Centre. It was a fitting tribute to Harry Wood, who had been Chairman of Governors during the difficult days of the '80s.

Not only did more facilities arrive, but also more boys; the school became four-form-entry throughout and a fourth house, Webb House, was created. An increasing number of boys transferred to Adams' sixth form from other schools, following the example of the girls whose numbers grew rapidly. By 2002 there were 776 on roll with 240 in the sixth form, of whom 52 were girls, taught by 48 staff.

In 1995 Alan Snead stepped down as Chairman of Governors. As his predecessors had done, he lived locally, but his successors, Bruce Hacking and then Bruce Powell, were both Wardens of the Company with no local connections. The message was clear: the school occupied an important place in the Company's long-term planning. The relationship between the school and the Company had never been better.

In May 1997, after 18 years in control, the Conservative government was replaced by a Labour one. Adams' was doubly vulnerable, being both a grammar school and also Grant Maintained. But the 'Old Labour' policy had now been replaced by a very different 'New Labour' one. Grant Maintained status was abolished but the school was not threatened with extinction. Under New Labour each grammar school could continue unless a special ballot, initiated by the local community, decided otherwise. At Ripon, in the only ballot so far, the anti-grammar campaign was defeated by a two to one margin. Adams' was able to return to Voluntary Aided status and from 1998 the newly formed Telford and Wrekin Unitary Authority became its maintaining authority. In practice it was still able to control its own budget in a way very similar to that under Grant Maintained status and it still controls its own admissions: there are currently four applicants for every day place in Year 7.

Adams' has continued to appear prominently in the lists of the top 250 schools in the country, its actual position depending on which method of calculation is used. The *Financial Times* uses a combination of the average A level points per candidate and the average points per entry to produce an 'FT index'. In 2000 Adams came 41st in the FT combined list of state and independent schools and third in the list of state schools, earning three paragraphs of praise and a Government 'School Excellence Award'.

A feature of recent educational policy has been the provision by central government of target-related extra finance for schools. Adams' secured such funding by achieving Technical College status in 1996 and continues to excel in the academic, sporting and artistic fields, winning many of the national awards now available in different disciplines. The science department has been particularly successful in winning awards for outstanding teaching. Philip Hunt, Head of Science, received a 'Teaching Award 2000' for his contribution to physics since 1986; Dr Samantha Moore reached the final six of the national Chemistry Teacher of the year award and Dr Tessa Hill (chemistry) was named as West Midlands Outstanding Young Teacher of the Year in 2001. A new Sports Hall is scheduled for completion in the autumn of 2002 with the subsequent conversion of the old gymnasium into a Performing Arts Centre and Lecture Theatre.

The school has never been more successful and it can rightly take its place as a school for the 21st century. William Adams would be proud of it.

Appendix A

Bequests of William Adams extracted from his Will made 6 July 1660

	Total
John Adams, nephew	£1500
already received	£500
	£2000
William Adams, nephew	£1000
already received	£500
	£1500
Walter Adams, nephew Iscoyd Hall	?
Margaret Tonna, niece, wife of Randall Tonna the younger	£250
William Justice, nephew executor & partner from William Adams' part of the store	£6000
Elizabeth Taylor, sister	£100
From rent of Cross Keys annuity per annum	£10
John Taylor, nephew, a house in Newport in which his mother is to live, 2 closes in Newport, plus £200, already received £300	£900
Elizabeth Lane, niece, and her husband, 'my cousin' John Lane, all my silver and gilt spoons	?
my house at lower end of Lawrence Lane near Guildhall	?
lease of Cross Keys, Lawrence Lane	?
Robert Taylor, kinsman,	£500
already received £1000	£1500
Luke Justice, nephew	£400
Ann Baddeley, niece, and her husband John	£400
Margery Ball and cousin John Ball her husband	£250
Ursula Adderley, kinswoman, towards her preferment	£50

209

Ann Baddeley, daughter of Ann and John paid to John Lane, interest only to her, principle sum when she is 21 or marries	£200
Elizabeth Pearson, cousin, and husband George	£250
Robert Allen of Brockton, cousin and my cousin his wife to buy each a gold ring	£6
Mary Allen, niece and cousin £10, having already given at marriage £200	£210
John Benbow, cousin	£20
His wife my goddaughter	£6 13s. 4d.
Thomas Adams Esq worthy friend and kinsman to buy a ring to wear in remembrance of me	£5
William Adams his brother, my loving kinsman, for the same purpose	£6
Richard Weiring Esq, my good friend, for like purpose	£5
William Melhuish, godson, now living with his uncle in Cornwall	£50
Doctor Thomas of Forton, my loving friend	£10
Mr Gace (?)	£5
Mr Cooper (?)	£5
Mr Martyn of the same parish	£5
John Malden, minister of Newport	£6 13s. 4d.
Thomas Chaloner the elder, head schoolmaster	£6 13s. 4d.
Thomas Chaloner the younger, his son	£6 13s. 4d.
Robert Blany, Clerk of the Haberdashers and my loving friend	£10
Thomas Sturge Esq	£5
Poor children of Christ's Hospital	£150
Apprentices belonging to my shop; John Gibbs, Thomas Peach, George Dixon £20 each at expiration of their apprenticeships to William Justice	£60

Prudence my maidservant	£5
Mary Tretton my old servant	£6 13s. 4.d
Goodwife Wilding	£2
My two waterbearers 20s apiece	£2
Poor of the parish where I dwell	£20
For the stock of the said parish	£100
Ten ministers' widows £5 apiece	£50
John Benbow messuage adjoining Lawrence Lane he now occupies on payment of £418 If he does not pay for it, William Justice and John Lane to have it for same payment	?
Dinner for Haberdashers	£35
Two pieces of plate to be bought for the Haberdashers by my executor	£50
Master and Wardens of Haberdashers, to pay in first year after my decease for my charity in Newport	£124
Master and Wardens of Haberdashers, woods on Knighton estate (but have to sell in 3 years enough wood to raise £400-500 to buy more land to lease out to Luke Justice for greater security to obtain £175 per annum for the charity)	?
Bayley and Burgesses of Newport, 2 closes in Norbroom, rent of £9 per annum to be used for the English School	?
In trust for building Market house with Town Hall above, in Newport	£550
To same trustees for removing and rebuilding Mr Barnfield's Market House	£20
William Justice, residue of estate	?
In a Codicil dated 18 March 1660/61 additional sums are left to several people, varying from £20 to £210, totalling	£480
New bequests are to	
Mary Francis, cousin	£10
William Lane, cousin	£5
Goddaughter (unnamed), daughter of John Powy	£5

Grand total in cash   £15719 6s. 8d.

The value of money has changed significantly since 1660 but there is no single multiplier one can apply because different items, such as food, clothing, land and wages, have changed in different ways. One set of statistics we have consulted, based on the modern Retail Price Index set of goods, puts £1 in 1660 equal to £73.77 in February 2002. This gives a modern equivalent value of William Adams' cash bequests as well over £1 million. The value of the property bequeathed is impossible to calculate.

Appendix B

Statutes, Constitutions, Orders and Directions made and appointed by William Adams, the founder of the free grammar school at Newport, in the county of Salop, the which are to be kept and observed for ever, touching the election, placing and displacing such person or persons, from time to time, who shall or may be made choice of, to supply the place and office of schoolmaster and usher in the said school.

2. *Item.* – It is ordained, that if any person or persons, so elected and appointed as master or usher, shall be afterwards, upon trial, found insufficient or remissly negligent, or if he or they shall, upon just accusation, be detected, or notoriously suspected to live incontinent in whoredom or adultery, to be a common swearer, a tavern or alehouse haunter, to discountenance religion or religious duties, or the practice of the power of godliness, or otherwise scandalous, or shall take upon him any other charge or employment, to the hindrance of his or their performing of the duty of the said place, the governors of the school for the time being, shall and may, upon their own knowledge, or certain information thereof given to them by the visitors, or the major part of them, or otherwise howsoever made known unto them, remove him, them, or either of them, found so obnoxious, and cease all further payments to him and them, and in their rooms elect and settle one other sufficient man or men into the said places and employments qualified as before.

3. *Item.* – It is ordained that the schoolmaster so elected and appointed to enjoy and supply the said place and office, shall be constantly resident and attendant thereupon, and if he, being in health, shall be absent above twenty and four school days, at one or several times, in any one whole year, or otherwise shall be observed to be absent from the school, as to neglect his due performance in the instructing and teaching of the scholars, so that there shall be just occasion for complaint, and so given to the visitors, or any of them for the time being, and the same, upon inquiry and examination, found to be true by any six of the said visitors, and thereupon the said master being admonished by any three or more of them, and upon so doing no amendment immediately shall follow, and so continue, that then in either of these cases, or the like at any time happening, the said visitors, or major part of them, are hereby desired to give notice forthwith, under their hands in writing, to the present governors, to the end that the said master, upon three months warning given to him, or left in writing at his house, under the said seal, may be removed and displaced, and all payments cease to be further made to him, and shall proceed to elect and settle one other sufficient and able man, qualified as before, in his place and office; and it is further ordained, that the usher of the said school shall be resident and attendant constantly at school times, and if he, being in health, shall

213

be absent above fifteen school days, at one or several times, in any one whole year, or otherwise shall be observed to be so absent from the school as to neglect the duty of his teaching, that for any of these things, or the like falling out and complaint as before made, and after admonition given him by two or more of the said visitors, and no reformation found as aforesaid, then the like certificate is desired to be made by the said visitors, to the end that the like warning may be given by the governors, and to cease any further payments to him, and proceed to a further choice of one other to supply his place, qualified as before.

5. *Item.* – It is ordained, that the schoolmaster for the time being shall have and enjoy for his dwelling the bigger house, adjoining to the said school, with the garden thereunto belonging, behind the said house, rent free. Provided, that the said school-master shall, and do, from time to time, upon his election, and before admission into the possession of the said house and appurtenances, intended for his habitation, by obligation under his hand and seal, become bound for himself, his executors and administrators, unto the said founder during his lifetime, and afterwards to the said governors and their successors for ever, in due and lawful manner, in the sum of one hundred pounds of lawful money of England, for the good and sufficient repair-ing, amending, sustaining, upholding, and maintaining the said house, with the appurtenances, in and by all manner of needful reparations, and for quitting and delivering up the possession thereof, when by death or otherwise the same shall become void, together with all such books that be or ought to be in the library, as also all such goods and utensils as are or shall be contained in any schedule or schedules, whereto the master's name for the time being shall be subscribed, and also of any other thing or things: whatsoever that now are or hereafter shall be justly belonging and appertaining to the said house and appurtenances, school and library; and that he shall peaceably and quietly permit and suffer the founder, governors or visitors for the time being, or any of them, with such workman or workmen as they or any of them shall appoint, to enter into and there view the premises so often as they shall think meet; and always upon such view, if it shall so happen that any default or want of reparations shall be found, notice shall be given or left in writing by the founder during his life, and after by any of the governors, or two of the visitors of the time being; and if the said house and appurtenances be not well and sufficiently repaired and amended within the space of three months next after such notice given or left, then the said founder during his life, and afterwards the said governors, shall appoint the same to be well and sufficiently repaired and amended, and shall and may deduct out of the said schoolmaster's salary, which shall be then due, or afterwards grow due, all such sum or sums of money as will fully satisfy and pay for the said amendments and reparations laid out. And it is hereby further provided and ordained, that the fairest room in the said house shall be reserved for the Governors and visitors for the time being, to make use of for their more con-venient meeting, so long and so oft as they please, with free ingress, egress, and regress thereunto and thencefrom, without any the let or molestation of the said schoolmaster, or of any other person or persons of his procuring or abetting.

8. *Item.* – The present master shall take a perfect and exact account, written in a book for that purpose, and fixed to one of the desks in the library, there always to remain, of all such books as shall be given by the founder towards the furnishing of the said library, together with the names of the authors, title and editions, together

with the number of the volumes of every the said books; and that the said master and usher, and their successors for ever, shall likewise take and keep in the said book the like account of all such other books as shall hereafter at any time be further given, together with the names of such that gave them, whereof at all times he or they shall be ready to give a true and perfect account to the founder, governors or visitors, or major part of them, when and so often as they, or any of them, shall require; and that none of the said books (upon any pretence whatsoever) shall be lent out or removed out of the said library at any time; and the master and usher for the time being shall, from time to time, appoint the scholars, or so many of them as he or they know fit, to repair into the said library, and make use of the said books, or so many of them as shall be useful for their better profiting in their respective way of learning; and that none whomsoever shall be suffered to write in, scratch or deface, with pen or otherways, any of the said books; and that once in a week, by the care and appointment of the master or the usher, the dust may be beaten from off the said books, and the like care to be taken by them for preservation and good usage of them the aforesaid books, as by experience they shall find best, or otherways shall be advised.

Appendix C

STATUTES, CONSTITUTIONS and ORDERS, made and appointed by William Adams, the founder of the Free Grammar School at Newport, in the county of Salop; and at all times to be observed and kept, for the better ordering and government of his said Free Grammar School.

First. – It is ordained that the said school shall be for ever free for the teaching of the Latin, Greek and Hebrew tongues, or any of them, unto fourscore scholars; whereof all such children as now are, or hereafter shall be born of parents inhabiting the town of Newport or Chetwyn End, thereunto adjoining, together with the children of John Badulie, Luke Justice, and Randell Tonna the younger, shall have the priority of admission into the said school; and if it shall so happen at any time or times hereafter, that the children aforesaid shall not amount to the number assigned, that then it shall be lawful for the master to admit and receive into the freedom of the said school, the children that now are or hereafter shall be born of such parents as do or shall inhabit within three miles round of the said town of Newport until the said number be accomplished; but if those, the children within the bounds aforesaid, shall yet fall short of the afore-mentioned number, then it shall be lawful for the visitors, or the greater number of them, appointed to meet annually in the month of February, and so from time to time, when they meet yearly, in that month, to admit into the like freedom, so many other children as shall be wanting of the said number; and in the first place, to be of those who were and shall be born, and live any where within the space of five miles distant from the said town of Newport; and if yet those last appointed shall not make up so many, that then, likewise, so many more children who now are, or shall be afterwards born, and live elsewhere, in the said county, shall be also admitted to the said freedom of the school, to complete and make up the full number of fourscore free scholars, respect being always had for the preferring of the poorer sort, and of those that live at least distance from the said school: provided that the children born in Newport and Chetwyn End, together with the children of the said John Badulie, Luke Justice, and Randell Tonna, be not thereby, in any kind, debarred of their intended privileges.

Secondly. – The due fee for admission shall be two shillings and sixpence for each scholar of the foundation first appointed, whereof eighteen-pence to the master, and twelve-pence to the usher, except it be of such children only whose parents are inhabitants and not assessed weekly towards the maintenance of the poor, who shall pay twelve-pence, to be equally divided betwixt the master and the usher; the like fee also shall be due, to be paid for those within the compass of three miles; and the poor to be alike respected; and what shall be there paid, in either way, shall be divided as aforesaid.

Thirdly. – No children that have upon them any noisome or infectious diseases, shall, during the same time, be admitted; or if after admission any shall fall into such maladies, they shall be removed until they are perfectly cured.

Fourthly. – The scholars shall have notice of the time of their repairing to school by the ringing of the bell, at some meet space before the hours hereafter specified when they ought to come, by some poor scholar, (to be by the master appointed from time to time for this purpose,) who shall have for his pains yearly twenty shillings, half-yearly paid him. The like sum shall be yearly paid for the sweeping of the school and library, and wiping the dust from desks and seats every school day, in both of them; and it shall be at the will and pleasure of the master, as he thinks meet, to appoint one or two scholars for the doing thereof.

Fifthly. – The hours of coming into and departing from the school, from the tenth day of March to the tenth day of September yearly, shall be from six of the clock in the morning to eleven, and from one of the clock until five in the afternoon and from the said tenth day of September until the said tenth day of March: from seven of the clock in the morning until eleven, except for two months when the days are at the shortest, when they shall repair to school by half an hour past seven at the furthest, and continue until half an hour past eleven; and from the said tenth day of September to the tenth day of March, they shall continue from one of the clock until five of the clock, or so long as the day light shall continue, it being ordained that no candles shall be used for teaching in the school at any time.

Sixthly. – The first duty entered upon every morning, after a short and solemn calling upon God by the master, or in his absence, the usher, for a blessing thereupon, shall be the distinct reading of a chapter, or some other portion of the Holy Scriptures, by one of the scholars, as the master shall direct and appoint; and afterwards prayer shall be put up unto the Lord for his further blessing upon their endeavours in teaching and learning; and before their dismission in the evening, they shall sing one of David's psalms, or a part thereof, as the master or usher shall appoint, and then close the day with prayer and thanksgiving; and hereof both master and usher are enjoined to take care that these religious duties be daily and diligently performed and attended by all the scholars, as doth become such holy performances .

Seventhly. – They shall not break off from school above four days before the time called the Nativity, and shall return to school the Monday next after Twelfth day; likewise they may intermit three days and no more, before Easter and Whitsuntide, but shall return and keep school the Monday next after the said Easter and Whitsun weeks are expired; and in those several days of relaxation, they shall not needlessly associate themselves with the apprentices of the town, or exercise themselves in the streets; but shall observe the directions of the master from time to time, both for the place of their recreation, and the exercises they shall use.

Eighthly. – The master may grant part of a day, and no more, for recreation in a month, except it be at the special request of two of the governors, or three of the visitors for the time being, provided the time be not on the market day; and also each Thursday in the afternoon, from three of the clock in the summer and from two of the clock in the winter half-year, shall be a remedy or time of recreation:

Ninthly. – The master and usher shall take special care that all the scholars do constantly repair to church every Lord's day, morning and afternoon, and other days of public fasting and thanksgiving and be placed together in the church, with or near unto the usher, if so there be, or hereafter shall be, any convenient place so to do; and that they decently and reverendly behave themselves under the public ordinances, and submit themselves to be publicly catechised, as the minister from time to time shall appoint them, or any of them; and that one or more scholars be appointed to view and take notice of such scholars as shall be absent, or not decently behave themselves during the time of the public ordinances; and that every Monday morning account shall be required by the master of any so offending, who shall be corrected as the nature of the offence shall deserve. And I do further order, that every Monday morning, after the reading of the chapter, some convenient time be spent by the master or usher, or both, in calling the scholars, or so many of them as they then well may, to give account of their profiting in the hearing of the word on the Lord's day before. And to the end, that catechising (being of such singular use for the training up of youth in the knowledge of the oracles of God) may be the better carried on, I do hereby order, that the master or usher, or one of them, shall spend one hour at the least, every Saturday in the afternoon throughout the year, in catechising of the scholars, teaching them first the Assembly's lesser catechism; and as any of the scholars have been sufficiently acquainted and instructed in that, and shall grow to maturity, and ripened in judgement, to instruct them in the said Assembly's larger catechism and if any of the scholars shall wilfully and stubbornly offend in any of the premises, after three admonitions, it shall be lawful for the master, with the advice and consent of three, or more, of the visitors, to expel and eject the said offender or offenders from the said freedom.

Tenthly. – The master and usher shall have a special care to the good manners and decent deportment of the scholars, and shall exemplarily punish all misdemeanors, especially the sins of swearing, cursing, lying, filching, filthy or obscene talking, or acting, gaming for any thing of price, and foul language to any person; and in an especial manner, shall diligently endeavour to see the Lord's day kept free from any profanation (as much as in them lieth,) as well after as under the public ordinances, by all their scholars.

Eleventhly. – No scholar, being in health, shall be absent above six days together, and that with the master's allowance; and if he shall be longer absent, after admonition of the scholar, or notice given to the parents or friends, unless in some extraordinary case, and the master approving the cause, he shall forfeit all privileges in the said school, and become incapable of re-admission, unless the visitors, or major part of them, hearing of the case, do otherwise order, who have also power, upon complaint, to call the master to give an account for any such licence to him given; and thereupon to take such order therein, as may most conduce to the promoting of the end of this order, viz. a diligent and constant attendance upon the school, for their better profiting in learning.

Twelfthly. – All disobedient stubborn youths, that are pertinaciously and exemplarily bad, after two admonitions, wherewith their parents or friends be acquainted, shall the third be expelled the school.

Thirteenthly. – The school shall consist of six classes or forms, or more, if in the discretion of the master and the visitors, or the greater number of them, that shall appear to be meet and necessary.

Fourteenthly. – The master shall read and teach classical authors, in order to grammatical learning and knowledge of the tongues, with a special regard to religion, morality, and pure language.

Fifteenthly. – No scholars that have attained to such a progress in learning, as to be able to speak Latin, shall neither, within school or without, when they are among the scholars of the same, or a higher form, speak English; and that the master shall appoint which are the forms that shall observe this order of speaking Latin, and shall take care that it be observed, and due correction given to those that do neglect it.

Sixteenthly. – Each scholar shall be placed according to his progress in learning, and without partiality, preferred by the master according to his desert; and in case of injury offered by the master herein, there shall be appeal to the visitors.

Seventeenthly. – That once in a month at least throughout the year, Saturday, in the forenoon, shall be spent by so many of the upper forms as shall be fitted for it, in such exercises as these: construing such authors of themselves as the master shall appoint, proposing grammatical or historical questions one unto another, and making declamations, or such like exercises, as may tend to the begetting of an emulation amongst the scholars in learning.

Eighteenthly. – No scholar, at any time, shall with knife, or otherwise howsoever, in stone, lead, or other materials, cut, notch, deface, or break the windows, wainscot, forms, seats, table of orders, desks, doors, tables in any part of the houses, school and library, neither deface, or in any kind abuse, any of the books in the said library; the master, upon conviction of such offender or offenders, shall give him or them exemplary punishment for deterring others so to do.

Nineteenthly. – And to the end, that the free scholars may not be neglected in their teaching, the master shall not, at any time, increase or suffer the number of scholars to be above what the master and usher are able diligently and thoroughly to teach and instruct; and the visitors are desired to be very careful that, if the number of scholars taken in, together with those of the foundation appointed to be free, shall be above the number of 130 at any time, then to appoint the master to take one other usher at his own charge, to assist him in the teaching of them; and in case the master shall not submit and so do, the visitors shall, or the major part, certify the same to the governors, to the end, such master may be removed from the said school, upon three months warning to him given.

Twentiethly. – All these statutes and orders made for the free scholars, privileged by the founder, shall be duly observed by all the scholars in the said school; and that no scholars not comprehended within the freedom shall be admitted into the school, but such as submit to one and the same government.

Twenty-first. – The usher shall stand to the master's direction for method and order of teaching; also the master shall examine the proficiency of the scholars under the usher's teaching, and by himself, or if it need be, by two of the visitors, take course for the regulating of what shall be amiss, if any such thing be.

Twenty-secondly. – The visitors shall be appointed by the governors from time to time, after the death of the founder, to meet together at the school, in some of the last ten days of February yearly, or as often as they, or the major part of them, shall find cause so to do, to examine the master's and usher's diligence, and the scholars due admission and proficiency; and to hear and determine all matters of difference that shall arise, either betwixt the master and the usher, or between the master and any of the scholars, upon appeal made unto them of the undue proceedings of the master or usher, contrary to these orders, or of any miscarriages of any of the scholars, contrary to the true meaning of the founder; and any determination made by the said visitors, or major part of them, upon such appeal, shall be binding to the parties concerned; and the visitors are further desired, as it shall seem good unto them, to inquire of the life and conversation of the poor people inhabiting the almshouses, and to use such means, as to them shall seem best, for the amendment of what, in school or otherways, they find amiss.

Twenty-thirdly. – These statutes and orders fairly written, shall be hanged up in a convenient place publicly in the said school, and the master shall cause them to be read or shewed to all such persons as offer children to be admitted, either as free scholars or otherways; and also shall be openly read in the said school once a quarter, from time to time, so none may plead ignorance; and if any of the parents or friends refuse to have their children or relations to submit to these statutes and orders, or any of them, let not such be admitted into the said freedom or benefit of the school.

Twenty-fourthly. – The visitors, or the major part of them for the time being, after the death of the founder, upon defect found in any statutes and orders herein comprized, and that other orders are necessary, and may further tend to the good of the said school, are desired to represent such defects to the present governors, to the end that, upon advice from the said visitors, or major part of them, such further statutes and orders for remedy therein may be provided, as the said governors shall make and approve of; and that if any question or doubts shall hereafter arise about the plain and true meaning of these articles, the visitors, or the major part of them, giving their sense upon such differences under their hands unto the present governors, the said governors shall have power, and are hereby empowered, to consider and judge of and so determine the same from time to time.

Twenty-fifthly. – The founder reserveth, during his natural life, full power of enlarging, altering, changing in substance or words, of adding or renewing what, by experience and prudent council, shall appear to be behoveful to the furtherance of his pious intentions, to the glory of the great God and the public good of the said foundation; and whatsoever is herein appointed and ordained, shall commence and take place from the five-and-twentieth day of March next, 1657.

Appendix D

ADAMS GRAMMAR SCHOOL MASTERS

All were ordained in the Church of England until Tom Collins in 1871

1657-1663   Thomas Chaloner

1663 July 23   John Wickens
never took up the post

1663 Nov 30 - Christmas 1666 Francis Potts

1666 - Midsummer1666-8   Timothy Wood

1668-1704 (died April 1704) Samuel Edwards
HM Whitchurch School 1664-1668
Rector of St Andrews, Weston under Lizard 1687-1704 and Donnington Co Salop
1703

1704-September 1722 John Greenwood
Rector of Newport 1700-1722

1722-1725 Robert Symonds

1725-1773 Samuel Lea

1773-1818 Joseph Scott
Curate in charge of Forton 1772-1776 (prior to usher E. Hughes)

1818-1819 John Langley
never certified by Visitors

1819-1846 Edward Meredith
Rector of ?

1846-1870 Charles Waring Saxton

1871-1903 Tom Collins

1903-1926 John William McLellan Shuker

1926-1946 Walter Samuel Brooks
ordained on retirement

1946-1952 Alexander Duncan Campbell Peterson

1953-1959 Robert Finlay Glover

1959-1973 Jeffrey David Roberts
ordained while in post

1974-1993 David John Taylor

1994 James Michael Richardson

ADAMS GRAMMAR SCHOOL USHERS

Most ordained in the Church of England until Mark Chattock 1866

1658 David Peirce

1658-1663 Thomas Chaloner Junior
Master at Nantwich 1655-58

April 1663-1667 Thomas Millington
Minister of Cheswardine 1655, Minister of Newport 1662-1667

1667 Thomas Wood son of Headmaster

1669   Ambrose Rea

1672-1674 William Turner

1674-1678 name not known, chosen by Samuel Edwards Headmaster

1678-1681 Francis Williams
born Lilleshall, educ Newport G.S., Headmaster of Wem School 1682

1681 Nov John Greenwood
becomes Headmaster in April 1704

1704-1727 John Haynes

1727-1752 John Dickenson
Held a living within three miles of Newport, not known where.

1752-1759 John Lea son of Headmaster
Curate in charge Forton 1754-1758

1759-1761 William Church

1761-1772 John Forrester

1772   Joseph Scott obtained MA 1773 so could become Headmaster
Curate in charge Forton 1772-1776

1775-1801 Edward Hughes
Curate in charge Forton 1776-1793

1801-1819 John Langley
officiating curate for Rector Dr Buckeridge Newport 1791-*c.*1820 nominated Headmaster 1818-1819

1818 Edward Meredith
becomes Headmaster 1819

1820-1853 William Sandford
officiating curate Newport then Rector 1827-1864

1853-1857 J.S. Benifold

1858-1864 John.R.Heawood
left to go to living in Suffolk

?-1866 I.W.Alloway

Dec 1866-Feb 1868 Mark Shattock

1868-1870 H.F Codd

1870   G.R.Burrows

1871-1875 Mr Hutt

1875-? A.M.Drennan After this too many to list

WRITING MASTERS

1784-1795 John Horton

1795-1837 Samuel Cobb

1837-1882 Richard Crowther

1878-1919 Frederick Finnis
master of the junior boys

NOTES

One WILLIAM ADAMS AND HIS FAMILY, pp.1-12

1. GL15842/2 p33.
2. SR&R Hinstock Local History Group, 'An Account of the Squires of Hinstock' (1981).
3. Thomas Horton Sermon, Haberdasher archives.
4. We are indebted for this information to Mr David Smith who has built on numerous wills and other original documents, and on the works of Percy W. L. Adams, *A History of the Adams Family of North Staffordshire* (London, 1914) and *Notes on some North Staffordshire Families* (London, 1914).
5. PRO PROB 11/305fo 239-243.
6. *Diaries and Letters of Philip Henry MA,* ed M. H. Lee (Kegan Paul, Trench & Co, London, 1882).
7. Papers of Canon M. H. Lee, Clwyd RO D/CL/51-53, p.99.
8. Ibid., p98.
9. *Transactions of the Shropshire Archaeological Society* Series 1 vol.9 p.163.
10. John Harvey, 'Aspects of Newport, Shropshire in the seventeenth and eighteenth centuries' (1994).
11. *TSAS* Series 1 vol.9 p.160.
12. *TSAS* Series 1 vol.9 pp.159-161.
13. Newport Parish Register.
14. Letter from P.L.Dickenson, Richmond Herald, 29 March 2000.
15. GL 15842/4 p.248 and GL 15842/5 p.2.
16. *Dictionary of National Biography.*
17. Ian Archer, *History of the Haberdashers' Company* (Phillimore, 1991), pp74-9.
18. Thomas Fuller, *The History of the Worthies of England* (London, 1662). New edition ed. P.A. Nuttall (London, 1840) vol.3 pp.67-8.

Two THE FOUNDING OF THE SCHOOL, pp.13-25

1. SR&R.
2. *TSAS* Series 1 vol.9 p.159.
3. Ian Archer, *History of the Haberdashers' Company* (Phillimore, 1991) pp.83-4.
4. HH 3/1/72.
5. Rosemary O'Day, *Education and Society 1500-1800* (Longman, New York, 1982) p.175.
6. TSAS vol.xlvii pp.12-13.
7. SR&R 1910/1762.
8. GL 15879 p.75.
9. HH 3/1/44.
10. *DNB* Charles Hoole.
11. GL 15842/2 pp.100v,105v,107v & 109.
12. Rosemary O'Day op. cit. p.57.
13. Godfrey Davies, *The Early Stuarts* (Oxford, 1949) pp.304-5.
14. W. E. Brown, *The History of Bolton School* (Bolton School, 1976).

THREE THE SCHOOL BEGINS, **pp.26-40**

1. K. Kenyon-Thompson, *Thomas Chaloner, Headmaster of Ruthin School* (The Coelian Trust, 1992); D. J. Taylor, *Thomas Chaloner*, AGS archive. Chaloner's moves 1645-1663 were: Shrewsbury (ejected), Ruyton XI Towns, Newnes near Ellesmere, Birchall near Ellesmere, Market Drayton (ejected), Hawarden, Overton, Stone, Emrall near Bangor on Dee, Ruthin, Newport, Shrewsbury.
2. G. W. Fisher, *Annals of Shrewsbury School* (Methuen & Co, London, 1899) p.161.
3. Thomas Fuller, *The History of the Worthies of England* (London, 1662). New edition ed. P. A. Nuttall (London 1840), vol.3, pp.67-8.
4. HH 3/1/45.
5. GL 15849/1 p334.
6. Sir George White, *English Lantern Clocks* (Antiques Collectors' Club 1989) and F. J. Britten, *Old Clocks, Watches and their Makers* (London, 1899).
7. GL 15879 p75 & HH 3/1/77.
8. GL 15843/9 p259.
9. HH 3/1/42.
10. Nicholas Rogers, 'Early History of Sidney Sussex College Library' in D.E.D.Beales & H.D.Nisbet (eds.), *Sidney Sussex College Cambridge Historical Essays* (Boydell Press, Woodbridge, 1996).
11. SR&R Blakeway ms.
12. Corpus Christi College ms 390.
13. SR&R Blakeway ms.
14. GL 15881 21 June 1818.
15. GL 15882 p.79.
16. GL 15882 pp.98-9.
17. GL 15881 pp.116ff.
18. GL 15881 25 September 1826.
19. GL 15849/1 pp.46-7.
20. GL 15849/1 pp.51ff.

FOUR THE KNIGHTON ESTATES: HOW THE SCHOOL WAS FINANCED, **pp.41-56**

1. GL15879 pp.9-15 & 65-65v.
2. Peter Rutter, *The Haberdashers' Oldest School* (Peter Rutter 1993) Chapter 2.
3. Ian Archer, *History of the Haberdashers' Company* (Phillimore 1991) Chapter 8.
4. GL 15842/4 pp.65ff.
5. GL 15843 vols 1-12 (1760-1912).
6. GL 15883/1.
7. GL 15843/1 p.163.
8. GL 15843/1 pp.63-74.
9. Information about Richard Whitworth comes mainly from J. S. Billington, *Adbaston* in the William Salt Library, Stafford and D. H. Robinson, *The Sleepy Meese* (Waine Research 1988).
10. *Transactions of the Old Stafford Society* (1931), pp.27ff, GL15843/1 p73.
11. GL 15843/1 p.73.
12. SR&R 81/332 ff.
13. SR&R 81/353.
14. GL 15843/1 p.147.
15. GK 15843/2 p.159.
16. GL15843/1 p.232.
17. GL15843/1 p.230.
18. GL 15843/1 p.279.
19. GL 15883 & 15884.
20. GL15843/2 p.175.

21. GL 15843/2 p.265.
22. SR&R 81/394.
23. GL 15843/3 p.329.
24. GL 15841 p.54.
25. GL 15881 pp.64ff.
26. GL 15881 p.83.
27. GL 15843/9 pp.242-253.
28. GL 15851/2 p.11 + loose leaf.

FIVE LATE SEVENTEENTH AND EIGHTEENTH CENTURY, pp.57-72

1. James Bentley, *Dare to be Wise* (James & James, London 1990), p.31.
2. GL15842/2 p.129.
3. GL15842/3 p.557.
4. *Dictionary of National Biography.*
5. GL15842/3 p.323.
6. GL 15842/3 p.474.
7. SR&R 81/403.
8. GL 15843/1 pp.58-78.
9. GL 15843/1 pp.269-70.
10. SR&R 81/408.
11. Notes and Queries vol.204, November 1959 pp.404ff.
12. Notes and Queries 4th SIII Feb 13 1869 p.151.
13. GL 15843/2 p.264.
14. We owe this information to Christopher Jobson.
15. SR&R 81/403.
16. GL 15842/8 p.405.
17. GL 15843/2 p.295.
18. GL 15842/3 p.303.
19. GL 15843/4 p.379.
20. HH 3/2/161/21 and GL15882 pp.19-21.
21. Wase ms, Corpus Christi College, Oxford.
22. SR&R 1910/1739.
23. GL15842/4 pp.48-50.
24. GL15843/1 p.62.
25. GL15843/2 pp.115 ff.

SIX THE EARLY NINETEENTH CENTURY, pp.73-85

1. GL15842/6 pp.175ff.
2. GL 15849/4 p.138.
3. GL15843/2 pp.160ff.
4. GL 15843/4 pp.545-8.
5. SR&R 81/408.
6. GL15843/5 pp.110-13.
7. GL15843/5 p.402.
8. GL15881 pp.51-2 & 61-2.
9. GL 15942/12 p.572 & GL 15942/13 p.261.
10. GL 15843/9 p.421.
11. GL 15843/9 p.253.
12. SR&R 81/410-13.
13. Information on the John Langley affair comes from HH 3/2/202, HH 3/2/161/ 1-13 and GL 15882.
14. Ledger acquired in June 2001 by Malcolm Miles, to whom we owe this information.
15. GL15842/10 p.631 & HH 3/2/161/20.

SEVEN THE NINETEENTH CENTURY TO THE 1860S, pp.86-100

1. SR&R 5141/6 1-4.
2. HH 3/2/161/25.
3. GL 155849/1 pp.45-53, 72-92, 108-121.
4. GL15849/1 pp.354-9.
5. GL 15849/5 p.4.
6. GL 15849/3 p.254.
7. GL 15849/3 pp.140-152.
8. GL 15849/3 p.139.
9. GL 15849/2 p.55.
10. GL 15849/3 pp.218-26.
11. GL15849/4 p.190.
12. SR&R1910/660.
13. GL15849/4 p.360.
14. GL15849/4 p.373.
15. GL15849/5 pp.72-6, 97-9, 116-18,139-142,173-7 & GL15843/9 pp.501-4, 543.
16. GL15849/5 pp.46ff.
17. GL15849/5 p.531.
18. GL15842/15 p.286.
19. GL15849/6 pp.148 & 151.
20. *Novaportan* July 1909 p.6.
21. *Novaportan* July 1925 pp.32-3, December 1928 p.11.

EIGHT THE TAUNTON COMMISSION AND REVIVAL UNDER TOM COLLINS, pp.101-16

1. *Parliamentary Papers 1867-8 Schools' Inquiry Commission (Taunton Report)* Vols XV and XXVIII.I, pp.594-5.
2. *Ibid* Vol XXVIII, p.595.
3. PRO ED27/3977.
4. *Taunton Report,* Vol XX, p.32.
5. Archer, *The Haberdashers' Company,* pp.195ff.
6. GL 15849/6, p.80.
7. PRO ED27/3977.
8. GL15849/6, p.380.
9. GL15849/1, pp.339-40, 354-9.
10. John Harvey, *Aspects of Newport Shropshire in the nineteenth century,* p.26.
11. SR&R 1910/656, 657, 659.
12. SR&R 5141/6.
13. GL 15842/12, p.542.
14. PRO ED27/3989.
15. GL 15849/6, p.153.
16. Much of the information in this section comes from Tom Collins, *School and Sport* (London, 1905) and from researches by Malcolm Miles, mainly in *The Newport and Market Drayton Advertiser.*
17. A Trott, *No Place for Fop or Idler* (James & James, London 1992), p.78.
18. *Newport and Market Drayton Advertiser,* 30 November 1878.
19. GL 15849/6 pp.211, 273, 296, 300.
20. GL 15849/6 pp.261-3.
21. GL 15843/10 p.206 & GL 15842/16 p.52.
22. GL 15849/6 pp.329, 360, 374, 387, 399, 403-4, 410.
23. *Newport and Market Drayton Advertiser,* 13 September 1884.

NINE 1903-1926, pp.117-36

1. GL 15842/18, p.625.
2. GL 15843/12, pp.395 & 493.

3. GL 24727 & GL 24719/1, p.437.
4. HH Haberdasher Company Manual 1901, supplement 1905.
5. Shropshire Education Reports April 1920, pp6, 7.
6. GL 24727 1907.
7. GL 15842/19, p.56 & GL 15852/2 pp.227, 231, 235.
8. GL 15852/2 pp.248, 258, 287.
9. GL 24719/5 p.188, GL 24719/6 pp.14, 42, 93, 127, 158, 161, 308, 322, 337, 432.
10. Interview with Tony Talbott (AGS 1933-41) and his sisters Betty, Peggy and Pat 1998.

TEN   1926 TO 1952 THE SCHOOL UNDER BROOKS AND PETERSON, pp.137-57
1. Doris M. Hawkins, *Atlantic Torpedo* (Victor Gollancz, London 1943).
2. Lamsdorf was the largest of the German concentration camps, with over 21,000 British POWs. It is now a Prisoner of War museum.

ELEVEN   1953 TO 1973, pp.158-72
1. GL 24719/15 Court of Assistants item 110.
2. GL 24719/12 pp.56 and *passim* and GL24719/14 item 557.
3. GL 24719/10 p.161.
4. GL 24719/12 item 375.
5. GL 24719/18 items 61/66, 2/67, 18/67ff.

TWELVE   1970S: RE-ORGANISATION, pp.173-87
1. *Shropshire Journal*, 2 April 1971.
2. Letter 11 September 1978 School Governors to Dept of Education & Science
3. *Newport Advertiser* 15 September 1978. Henry Wollaston, a Haberdashers' Company Governor, played a vital role in negotiations throughout this period. A Home Office lawyer by profession, he was responsible for drafting many of the Governors' statements.
4. SCC Education Committee minutes, 17 November 1979.
5. In November 1980 a meeting attended by about 300 primary school parents affirmed its support for comprehensive education and voted to send a delegation to Baroness Young. She declined, saying that the earlier delegation had given her a very clear view of local feelings.
6. My family and I were on holiday in France and read about it in the *Daily Telegraph*!

THIRTEEN   1982 TO 1987 THE FIGHT FOR SURVIVAL, pp.188-96
1. *Newport Advertiser*, 9 March 1984.
2. *Shropshire Star*, 28 March 1984.
3. *Newport Advertiser*, 28 September 1984; see also *Shropshire Star* 24 and 26 September 1984.
4. Ian Dobson, Deputy Chief Education Officer LEA at meeting with Newport teachers, 7 January 1986.

FOURTEEN   1988 AND BEYOND, pp.197-206
1. *Shropshire Star* of November 1989 and *Newport Advertiser* 10 November 1989.

GLOSSARY

ADVOWSON
The right to appoint a clergyman to a church living, e.g. as a parish priest.

CURRENCY
Before 1971, when decimal currency was introduced, the system used was pounds (£) shillings (s) and pence (d). There were 20 shillings in a pound and 12 pence in a shilling. There was also the halfpenny (½d) and farthing (¼d). Prices were often quoted in guineas (21 shillings). In the seventeenth–century the mark was still used; this was two thirds of a pound, 13s4d. Half a mark, 6s8d, was also commonly used.

DES, DfE, DfEE
Department for Education and Science, Department for Education etc. Successive titles for the government department responsible for education in the twentieth century. First called Board of Education when established in the nineteenth century. Headed by a Secretary of State and one or more Ministers.

ELEEMOSYNARY
from Latin eleemosyna – alms. Concerned with almsgiving or charity.

ENDOWED SCHOOL
A school provided with an endowment by its founder (usually property). Most were founded in the sixteenth and seventeenth centuries. Those that attracted pupils from a wide area became known as public schools.

EXEAT
(Latin) 'let him leave.' Permission for a pupil to leave the School site, given by a master or prefect.

FE
Forms of Entry. The number of forms entering a school in the first year, (usually taken as 30 pupils in each) was used to calculate total numbers in a school during reorganisation discussions.

GLEBE LAND
belonging to the parish priest.

GOVERNOR
a) The Governors of William Adams' Free Grammar School established in 1656 were the Master and Four Wardens of the Worshipful Company of Haberdashers.

They remained as Governors of William Adams' Charity after their right to oversee the School was transferred to the local Managers in 1878. Also known as Foundation Governors.

b) Governors has been the term used to describe the local managers of the School since the 1944 Education Act. See Visitor and Manager.

GRANT MAINTAINED STATUS
New type of status available to schools under the 1988 Education Reform Act whereby schools received their allocation of money direct from the Department of Education instead of the LEA. They therefore had complete control of how the money was spent. Adams' was grant maintained from 1990 – 1997.

FOUNDATION
Another term for the Charity founded by William Adams in 1656.

LEA
Local Education Authority. The 1902 Education Act appointed the County Council to be the LEA in charge of all education in its area. Since 1998 Telford and Wrekin Unitary Authority has been the LEA for Newport.

MANAGER
The name given to members of the committee which controlled the running of the School from 1878 to 1944.

MASTER
a) the title of the chief master of a grammar school until headmaster came into use in the nineteenth century.
b) the title of the head of the Haberdashers' Company who holds office for one year.

OFSTED
Office for Standards in Education set up in 1992 to inspect schools.

PUBLIC SCHOOL
Former term for an independent fee paying secondary school.

SCC
Shropshire County Council. Elected council to run the county established by the County Councils Act of 1888.

SIZAR
student who helped pay for his university education by acting as a servant to another student, mostly in sixteenth to the eighteenth centuries.

TITHES
A tenth part of a person's income or produce, contributed to support the parish priest, from mediaeval times to the 1830s. In certain circumstances they could be held by non-churchmen.

USHER
The title of the under or second master at a school, used until the second half of the nineteenth century.

VISITOR
Ten local men, four of them laymen important in the locality and six of them clergymen, appointed to supervise the Grammar School in Newport. The first Visitors were chosen by William Adams and they were replaced when necessary by the Haberdasher Governors on local advice. They were responsible to the Haberdasher Governors. The term was dropped in the 1878 reorganisation scheme.

VOLUNTARY AIDED STATUS
Arrangement set up by the 1944 Education Act, by which the voluntary body (the Foundation), appoints the majority of governors and is responsible for maintaining the exterior of the school buildings, and for improvements and alterations. A percentage of approved expenditure can be recovered from central government. This started at 50 per cent but is now 85 per cent. The LEA appoints the other governors, pays for internal maintenance, salaries and general costs. Adams' was Aided from 1944 to 1990,and after 1997, when Grant Maintained status was abolished.

WILLIAM ADAMS' CHARITY
The charity set up by William Adams in 1656 to distribute money from the rents of property on the estates at Knighton, Staffordshire, as set out in his Deed of Uses, 1656. From 1656-1784 this was £175 a year but increased from time to time thereafter. The Master and Four Wardens of the Haberdashers' Company were Governors of this charity. In 1906 it was split into two: Adams' Newport Charity which supported the School and the Eleemosynary Charity which administered the other items.

YEAR NAMES
For most of the twentieth century boys entering school at 11 went into Form 1. Since the introduction of the National Curriculum in the late 1980s this has been known as Year 7, as years are dated from first entry into primary school. What used to be called the lower and upper sixth form are now officially years 12 and 13.

BIBLIOGRAPHY

REFERENCES TO MANUSCRIPT SOURCES
GL Records of the Haberdashers' Company from earliest times to the 20th century are held at the Guildhall Library, London. They are mainly committee minute books. Details are given in W. Le Hardy *The Worshipful Company of Haberdashers. The Descriptive Class List of Records* (1954), which can be consulted at the Guildhall Library.
HH Records kept at Haberdashers' Hall, London
SR&R Shropshire Records and Research Centre, Shrewsbury
PRO Public Record Office, Kew
Staffordshire Record Office and William Salt Library, Stafford
Archive material collected at Adams' Grammar School has not yet been fully catalogued. It includes headmaster's speech day reports, annual reports to governors, end of term letters to parents, governors reports to parents, school development plans, school magazines (the *Novaportan*) as well as governors' meeting and committee reports.

UNPUBLISHED SECONDARY SOURCES
John Harvey *Aspects of Newport, Shropshire in the Seventeenth and Eighteenth Centuries, Aspects of Newport, Shropshire in the Nineteenth Century* (1994) *and Aspects of Newport, Shropshire in the Twentieth Century* (1995)
J. L. Turnock *The Endowed Grammar Schools of Shropshire. The Careswell Exhibitions and the response of local communities to educational reform.* Manchester PhD Thesis 1998

PUBLISHED WORKS RELATING TO NEWPORT AND THE GRAMMAR SCHOOL
Ian W. Archer *The History of the Haberdashers' Company* (London 1991) Phillimore
N. Carlisle *Concise Description of the Endowed Grammar Schools in England and Wales* (1818)
Charity Commissioners' Report for Salop 1829
Tom Collins *School and Sport* (London 1905)
J. Foster (ed) A*lumni Oxonienses*
Oliver J. Lodge *Past Years. An autobiography by Sir Oliver Lodge* (Hodder and Stoughton, London 1931)
J. R. Meredith *Adams' Grammar School Newport 1656-1956 A Short History* (Newport, Shropshire 1956)
Papers of the House of Commons 1867-8 Schools' Inquiry Commission (Taunton Report) vol XV West Midland Division HMSO 1869
TSAS Transactions of the Shropshire Archaeological Society
J. A. Venn (ed) *Alumni Cantabrigienses*
*The Victoria History of the Counties of England: Shropshire,*vol 2 (1973)
Ann Warner *Newport, Shropshire, past and present* (Newport 1983)

GENERAL BACKGROUND READING

W. K. Jordan *Philanthropy in England 1480-1660* (London 1959)

Rosemary O'Day *Education and Society 1500-1800* (Longman Inc, New York 1982)

David Owen *English Philanthropy 1660-1960* (London OUP 1965)

R. S. Tompson *Classics or Charity? The Dilemma of the Eighteenth Century Grammar School.* (Manchester UP 1971)

Foster Watson *English Grammar Schools 1460-1660* (Cambridge UP 1908, new impression 1968)

Other works used are referred to in the endnotes

OLD NOVAPORTAN CONTRIBUTORS

Akerman, Carl, 1920
Allman, Geoff, 1929-35
Banks, Elizabeth, 1993-95
Banks, Victoria, 1996-98
Barnard, Joan, née Dawbarn (NHS)
Basford, David, 1945-52
Bourne, M. J., 1931-38
Bowles, Ian, 1955-63
Broad, Ken, 1942-49
Brock, Ted, 1910-20
Bromage, Nigel, 1942-51
Brown, Frank, 1942-50
Byrd, Ian, 1944-51
Casewell, Andrew, 1943-49
Cooper, Harold, 1939-46
Coulson, Kenneth, J. 1941-46
Davies, John
Dawbarn, Peter, 1929-38
Dillamore, Alfred, 1917-25
Edwards, Arthur, 1934-39
Elkes, Raymond, 1922-31
Everall, Stuart, 1968-75
Goulson, Gavin, 1944-49
Gourdie, Ian, 1955-62
Griffiths, Ken, 1939
Harrison, Stanley T., 1938-46
Henderson, David, 1940s-50s
Holland, Alan, 1940-51
Home, Jim, 1943-53
Jones, Maurice, 1935-39
Koenigsberger, Helmut G., 1934-37
Koenigsberger, Konrad, 1939-40
Koenigsberger, Peter, 1936-39

Lees, Reg, 1921-28
Lewis, K. Bryan, c.1946-56
Lucas, Evelyn Headmaster's Secretary, c.1948
Malone, Paul, 1975-82
Martin, David, 1969-76
Mellor, Rosemary, daughter of Claude Perry, 1908-12
Midgley, Michael, 1945-52
Millington, Graham, 1952-61
Newton, Frank, 1942-48
Oliver, Richard, 1981-88
Pemberton, John, 1978-85
Pendlebury, John, 1941-46
Poppitt, Sydney, c.1914-16
Preston, T. S. (Syd), 1939-43
Preston, W. (Bill), 1939-43
Quant, Charles, left 1936
Shaw, Ian, at Adams 1926
Shuker, Alan, 1941-47
Smith, John D., 1948-56
Speake, G. David, 1929–38
Speake, J. G. (Guy), 1923-31
Talbott, Tony, 1933-41
Thompstone, Stuart, 1923-29
Watson Jones, Peter, 1934-44
Walker, Edgar, 1940-45
Warrillow, Cerdic, 1948-55
Wilson, Jim, 1933-41
Woods, Bill, 1939-45
Wright, Geoffrey, left 1928
Wright, W. (Bill), 1938-46

INDEX

Page numbers in **bold** denote text illustrations. Plates are indicated by Plate numbers in **bold**. The following abbreviations have been used in this index: b. – born; C – century; d. – died; fl. – *floruit*; m. – married.

DJT 4 02